MIXED RACE IN

Our family polit
roots, and rev

Spartaca Chevannes-Reeves

BLUE ROOF BOOKS

Published by Blue Roof Books, 53 Woodthorne Road, Tettenhall, Wolverhampton, WV6 8TU.

The events described in this book are true, but some names, locations, and other details have been changed, or omitted, to ensure people's identities, anonymity, and right to privacy are protected.

ISBN 978-0-9570042-0-7

Format and design by Freda Edwards and Sarah Moss Designs Ltd. Front cover photograph courtesy of James Price of Penkridge, Staffs.

Dedicated to my mother and father for raising three mixed-race children, each with a steely determination to oppose injustice and the abuse of power.

CONTENTS

		Page
Preface: Bandana in the wedding photographs		1
Part I	**After they met**	
1.	Married to protest	10
2.	My father's testicles	24
3.	The black man's bar	36
4.	A brick through the window	47
5.	Rex, rum and research	60
6.	Poetry and sweet tea	69
7.	Not a scintilla of evidence	77
8.	Commanding the Empire	89
9.	A whistleblower	98
10.	Gobby Wulfrunians	110
Part II	**Before they met**	
11.	Growing up barefoot	123
12.	Growing up on chocolate	131
13.	From Spanish Town to KT	141
14.	Pietas in the coal hole	150
15.	On telephones and tapping	160
16.	The laying on of black hands	166
17.	A quick word in the kitchen	176
18.	Disembowel Enoch Powell	190
19.	An unconventional cure for asthma	202
20.	Message on a windscreen	214
Part III	**When we meet now**	
21.	De higher monkey climb!	226
22.	Capacity! What capacity?	237
23.	Under the shade of the family tree	253
24.	The House of Terror	265
25.	Rhodes to Zim and back again	278
Postscript: What happened to the wedding guests?		294
Glossary		306
About the author		312

Preface

Bandana in the wedding photographs

A pretty black woman and handsome white man smile into the camera. She is dressed in an embroidered white peasant blouse, brightly-patterned skirt and head wrap. Her large silver earrings sparkle in the sun. She grasps a bouquet of red and yellow roses. He wears a light grey suit, colourful shirt, broad yellow tie, and a red carnation in his buttonhole. He squeezes her tightly around her slender waist. Specks of confetti are caught in their hair.

Children are often curious about their parents' identity, and relationships. Our Aunt Annie was adopted at the age of six weeks but in adult life still sought out her natural mom and tried to establish contact with her, only to be refused the quintessential maternal recognition she craved. The three of us spent what we understood to be a normal childhood in an ordinary, happy and stable nuclear family. Our version of normality, however, had to take into account mom and dad's extensive work commitments and their ever-active campaign to make the world a better place. Their political activities, especially, turned out to be an interminable business, leaving us for hours in the company of babysitters, albeit loving and devoted ones.

We, too, were intensely interested in how our parents met, why they married, and whether they loved one another. Just as importantly, why did they decide to have us? Perhaps all children want to ask their parents the same questions. Or were we just a little more inquisitive than most because we happened to be of mixed race, with a black Jamaican mother and a white English father?

Our mother, Melhado Chevannes, was born and brought up in Jamaica. She is brown-skinned, 168cm tall, and slimly built, with beautiful long shapely legs. Her attractive face is distinguished by dark inquiring eyes and high cheek bones, giving her an air of gentle serenity. She possesses an elegant ladylike demeanour, belying her steely determination to achieve the ambitious goals she sets herself.

Our father, Francis Reeves, was brought up in Bournville, Birmingham. He is white, 180cm tall, broad-shouldered, and of medium built. He has a swarthy complexion, long face, and pronounced nose. His head still sprouts a tuft of dark brown hair.

For as long as I can remember, he has worn a beard. It used to grow so wild that it made him look like Fidel Castro but, in recent years, he has trimmed it to be short and neat to comply, I suspect, with the expectations of a management role. Our parents, incidentally, prefer to be known as 'Mel' and 'Frank', rather than by the names on their birth certificates.

There are three of us children: two daughters and a son. My sister, Toussaint, is the eldest, born on Boxing Day 1979. I arrived next on St Valentine's Day 1981. I'm called Spartaca. Robeson, the youngest appeared just before Christmas in 1983.

When we first went to see our new brother in the maternity ward at New Cross Hospital in Wolverhampton, the midwife asked us what we were going to call him. "The baby Jesus," we replied in unison. Toussaint had been cast at the time as the Angel Gabriel in the Merridale Primary School nativity play.

Now, in an age of emails and texts, we are tagged respectively, 2s, Sparx, and Robo. But more on our distinctive names later!

When we were very young, we would search the bottom of the bedroom wardrobe where the family photograph albums were kept. We would extract the leather-bound collection of wedding pictures – a standard professional job lot by James Price of Penkridge. We pored over them eagerly, marvelling at the pictures of a youthful-looking Mom and Dad standing close together on a parched brown lawn with ornamental flower beds beyond.

As tiny tots, long after bed time, my sister and I would stagger downstairs with the heavy album, guessing that our parents would excuse the hour and make time to explain their wedding photographs in proud detail as we turned the pages for them.

Mom always started us off with: "This is Daddy and Mommy just after we married at the register office on Broad Street in Birmingham. I'm wearing my traditional Jamaican costume: a red bandana skirt and head wrap, with a white embroidered peasant blouse. Look! Daddy's shirt has been made in bandana cloth to match."

Bandana is a plaid cotton material in shades of red, yellow and white, traditionally worn by Jamaican peasant women as a head-tie, skirt, or apron, and seen as the badge of a woman market trader, or 'higgler'. More recently, bandana cloth has been adopted as the national dress, or folk costume, of Jamaica.

"The wedding photos," Dad explained, "were taken across the road in the gardens next to the Hall of Memory. I shall never forget the date: it was the 7th of August 1976. You can see from the lawn that it was a hot dry summer."

"Did you go away on honeymoon?" I asked innocently.

"We went camping in the Savernake Forest. The ground was so hard that the mallet wouldn't bang in the tent pegs."

"Daddy, your hair was ever so long," I remarked. "Mommy, did you like his hair long like that?"

"Yes," she replied, "I thought he looked romantic."

"Mommy, how old were you when you got married?" Toussaint wanted to know.

"I was 31 and your dad was 30."

Sensing we were about to be sent back to bed, Toussaint quickly turned the page and began to describe the content of the next picture.

"Those are your bridesmaids, aren't they, Mommy? That's Pat from London and that's Auntie Carmelita, your sister. They're holding bouquets of white roses to match their blouses. Yours are red and yellow to match your dress."

Pat, who lived in London, was Mel's best friend. She was a strikingly good-looking Jamaican woman of Indian descent, and the girlfriend of Mel's cousin, Lionel. Their first child, Fabian, born in 1972, was severely disabled. Pat had to make special arrangements for Fabian's care in order to attend the wedding and fulfil her duties as a bridesmaid.

Carmelita, Mel's sister, looked tall and ladylike in the photograph, despite being only sixteen and having just left school. When we were older, we came to know her as a generous and kindly-spoken aunt.

Toussaint turned another page: "And that's Grandma – all dressed up in her blouse and bandana skirt. What a big straw hat she's wearing!"

"Mommy, you look so happy with Daddy in that picture. Were you in love?"

Moving rapidly on to the next photograph, Mom explained: "This is Daddy with his 'best men'. The tall white man is Ryman Reece Roper, and the small Sri Lankan man with the beard is Sadun Perera. Daddy couldn't make up his mind which of them to choose, so they took it in turns to make the best-man speeches at the reception."

"We held it at the Strathallan Hotel on the Hagley Road in Birmingham," Dad added. "We invited eighty guests. After lunch we had speeches and a play. Your mother made a speech as well, because we thought the traditional wedding arrangements were sexist – what with the woman being given away by her father. We didn't want Mom's father or step-father to make their routine 'praise the Lord' speeches."

He continued to reminisce: "The Banner Theatre Group put on a play called 'Womankind'...Mel's dad was horrified with the scene about a woman's right to choose."

What's a woman's right to choose?" Toussaint's question was left unanswered as the page was briskly turned to the next photograph.

Frank, our dad, stood next to our two white English grandparents, and Mel, our mom, was lined up with three black Jamaican grandparents. The relationships on the English side of the picture were fairly obvious. Frank Reeves, stood next to his mother, Phyllis Reeves, who had her hand on the arm of her husband, Norman Reeves.

For those unacquainted with Jamaican family relationships and naming customs, the Jamaican side of the photograph was somewhat more difficult to decipher. Our flamboyant grandma with her big hat and long bandana skirt was pre-eminent indeed, standing between a slim wiry man in a brown suit, and a more stoutly-built fellow in a pork-pie hat. The man in the brown suit we knew to be the ebullient Mr Chevannes, father of Mel and her brother, Lloyd. The man in the pork-pie hat we recognised as the mild-mannered Mr Clarke, father of Mel's sister, Carmelita. Guests who weren't family had far greater difficulty fathoming Jamaican relationships when, in true Jamaican style, almost everyone in the wedding party was referred to by a title of respect, or nickname.

For example, our mother, Mel, has never called her mother 'Mom', or 'Epsi', or even 'Mrs Clarke', but 'Aunt Epsi'. In the Jamaican context, in addition to meaning 'aunt' in the English sense, 'aunt' is used as a title for any respected older female family friend or relative. Stepmothers, of which there are many, are also addressed as 'Aunt'. To confuse matters further, Mel has always called her natural mother 'Aunt'. My theory is that when she was growing up she heard all the other children calling her mother 'Aunt Epsi', and did the same.

We learned from a very early age that most Jamaican members of our family had a nickname that rarely bore any relationship to the name on their birth certificate. Thus, my mother always explained the part of the photograph showing my three Jamaican grandparents in the following way:

"There's Aunt Epsi, arm in arm with Uncle Riley and Mr Son." This could be decoded as: "There is my mother, Mrs Epsi Clarke, arm in arm with my father, Mr Fitzroy Chevannes, and my stepfather, Mr Clarence Clarke." The 'Aunt', 'Uncle' and 'Mr' were invariably added as a mark of respect for older relatives.

Likewise, my Jamaican grandmother, in common with all the older members of the family called Mel, her older daughter, 'Coolie', and Carmelita, her younger daughter, 'Blossom'. So Uncle Riley was Coolie's dad, and Mr Son was Blossom's dad.

When we asked our mother why she was called 'Coolie', she said it was probably because her hair was longer and looser than that of other family members, and made her look 'Indian' – 'coolie' being a derogatory term for East Indian indentured labourers brought to Jamaica in the nineteenth century.

The Jamaican scene was a world of multiple aliases or, as I imagined it then, a kind of extended spy or detective story.

At this point, Toussaint, still anxious to prolong the conversation and to avoid being sent back to bed, knowingly inquired: "Was everyone happy at your wedding?"

"I think everyone who turned up to the wedding," Dad said, "was genuinely happy and pleased for us. Those who didn't approve - not many - weren't invited, or didn't bother to turn up."

Tellingly, at such a young age, we pursued the question of which of our numerous relatives hadn't bothered to turn up, and why.

"Mel's cousin, Lionel, didn't come," Dad said. "He didn't like the idea of his favourite cousin marrying a white man. He thought she was making a big mistake."

When we were older, we realised that there may have been reasons other than our parents' racial difference for objecting to their marriage.

Dad's parents, Norman and Phyllis, thought Mel "a lovely girl with a sensible head on her shoulders", but were reluctant to lend their support to the proposal because their son had been married once before and divorced. As Catholics, they reasoned that marriage was for life and that their attendance might signal approval for Frank's reprehensible behaviour. Frank pointed out in his defence that they had never recognised the legitimacy of his first marriage because it hadn't taken place in a church, but to no avail. They were adamant they wouldn't be coming, until it was suggested that Mel's family would see their absence as a gesture of their disapproval of his decision to marry a black woman and not of his divorce. This consideration played on their minds and persuaded them to relent on the day before the wedding took place.

Frank had also fallen out with Mel's father, Fitzroy, over the literal truth of the Bible creation story. Fitzroy was convinced that Adam had one rib fewer than Eve, and that this was true of all men, a view that Frank had told him was absurd. This incident, along with the register office wedding, gave Fitzroy grounds for fearing he was about to acquire a godless atheist as a son-in-law.

We insisted on counting the people in the next photograph one by one. There were sixteen of them. Once again, at the centre of the picture, were the groom and bride, flanked on the left by the Reeves family of parents, Norman and Phyllis, and Frank's three sisters, Margaret ('Maggie'), Angela ('Annie'), and Philippa ('Pip') – now our paternal aunts. On the right were ranged the combined Chevannes and Clarke clan, including Mel's brother, Lloyd, and sister, Carmelita, and three children by Mom's stepmother.

As the pages turned, the number of faces in the photographs increased. The next picture was of all the relatives, many of them my English grandmother's brothers and sisters and nephews and nieces, who referred to themselves as 'the Fortey clan'. I couldn't remember all their names, although Great Aunt Meg and Great Aunt Edna were there, and Edna's daughter, Janet.

And then came the picture of staff and students from Bilston College where Mom and Dad first met and fell in love. Ryman Reece Roper and Sadun Perera, the 'best men', were present, as were David Warm and his wife Denise, and Betty Simms. Dad pointed out two black men with Afro-hair styles: Pasvil Plummer and Trevor Coote, both students at the college. They were easy to recognise because they still called at our house, although they had long since dispensed with their Afros.

"Why aren't there any pictures of you cutting the wedding cake?" Toussaint demanded. "You did have a wedding cake, didn't you?"

"We could only afford the photographer for an hour at the register office," Mom confessed, "but we had a lovely white three-tiered cake given to us as a present by my friend, Claudette Blackwood."

"Is she in the wedding photos?" Toussaint inquired.

"No," Mom confirmed. "She didn't want to show herself because of how she looked and felt. Her face was swollen from the steroids she was taking for her illness. She suffered from systemic lupus erythematosis."

"That sounds serious," Toussaint remarked. "What happened to her?"

"Shortly after our wedding, she decided to go back home to live with her mother in Jamaica," Mom explained.

In the final photograph, our parents appeared with their four Zimbabwean friends. Dad pointed them out:

"This is Joshua Mpofu and his young daughter, Nonhlanhla. Unfortunately, Ratie, his wife, couldn't come. This is Herbert and Agnes Taruvinga. They've now all gone home to build the new Zimbabwe."

I thought at the time that they must have been bricklayers.

Toussaint was five years' old, and I four, when this conversation took place. Our two-year-old brother, Robeson, was asleep upstairs in his cot. That's why he doesn't feature in the preface, although, like us, he is central to the story that follows.

Ten years had already passed since the photographs were taken. Our parents still kept in touch with their guests, although by that time some of them had died, and others had left the area and, in a few cases, the country, too. Little did we realise at our young age the significant part that these characters had played, or would soon come to play, in our parents' lives. They crop up again and again like the dramatis personae of a Shakespeare play, some noble, some ignominious.

The chapters that follow are grouped into three sections, the first describing our parents' activities after they married, the second providing an account of their lives before they met, and the third recounting their most recent adventures and insights. When I tested what I had written on Patrick, my American partner, I became aware that some readers might not always share my taken-for-granted vocabulary. I have taken the decision, therefore, to include a short glossary of terms.

Our shared regret as we went to bed, leaving our parents and the album in the bright warm living-room, was the absence of any photograph of us at the wedding. In August 1976, of course, we had yet to be conceived or born. It is difficult for young children to accept that there was a time before they were conceived when they did not exist, just as the elderly find it hard to face up to the finality of death and extinction.

Toussaint used to ask Dad the question: “Where was I before I was in Mommy’s tummy?”

I remember being as dissatisfied as she was with his answer:

“Nowhere: you just didn’t exist!”

“But I must have done, Daddy!”

PART I AFTER THEY MET

Chapter 1

Married to protest

A black woman, tall and light-skinned, and crowned with a definitive dome of Afro hair, stood upright and confident on the stage in front of the mike. As she began her address, her rowdy racially-mixed Brummy audience, jam-packed into Digbeth Town Hall, fell uncharacteristically silent to hang on her every word. She spoke clearly, simply and precisely, with only a hint of an American accent, about a universal struggle for racial justice, equality, and socialism. Was this the Angela Davis who befriended the Black Panthers? The brazen propagandist who Governor Ronald Reagan of California wanted to have sacked from her university post? Was this the criminal whose name was on the FBI's 'Ten Most Wanted Fugitives' List'? The very same person who President Richard Nixon had called a 'dangerous terrorist'? Had she really spent time in a US prison on a charge of 'aggravated kidnapping and first degree murder'? Yet her oratory was so level-headed, rational, and compelling. Angela drew forceful comparisons between race relations in Birmingham, Alabama, where she had been born and brought up, and the Birmingham in England which she was visiting. Ending her address with a distinctive high-fisted Black Power salute, she received an exuberant standing ovation from the appreciative crowd.

When Mom and Dad returned from honeymoon in 1976, they went to live at Dad's Oak Street address, a modern three-bedroom detached house like others in the road. The extension, of two extra bedrooms, study and wash area, wasn't completed until 1981 when I was born.

Our home was situated about one hundred yards from where Enoch Powell, the former MP for Wolverhampton South West, had stayed when visiting his constituency. We were told that he had vehemently opposed the immigration of black and Asian people, and imagined from this that he'd wanted personally to deprive us of our mom. Obviously, he was a very bad man! Our parents were keen to point out his former property on Merridale Road. Dad thought it very droll that the current owners of Enoch's old house were a black

Caribbean family who also happened to share the surname, 'Powell'. Of greater relevance from our point of view was the fact that Oak Street was near to a bus route and within walking distance of Wolverhampton town centre.

Having gained her Health Visitor Tutor's Certificate, Mel began work teaching health visitor students at Birmingham Polytechnic, now City University. Frank divided his time between his work as an Assistant Senior Counsellor with the Open University in Harborne, Birmingham, and attending the University of Warwick in pursuit of first, an MA, and then, a PhD. They both had to travel out of Wolverhampton to work. Mel wasn't to be employed again in Wolverhampton for another thirty years, Frank for another nine. Yet they went on living at the house in Oak Street until 2007, before moving to their current address in Tettenhall, three miles away.

"Why did you choose to stay at Oak Street," Toussaint wanted to know, "when both of you worked away?"

"It was a working-class, multi-racial area and, as a black and white couple, we found it convenient living there," Dad said.

"It was very multi-racial," Mom explained, "and turned out to be an ideal location for bringing up a mixed-race family. We fitted in. Curtains didn't twitch when we held arms together along the street."

"Another major consideration," Dad added, "was our involvement in local politics."

It was obvious that our parents' marriage was as much a political as a social matter. Their account of this period in their lives reads more like a campaign journal than a romance.

At the time, Mel and Frank were active in the Communist Party. Mel, as a black woman 'comrade', was given a lead role in the West Midlands in the struggle to win the black Caribbean community for the Left.

In common with others of our age, when hearing the word 'communist', we conjured up images of bloodthirsty dictators keen to snuff out all stirrings of democracy. How could our parents have sided with such people? As Mom and Dad evidently weren't bad or mad, we somehow had to get a grip on their perspective.

“Why did you become communists?” was a question we asked them repeatedly.

The first explanation we were offered related to the Communist Party’s unequivocal record on opposing discrimination against New Commonwealth immigrants at home and colonial exploitation abroad. Whatever that meant, it mollified us at the time.

Invariably, Mom would draw our attention to the exemplary lives of black communists. She was fond of three in particular. There was Paul Robeson, the American singer, film star, sportsman, and early civil rights leader, who died in 1976, in the year she had married. Claudia Jones, a Caribbean, was another lifelong communist, deported from the United States. She had fought discrimination from the time she arrived in Britain in 1955 until her death in 1965, and had the distinction of having started the Notting Hill Carnival. Finally, there was Angela Davis, the American black civil rights activist and an associate of the Black Panthers. Our parents’ admiration for these people extended as far as naming our younger brother, ‘Robeson’.

We also learned that ordinary members of the Communist Party and the Young Communist League were often prepared to go to extraordinary lengths to support the causes in which they believed. Mel was asked by Tony McNally, the Party’s regional organiser, to visit the parents of Sean Hosey, who lived in Coventry. The aim may have been to comfort and reassure the Hoseys, but Mel and Frank came away overwhelmed by the family’s resolve and commitment to the anti-apartheid movement.

Sean, their son, had been arrested in South Africa in 1972 while acting as an undercover courier for the African National Congress. As one of the ‘Pretoria Six’, he had been sentenced, in effect, to six years’ imprisonment for possessing false passports and money en route for the ANC. Despite the Party and League’s campaign to free the Pretoria Six, and appeals from MPs and the Labour Party, the apartheid regime never reduced their sentences.

Mel and Frank were constantly mixing with people who shared their beliefs. In the course of campaigning, they made friends with Left-leaning South African and Zimbabwean refugees, and members of the communist Indian Workers’ Association, especially the factions led by Jagmohan Joshi and Niranjan Singh Noor. Mel appeared on platforms alongside Mick McGahey (vice-president of the National Union of Mineworkers during the 1974 miners' strike), and Derek Robinson (otherwise known as Red Robbo, the shop stewards' leader at British Leyland), who was on the Party's regional committee.

Mel was introduced to Angela Davis during her visit to Britain at the invitation of the Communist Party. She discovered they were of the same age. When Angela came to Digbeth Civic Hall to meet the people of Birmingham, Mel formed part of the welcoming delegation and platform party and helped to warm up the audience in readiness for her speech. When I was older, my parents induced me to read Angela's autobiography. They admired the fact that she had succeeded in combining the life of an intellectual with that of a revolutionary. What's more, she had been a student of Herbert Marcuse, one of the most incisive neo-Marxist social philosophers of the twentieth century.

Mel developed a reputation, in her own right, for delivering fiery speeches denouncing discrimination and urging community mobilisation in the face of racialist attacks. She was asked by black Caribbean groups, the Indian Workers' Association, trades councils, Labour and Communist Party branches, the African National Congress, the Zimbabwean African People Union, and others, to address meetings and rallies across the West Midlands.

On these occasions, she used to wear a khaki shirt and trousers and a red beret or headscarf, giving her a distinctively military appearance. Audiences saw the slight young woman urging them on to defend their rights as their local answer to Stokely Carmichael and Eldridge Cleaver, the American Black Power leaders. Many years later, a senior police officer with whom Frank was friendly, expressed his admiration for Mel's performance and let drop that many of those listening to her had been plain-clothed police officers.

Shouting, chanting, police sirens, red banners and flashing lights! Placard-carrying organisers of the anti-racist protest against the Nazi National Front find themselves crushed against the shields of a double line of police officers who repel them with truncheon blows. From the back of the demonstration, an unruly mob lobs ill-aimed cans, bottles, stones and sticks at the barely-visible National Front parade. The hail of missiles rarely reaches its intended target, and falls indiscriminately instead on police and front-line protestors. The injured - bloody, bruised, cut, and broken nosed - are led to ambulances parked some distance from the melee. As if from nowhere, gangs of youths and children emerge from the demonstration to charge down surrounding streets, smashing windows and doors of shops and offices, before returning to seek refuge in the anonymity of the crowd. In their wake, older men and women can be seen furtively removing goods through broken shop windows and doors. This is how Dad recalled the chaotic repercussions of an anti-racist demo he'd been on.

In 1976, Mel and Frank's main political concern was the rise of organised racism, which came in the form of the National Front, a party set up in 1967 from a rag bag of Far-Right groups, including the League of Empire Loyalists, the (old) British National Party and, later, the National Socialist Movement. Its supporters could quite accurately be referred to as 'Nazi scum', the term of abuse frequently hurled at them by members of the Anti-Nazi League, an umbrella organisation formed in 1977 to make it difficult for the National Front to stage street demonstrations without incurring public protest. In Wolverhampton, the longer-standing Anti-Racist Committee eventually merged – or held meetings in common – with the Anti-Nazi League.

In 1976, the National Front demonstrated in support of Robert Relf who was being held in Birmingham's Winson Green prison for contempt of court. He had disobeyed a judge's order to take down a sign advertising his house for sale exclusively to a white English family. Mel and Frank joined an anti-racist counter-demonstration made up mainly of black people living in Handsworth and held in the vicinity of the prison. The police tried to keep the two factions separate, but the situation quickly got out of hand as bricks and timber from nearby derelict properties were used as missiles.

The following year, 1977, the tension on the streets between black and Asian communities and the National Front, protected by the police, came to a head in the events leading up to the Ladywood by-election. The National Front organised a meeting at the Boulton Road School to be addressed by John Tyndall in support of its candidate.

"We arrived early," Dad said, "to dissuade people from going in, but the police were there in their hundreds and wouldn't let us talk to them."

The demonstration grew in size and began to push forward. It was joined by large numbers of young black people who began to shower the police with bottles, cans, sticks, and masonry ripped from garden walls. For the first time, the police in Birmingham were issued with riot shields.

"It got completely out of hand," Dad said. "I could see it was going from bad to worse. We couldn't do anything, so we left."

Crowds of young people ran down the Soho Road smashing shop windows and looting. Police cars and vans were overturned and set on fire. People attacked the police station with bricks and broken paving stones to try to release demonstrators who had been arrested, but they were driven back by police baton charges.

As expected, the election was won by the Labour candidate, with the Conservative coming second, but the National Front came in third.

In February 1978, the National Front organised a meeting of its newly-formed youth movement at Digbeth Civic Hall in Birmingham. The Wolverhampton Anti-Racist Committee joined the mass picket of many thousands outside the venue, which was protected by an enormous phalanx of police. Once it became clear that the Front had eluded the protestors, the demonstration deteriorated into a major disorder, resulting in serious damage to shop windows and offices.

"What was the point of holding these demonstrations?" Toussaint inquired sceptically. "As far as I can see, they just caused trouble and inconvenience for local people and the police. They must have given the National Front publicity it didn't deserve, if its candidate came in third."

"No," Mom said exuberantly. "Local people had to be seen to be standing up to these racist hooligans. We couldn't allow them to march through a multi-racial area and get away with it. It would have been as if we didn't care. Remember that these people saw us as sub-humans, passively awaiting our deportation. We had to show the world we wouldn't tolerate such treatment. We might have ended up like the Jews in Nazi Germany if we'd sat at home doing nothing."

In the course of their activities, Mel and Frank made alliances with other West Midlands anti-racist campaigners, such as Maurice Ludmer from *Searchlight*, the Indian Workers' leaders: Jagmohan Joshi and Niranjan Singh Noor, and some prominent black Caribbeans, among them Lance Dunkley, Ivan Henry, and Maxi Hayles.

Maurice Ludmer was President of Birmingham Trades Council and founder member of the Coordinating Committee (later Campaign) Against Racial Discrimination. His experience of visiting the Belsen concentration camp when serving as a soldier in the Second World War had given his life an overarching purpose. In 1975, he set up *Searchlight,* a magazine to expose racists, fascists, and the machinations of the Far Right. It is still in existence, informing the current struggle against the British National Party. Mel and Frank used to visit his pokey Birmingham office, stacked high with yellowing records of extremist activity, to exchange information on National Front candidates standing in the Wolverhampton Council elections. Maurice was a member of the Communist Party until it ordered the Indian Workers' Association to dissolve its branches and merge with the CP proper. Along with most of the Indian comrades, he'd ripped up his party card in protest. He died suddenly in 1981.

Maurice was a friend of Jagmohan Joshi, a key organiser of the pro-Chinese faction of the Indian Workers' Association, an organisation set up to protect Indian immigrant factory and foundry workers against ill-treatment and discrimination. In 1967, it had split into two factions, supporting, on the one hand, the Communist Party of India (Marxist) and, on the other, the Maoist Chinese Communist Party line. As general secretary, Jagmohan believed in the unity of the international working class and mobilised people across national, religious, and caste lines to oppose racialism and fascism. He'd been beaten up by fascist thugs and was keen on community self-defence.

In 1979, aged 43, he collapsed and died on a rally against racial violence, police brutality, and new racialist immigration laws. Mel and Frank, who had campaigned alongside Jagmohan, went to his funeral at Sandwell Crematorium, which was attended by thousands of people who had admired and appreciated his commitment to working-class internationalism. Mel was a colleague of Jagmohan's wife, Shirley, who lectured in sociology at Birmingham Polytechnic. At a packed memorial meeting held in Birmingham Town Hall, Mel gave a message of sympathy on behalf of Wolverhampton anti-racists and the Caribbean community. Jagmohan had always lent his weight to their campaigns.

In January 1978, Exeter City and Wolverhampton Wanderers drew 2-2 in the FA cup third round. Wolves supporters invaded the Exeter pitch and caused havoc in the streets afterwards. Some of them were seen wearing Ku Klux Klan-style hoods. In the build-up to the replay in Wolverhampton, the hood idea caught on and gangs were seen wearing Klan costumes and daubing racist slogans on houses and pubs. A member of the Wolverhampton National Front was arrested for using threatening behaviour and wearing a hood with intent to provoke a breach of the peace. He was reported as saying: "I decided to make a white Ku Klux Klan mask because I knew it scares the coons".

Rumours spread quickly of a spate of unprovoked attacks on black youngsters by white gangs. One girl was said to have suffered brain damage as a result of a particularly brutal assault.

Black youngsters in Wolverhampton were in the habit of attending a youth club in the town centre known as 'The Crypt'. One night, soon after the Klu Klux Klan incidents, they learned that National Front members were meeting in a nearby pub (The George, now known as the Varsity) and were about to launch an attack on them. The black youths poured out of the club to confront a gang of a hundred whites chanting 'kill the niggers' and 'National Front'. Police intervened to keep the two factions separate. Most of the whites ran off as police reinforcements were brought in.

Witnesses disagreed as to what happened next. The black youngsters were reported to have marched aggressively around the town centre, throwing bricks, breaking windows, denting cars, and chanting 'kill the pigs'. Others claimed that the police encircled the young blacks and prevented them from dispersing. When some tried to make off down side streets, they were pursued and beaten with truncheons. Seven youths were arrested, six of them charged and detained.

A few of the young people approached Mel for help. One of them told her that he'd been punched and kicked at the police station. Mel decided to set up Black Arrow, a new organisation for black youth. Its aims included opposing racialism, encouraging self-confidence and self-reliance, and developing awareness of black-Caribbean and Asian cultures.

Mel arranged for some of the young black people who had been present on the night to describe what had happened to the Wolverhampton Anti-Racist Committee. The Committee decided to compile a dossier of attacks on black people and to organise a march to draw attention to racial harassment by Far-Right organisations and the minority communities' loss of faith in the police's willingness to protect black people.

It was thought that the march would demonstrate solidarity with the black youths' cause and help to diffuse tension by giving political direction to their grievances. Nevertheless, the plan was vehemently opposed by the town's Community Relations Officer and the Education Department – which contacted headteachers in a futile effort to dissuade young people from attending. Possibly because of this intervention, turn-out on the day swelled to over 1,200 – the majority, young black Caribbean and Asian. Though tense and volatile at times, the march passed without major incident. (One man who hurled a brick at the marchers had to be rescued by the police from an attack by three black teenage girls.)

The recently-formed Black Arrow, which had helped mobilise the young people for the march, issued its first leaflet, jointly with the Anti-Racist Committee, calling for police protection against racist attacks, proper investigation of cases reported, and action to be taken against attackers.

The Wolverhampton Ant-Racists busied themselves interviewing members of the racial minorities to gather information on racialist incidents and police neglect or abuse of black people. Frank helped to compile a dossier of eighteen case studies which was handed to the Deputy Chief Constable as a direct response to his challenge to produce evidence of racial attacks.

One of these cases involved Frank's friend and former colleague at Bilston College, Raj Mitra. In an unprovoked attack by a van driver in the street and in front of witnesses, Raj had been kicked in the stomach and punched in the face – cutting his lips and soaking his shirt in blood. He had been advised by the policeman called to the scene that if he wished to take the matter further he should see a solicitor.

The Anti-Racists' conviction that racial harassment was a pervasive aspect of life in Wolverhampton was given sensational confirmation three months later in May 1978 when eight black-Caribbean youths, on their way home from watching a late-night film, were chased and blasted with a shot gun. Seven shots were discharged and two of the youths hospitalised, each with multiple pellet wounds to his back.

This time the police took no chances. Mel and Frank, along with other community leaders, were roused from their beds and asked to attend the police station early on Sunday morning. There, they were briefed on the incident in an attempt to allay rumour and calm possible reaction. Soon after, three white men, all aged 23, were charged with attempted murder, wounding with intent, and assault. Two of them were sent to prison for six years.

In 1979, the Conservatives won the General Election with a majority of 43 seats. The new Prime Minister, Mrs Thatcher, pledged to turn back the tide of socialism by adopting free market policies, privatising nationalised industries, and curbing the power of the trade unions. Interviewed for *World in Action* in 1978, she revealed her hostility towards the black and Asian community by saying "some people have felt swamped by immigrants: they've seen the whole character of their neighbourhoods change". She then called for a halt to immigration in all but compassionate cases.

The eleven years that followed of Mrs Thatcher's premiership weakened the power of the trade union movement and opened divisions on the political Left from which it has never recovered. Labour suffered a series of disastrous electoral defeats and the defection of some of its senior members to the Social Democratic Party, while the Communist Party split into factions and virtually disappeared.

"You weren't in the Communist Party when we were growing up," Toussaint observed. "You were both members of the Labour Party."

"That's right," Dad said. "We joined the Labour Party soon after it lost the May 1979 General Election, and Mrs Thatcher became

Prime Minister. We knew the Tories were out to smash the trade unions and slash working-class living standards."

"But why," Toussaint persisted, "did you leave the Communist Party?"

"It was more a question of the Party disintegrating around us," Mom explained. "It divided into two warring camps and we didn't feel comfortable with either of them."

As the 1970s drew to a close, the Communist Party became increasingly polarised between the so-called Euro-communists associated with the journal, *Marxism Today,* and hard-line industrial and trade union comrades whose mouthpiece was the Party's newspaper, *The Morning Star.* In crude terms, the *Marxism Today* people, headed by Martin Jacques, wanted to form 'a broad democratic alliance' based on the working class, women, ethnic minorities and gays, while the *Morning Star* faction, led by Tony Chater and Mick Costello, believed that the Party's work had to focus on class struggle - narrowly defined – and the trade union movement. It didn't help matters that the Euro-communists were highly critical of the Soviet Bloc's political and economic record, while *The Morning Star* faction was unashamedly pro-Soviet. With all the in-fighting between its members, the Party soon lost sight of its traditional class enemy: the Conservatives who, under Mrs Thatcher, had become far more extreme.

"Which faction did you support?" Toussaint asked.

"Neither," Dad replied. "We knew from our own involvement that the organised working class, in the form of the trade unions and the Indian Workers' Associations, was the key to the struggle against racialism, but we were most unhappy about *The Morning Star* faction's authoritarian tendencies. The *Marxism Today* people, on the other hand, were little more than a set of Left Liberals who couldn't see that the cause of ethnic minorities and women, or gays, for that matter, was inextricably bound up with the class struggle."

"We had to ask ourselves," Mom explained, "whether the Communist Party was any more likely than the Labour Party to bring about our vision of racial equality and socialism. Our kind of anti-racist campaigning was treated by the *Morning Star* faction as peripheral to the class struggle and by the *Marxism Today* people as an alternative to it. On balance, the Labour Party, with its long-standing relationship with the trade unions, seemed to be the better option."

"Labour became more attractive," Dad added, "when Michael Foot, who'd been a member of the CND, replaced Jim Callaghan as Labour Leader. We'd both read and appreciated Foot's life of Aneurin Bevin, the Labour architect of the National Health Service".

Conservative economic policies increased the number of unemployed people, dramatically. By 1985, more than one in five of the adult population was out of work. Mrs Thatcher's early years as Prime Minister are now remembered principally for the civil unrest that broke out in urban industrial areas, starting in Bristol in 1980 and spreading to Brixton and Southall in London, Toxteth in Liverpool, and Moss Side in Manchester. Although involving significant numbers of ethnic minorities and frequently referred to as race riots, the crowds out on the streets were from different racial groups and engaged in a complex mix of anti-authority protest, defiant exuberance, vandalism, looting, and gang fights. Publicised nightly on television, the disturbances spread to other urban areas.

In Handsworth in Birmingham, gangs of white and black youths smashed their way into shops, pubs and banks. Police officers in full riot gear counter-attacked with baton charges.

Events in Wolverhampton by comparison were perfunctory. In the town centre, young white men threw bricks and bottles and looted shops, while in the suburb of Whitmore Reans, black youths stoned the police station and smashed windows in a shopping centre.

"And what good did any of the rioting do?" Toussaint quizzed.

"The rioting wasn't consciously planned like a protest demonstration," Dad replied. "The riots were spontaneous – an expression of anger, frustration and hopelessness by people with no obvious stake in the wider society."

"But they ended up destroying their own neighbourhoods," Toussaint persisted. "It just made their situation worse."

"I think you're right," Dad acknowledged, "But the government was forced to take note. In the years that followed, it poured millions of pounds into regeneration and training in the Handsworth area."

"It couldn't have had much effect," Toussaint retorted. "That part of Birmingham looks as run down as ever to me. There was another riot there in 2005."

"But for a different reason," Dad rejoined.

Lord Scarman was appointed by William Whitelaw, the Conservative Home Secretary, to conduct an inquiry into the Brixton disorders, a remit extended to include the other outbreaks of lawlessness in Southall, Toxteth, Moss Side, and the West Midlands. When Scarman sought evidence in Wolverhampton, Black Arrow submitted a written report on the rising levels of unemployment disproportionately affecting black and Asian school leavers, and the discriminatory and abusive treatment they received at the hands of the police. Mel added a long list of demands, headed by a proposal to create an independent body to investigate complaints against the police. It wasn't until 2004, over twenty years later, that the Independent Police Complaints Commission came into existence.

In his 1981 report on the disorders, Lord Scarman concluded that the relationship between local communities and the police in the West Midlands was more favourable than in Brixton, Toxteth, and Moss Side. Mel and Frank thought at the time that this was nonsense. The intense violence of the subsequent rioting in Handsworth in September 1985 was to prove them right.

They went to see the aftermath for themselves and were appalled by the scale of the devastation: the burnt-out shops, and streets strewn with debris. The arson had resulted in two people being burned to death in the post office on the Lozells Road. A former Chief Constable, David Webb, blamed a mix of mass unemployment, social deprivation, lack of amenities, diversity of racial background, and cultural ignorance. Mrs Thatcher insisted that moral responsibility lay with the rioters – not with the unemployment caused by her government's economic policies.

"Have you yourselves ever actually been in a riot?" Toussaint inquired, sceptical of Mom and Dad's first-hand knowledge.

"We've been on demonstrations that have ended in chaos and widespread lawlessness," Dad revealed. "First, the organisers, and then the police completely lose control. The police mass in large numbers to deal with the more unruly demonstrators, but often this results in the withdrawal of normal police cover elsewhere, giving people without any overt political motivation the opportunity to charge around, break into shops, and make off with their contents. I've witnessed quite terrifying levels of violence, intimidation, and destruction of property on these occasions which, in my view, amounted to full-scale rioting."

"Were you frightened?" Toussaint asked.

"What I found most disconcerting," Dad observed, "was the speed with which a situation that starts off peacefully can descend into chaos. You simply don't know what's going to happen next!"

"Why do so many people join in the rioting?" Toussaint quizzed.

"Perhaps a better question to ask is why more people don't get involved," Dad said. "Through my work at the College, I knew some of the young people who had been on the rampage. They found running around the streets and stealing from the shops a very exhilarating exercise – a bit like some well-to-do people get a 'high' from a shopping spree. Remember many of the youngsters lead dreary lives and are hard up. Many are students, or unemployed, or low paid, with poor prospects and little to lose. Even as a lecturer, I found it very difficult to convince them that the path to prosperity lay through education or training."

"'Mindless vandalism' and 'wanton thuggery'! That's how the newspapers describe it." Toussaint remarked.

"Nonsense!" Dad said. "They're as rational and purposeful as you and I! Journalists just lack the will or imagination to read the rioters' mindset. Understanding their motives, of course, is not the same as condoning their actions. One obvious consequence is the destruction of the community facilities that all of us benefit from. If only they'd factor that in before they start!"

Chapter 2

My father's testicles

"Is that Mr Reeves?"
"Yes that's right."
"You're the chairman of the Race-Mixing Association?"
"Yes. Whom am I speaking to?"
"You're speaking to the National Front."
"Why are you phoning?"
"You race-mixing bastard!"
"Why did you swear like that?"
"We're going to kick your fucking balls in for you, OK?"
"Why do you want to do that?"
"Don't go out of your house. We know where you live."
"Why take that attitude?"
"We're going to pull your fucking bollocks off."
"Why?"
"Wolverhampton's been fucked up enough with wogs."
"What's your name?"
"Never mind my name."
"Are you threatening me with physical violence?"
(Phone call ends.)

Fortunately, especially from my point of view and that of my brother, the National Front never succeeded in castrating my father!

My sister, Toussaint, was born on the maternity ward at New Cross Hospital on Boxing Day 1979, thus initiating the train of events described in this chapter. As Mel had suffered a late miscarriage previously, our parents were delighted and relieved at her arrival. Mel had been very careful with this pregnancy to the extent of seeking medical advice on the advisability of taking a plane flight. The doctor told her that a holiday in Jamaica would do her and the unborn child a power of good. Frank recounts how, in Jamaica, Mel gorged herself ravenously on land crabs in her friend Sonia's garden. He jokes annoyingly that that's what little girls are made of, referring, I hope, only to Toussaint.

Mel and Frank went to Aunt Epsi and Mr Son for dinner on Christmas Day. Mel complained of feeling uncomfortable. She put it down to the amount of food she'd eaten, or to the excitement of watching Robert Redford in *The Sting*, a film showing that evening on television but, on the way home, she realised that the baby was on its way.

Toussaint was named after Toussaint L'Ouverture, the black slave who led the first successful slave rebellion in St Domingue, now Haiti, and who believed that the values of the French revolution – liberty, equality, and fraternity – applied to black citizens as well as white. My parents, I understand, were inspired by CLR James's book, *The Black Jacobins,* penned, as one reviewer put it, "with the flame of ardent personal feeling."

Grandma Phyllis Reeves was initially shocked by the name, but consoled herself with the thought that it translated as 'All Saints (day)'. Curious, she soon discovered William Wordsworth's famous sonnet, written in honour of Toussaint, part of which reads:

'O miserable Chieftain! where and when
Wilt thou find patience? Yet die not; do thou
Wear rather in thy bonds a cheerful brow:
Though fallen thyself, never to rise again,
Live, and take comfort.'

She copied the poem out in a letter of congratulation to her daughter-in-law, but couldn't resist adding at the end: 'I think it's a bit much of Wordsworth to advise him to 'wear a cheerful brow' when he's dying of pneumonia in a freezing French chateau. Do your best to keep my grandchild warm.'

The experience of bringing Toussaint into the world led Mel and Frank for the moment to focus their campaigning zeal on the reform of hospital practices. When Frank accompanied Mel on her ante-natal visits to the hospital, he was asked to stand outside the waiting room. On inquiring why, he was told curtly that these were the rules and that he must leave. This provoked him into writing a letter of complaint, pointing out the inconsistency between the women-only waiting-room policy and the health service's stated aim of encouraging men to participate in parenting, and to attend their baby's birth. The policy of excluding fathers was changed soon afterwards.

When Toussaint was born, Frank was asked by the midwife to provide missing details on the Notification of Birth form. He noticed over her shoulder that she'd already entered Toussaint's ethnicity as West Indian, and challenged her decision, but she refused to change it. He decided to send a letter to Reginald Prentice, the Minister of State for Health, to seek clarification on the legal aspects of the Notification of Births ethnic classification. Many months later, he received a bureaucratically-framed reply from the Department of Health informing him merely that there was no statutory obligation to supply information about the ethnic origins of the child, and completion of the monitoring form was entirely optional. Only a very few hospitals, of which Wolverhampton was one, were monitoring by ethnicity at the time. None of this had much bearing on Frank's quarrel with the midwife.

Fourteen months after Toussaint was born, I arrived on the maternity unit at New Cross. It was St Valentine's Day 1981. Like Toussaint, I was called after the leader of a slave revolt, this time, the mighty Spartacus, the white gladiator from Thrace, who caused the Romans so much grief. In deference to my being a girl, the name was feminised to 'Spartaca'.

When I was older, I wanted to know whether my parents had been watching the Hollywood blockbuster featuring Kirk Douglas or, at least, reading the Howard Fast novel on which it was based. No, they said, they'd been inspired by an historical account of the life of Spartacus written in 1944 by Frank Ridley, a member of the Independent Labour Party and National Secular Society. Looking through Dad's copy, I discovered that Ridley had dedicated his little book to 'the immortal memory of Rosa Luxemburg, Karl Liebknecht, and the German 'Spartacists' of 1919'. What was more, Dad had bought the book directly from Ridley whom he had met on the street in London. The author had rewarded him with his autograph - F A Ridley - scrawled on the title page.

I'm often asked whether I'm satisfied with my parents' choice of name. People recognise why they chose it, but assert that they would never do it to their own children. I think my parents wanted my name to have an effect on me and had high hopes that their children would join them in campaigning for a fairer world. But my name didn't make me who I am. My parents did that by shaping my values and opinions.

I am happy to have an unusual name that can be remembered easily. Whenever I'm introduced, people always react with remarks like:

"No, I am Spartacus!"
"That's an unusual name!"
"Where's that from?"
"Are you of Greek descent?"

Some people's eyes light up when they hear my name, typically those of a Left-wing disposition. Invariably, I have to spell my name and sometimes to argue to ensure that it's spelled correctly. Once, when I gave my name to hire a taxi to pick me up from Cineworld in Wolverhampton, the operator retorted: "I want your name, not the movie you've been watching".

My brother was born nearly three years after me in December 1983. He was named Robeson Mandela, after Paul Robeson, as previously mentioned, and Nelson Mandela, who was to become the first black president of South Africa. Mandela was at the time imprisoned on Robben Island, and, according to Mrs Thatcher, a member of a terrorist organisation: the African National Congress. Initially, Dad worried about the choice of name, not because Mrs Thatcher thought Mandela to be a terrorist, but because, unlike Robeson, he was still alive and had time to renege on his principles. Fortunately, Mandela has grown ever since in moral stature, leaving my brother with more to live up to than either of his sisters.

When I asked Robeson recently whether he liked his name, he replied that he was proud to be called after such a brave and multi-talented man as Paul Robeson, but he had yet to meet someone of his generation who'd heard of him. His middle name 'Mandela', however, was instantly recognisable and always provoked a reaction, sometimes including questions about his parents' politics. My brother's name, like mine, was always misspelled, which led him to abbreviate it to 'Rob', whenever he made telephone calls.

Mom worked as long as she could before her confinements to have more time with us but, as soon as her period of paid maternity leave came to an end, returned to her job teaching health visitor students at Birmingham Polytechnic. In those days, 'paternity leave' was a sarcastic taunt levelled at the work shy.

From a very young age, Toussaint was transported from Monday to Friday in her carrycot to the nursery at Aston University where Dad was employed at the Research Unit on Ethnic Relations. This arrangement lasted until I was born. At that point, my parents decided to find someone to look after the two of us at home.

Our first nanny was an older Jamaican woman with grown-up children of her own. Despite her old-fashioned ways, she managed her responsibilities well until her rising blood pressure forced her to stop. After she left, we experienced a succession of poor, unreliable, and potentially irresponsible carers, none staying for more than a couple of months. When Robeson arrived, Mom was only able to stabilise the situation with her maternity leave. Fortunately, it was then that she hit upon a permanent, convenient, and reliable solution to her day-time child care requirements.

Our next-door neighbours were a Sikh family: Gurnam Singh, his wife Gurbax, and their four sons, Baldip, Baldish, Jaswinder, and Jagwinder. Mom and Dad had always got on well with them, despite the fact that neither parent spoke much English, and had to rely on the older children to translate. Almost every month, but especially at Diwali and other festivals, Gurbax would send round plates for us all, piled high with samozas, meat and vegetable curry, chapattis, sweet rice, and other food. Dad used to reciprocate by calling in at Christmas with a bottle of whisky to share with Gurnam, until he became religiously devout.

Gurbax had an industrial sewing machine at the house and would make up clothes from the bags of cut materials delivered to the door. The idea that it might be more economical to make a living from caring for the neighbours' children dawned on both women simultaneously. From then on, we spent weekdays with Gurbax and the boys next door, until our parents, on returning from work, came to collect us.

Toussaint and Jagwinder were of a similar age and Gurbax would walk them together to Merridale Primary School at the bottom of the road. Soon afterwards, I, too, went along, followed by Robeson a few years later. Gurbax treated Robeson like another son, referring to him as "my youngest child".

To enable them to pursue evening and weekend activities, Mel and Frank had to make additional baby-sitting arrangements. Following a period of trial and error, they were introduced fortuitously to the Potter family, who lived in Burton Crescent. After her husband died, Mrs Muriel Potter, who was born in St Kitts, brought up her twelve children - ten of them girls - by herself. One reason for the size of the family was that she'd had three sets of twins. Pat Potter was our regular babysitter to begin with, followed by her younger sister, Margaret, who, from the age of fourteen, looked after us until we were able to manage for ourselves. Margaret, too, had a twin called Venetta, but she was less keen on the babysitting.

After Margaret left home, she came to live in a one-bedroom flat in Oak Street. Now aged 45, with a degree in sociology and philosophy, and a Diploma in Nursing, she works in a GP surgery. Margaret and her sisters remain close and ever-helpful friends of the family.

Mel and Frank grew to know most of their immediate neighbours in Oak Street, and still stay in touch with them. A spare bedroom at Oak Street meant that Mel and Frank could provide accommodation overnight, a facility made use of by many of our parents' friends and colleagues, often for months at a time.

When we were young, our most frequent overnight visitor was Sadun Perera, one of 'the best men' at our parents' wedding. Sad and Frank would drink tea or beer, depending on the time of day, and engage in interminable discussions about politics, philosophy and sociology, of which we, as children, understood nothing. Sad was always kind to us but couldn't be trusted to baby-sit because he was so impractical. He scarcely knew how to draw the curtains or turn on the gas fire, let alone prepare food for children or change nappies. We had to show him how to work the washing machine and cooker.

Trevor and Jackie Coote, another black and white couple, recognisable in the wedding photographs, lived further along the street. Frank had taught them both at college and helped them when their respective parents had tried to put a stop to their relationship. Sadun also knew the Cootes, and stayed overnight at their house, too. As children, we imagined him as a stray cat, visiting any home that put out cream.

Our neighbours at number 7 were Wilfred and Violet Adams, who were both severely deaf. They frequently needed help in dealing with casual callers. When I decided to learn sign language, they invited me into their house to practise. They gave us toffees or chocolate biscuits at Christmas.

Icylyn, Sonson, and their son, Craig, lived across the street and were on good terms, despite Sonson's habit of parking his truck on the street outside overnight. When he went on holiday to Jamaica, he would bring Frank back a flask of rum. Mel and Frank were on first name terms with many of the other families in the street: Asian, black, and white, and we knew the local children who, like us, attended Merridale Primary School.

Our parents did their shopping on Saturday mornings. We walked into town, Mom holding our hands, Dad pushing Robeson along in his push chair. Most of our food was bought at Wolverhampton market, meat and fish inside, and vegetables in the outdoor section. The place teamed with Asian, black, and white people, of all shapes and sizes. The crowded aisles were cluttered with boxes and trolleys, making it easy for us to become separated and lost. Mom visited the stalls of the Indian and Jamaican traders for the ingredients she needed for Caribbean cooking. By the early 1980s, there was an immense choice of exotic foodstuffs, although yam, dashine, sweet potato, green bananas, breadfruit, chocho, ochra, and chilli peppers were expensive compared with the locally-grown produce. Spices, such as chilli, coriander, garam masala, and curry powder, could be bought cheaply and in large quantities from the Indian stalls.

In 1981, John Jones, a County Councillor and member of the Graiseley Ward Labour Party, told Frank that an allotment had become available near Jeffcock Road. John rode a bicycle about town, built a compost heap in his garden (which he peed on regularly), and spent his spare time cultivating his allotment. He advised Frank to go on his own to see the secretary of the Graiseley and District Co-operative Allotment Society. Frank did as he was told and, on paying the membership fee and acquiring his shares in the gardening co-op, took possession of plot 57, together with its tumbledown shed and ancient fruit trees. The gardener in the family, of course, was Mom, who, in Jamaican family tradition, had always wanted to produce her own food. Dad, being more of an artist than a peasant, was mostly interested in planting flowers.

The much-neglected allotment was overgrown with weeds and urgently needed clearing. Mel decided to organise a traditional Jamaican digging party, involving the mobilisation of a team of young men to turn over and clear the ground in return for a plentiful supply of food, alcohol, and entertainment. Historically, the men would hoe in time to digging songs, but in the era of the ghetto blaster they preferred to listen to the latest reggae music.

The subsequent Black Arrow digging party, fuelled by an adequate supply of Red Stripe beer and Breakers, rice and peas, and curried mutton, achieved more than the clearance of the land. A special meeting of the Co-operative Association's committee was called to discuss how one of its allotments had ended up in the hands of a gang of young black hooligans and whether anything could be done about it. Up until that point, the Co-op had managed to maintain an all-white membership.

On Sundays and holidays, our parents would take us with them to the allotment, where we would pick the strawberries, dig for worms, and play games, while they worked. Robeson would sit and watch us in his bouncing chair.

On more than one occasion, Mel was asked by people whose gardens bordered on the allotments how she'd managed to circumvent the white-men-only rule.

"We've been trying for years to get an allotment for our Indian neighbours," one man confided, "but the committee's never approved."

As members of the committee grew older and relinquished their honorary positions, the de facto colour bar gave way and Asian and black gardeners were admitted in increasing numbers to the Coop. By the time Mel and Frank gave up their allotment in 2009, thirty years later, ethnic minorities were far better represented and were starting to grow noticeably different crops, such as coriander, pumpkin, peppers and sweet corn. A long-term decline in tobacco growing in favour of the cultivation of purple poppies seemed to reflect the demographic shift from pipe-smoking white men in wellies, to Asian patriarchs in baggy trousers and sandals.

Shortly after Toussaint was born, Mel and Frank held the inaugural meeting of the Mixed Race Support Association at the Posada pub in Lichfield Street, Wolverhampton. An invitation was extended to people whom they knew were in mixed-race relationships, of mixed-race descent, or had adopted children from a different race. About thirty people turned up, some coming from as far away as

Birmingham and Shrewsbury. It was agreed that the new association would promote the interests of families with members from different racial or ethnic groups and racially-mixed children. It would campaign against racial discrimination, particularly as it affected people of mixed race.

Members took on the job of challenging the racial myths and propaganda surrounding mixed social, sexual, and marital relationships and the use of ignorant and insulting names like 'half-caste', half-breed', 'mixed blood', or 'mulatto'. The new group sought to celebrate the merits and advantages of being of mixed race and to show public pride in trans-racial relationships, mixed-race descent, and the birth of mixed-race children. It adopted the slogan, 'the best of both worlds'.

The constitution of the association included the aim of campaigning against racist and fascist organisations in recognition of the threat they posed to a multi-racial future. No prizes for guessing who'd added that in. There was some debate, however, over the key term 'mixed race'. Why not 'melting pot' or 'harmony', like similar organisations elsewhere? Mel and Frank were adamant that these were euphemisms: polite ways of avoiding the social reality of racial difference, in the same way that white people preferred to call black people 'coloured'. For like reason, our parents have always refused to use the terms 'dual' or 'mixed heritage', arguing that it is racial, not cultural, prejudice and discrimination, that has made life more difficult for us and them. The Mixed Race Support Association began to challenge the prevailing stereotypes of mixed-race people.

The death of three-year-old Adam Bunsie, drowned and put in a rubbish bin by his mother because of her shame at giving birth to a 'half-caste' child, provided the Association with the opportunity to send a letter to the local newspaper. Readers were told that many people in Wolverhampton were proud to be the parents of mixed-race children, or proud to be of mixed race themselves. The Association also called on reporters to refrain from using the insulting term, 'half-caste'.

Annoyed by police officers' habitual use of 'half-caste' to describe crime suspects, the Association wrote to the Chief Constable asking that, if race was relevant to identification, the term 'mixed-race' should be used instead. The Chief Constable responded with the reminder that 'half-caste' was in common use to mean a person who had parents of different races. He believed that no-one, police officers included, had any intention of using the expression deliberately to insult. He personally hadn't been able to find any independent evidence of it carrying a negative connotation.

With the approach of the local elections, Frank, on behalf of the Association, wrote to the *Express and Star* to point out that the National Front, with its slate of local candidates, was a self-acclaimed racist party with a programme of repatriation, or rather, the mass-expulsion, of British citizens. Not only did they want to throw out black immigrants, but black people born in Britain, their white husbands or wives, and mixed-race children. Furthermore, the Front had insulted the Association's members by describing the personal relations between people of different races as 'mongrelisation', 'race treason', and 'race genocide'. Frank asked voters not to support the Front or its policies.

Immediately after the letter's appearance, the abusive telephone calls began, night after night for the first week, and then less regularly for a further month or so. The callers were consistent:

"Mr Reeves?"
"Yes."
"Frank or Francis?"
"None of your business."
"You fucking wog-loving bastard…
"You nigger loving fucking bastard, you…
"A fire bomb through your window tonight."
"Why?"
"Because you're a fucking nigger-loving cunt."
"Why do you say things like that?"
"You're a race-mixing bastard for a start."
"That's true!"
"You called us Nazis."
"Nazis behave exactly like you're doing now."
"We're not Nazis."
"Nazis put fire bombs through people's windows."
(Phone call ends.)

And many more of like ilk, many dwelling on the damage they would do to my Dad's testicles. Frank always argued back, rather than put the phone down, in the hope of identifying the callers by tape recording their voices and the threats they were making. He'd recently acquired a miniature tape recorder with a telephone adapter to assist him in his job as a research worker.

He went next to lodge a complaint with the police about the abusive calls and the threats of violence. The police showed little interest. They couldn't do anything, they said, and advised him to go ex-directory. On learning that there was supportive taped evidence, however, they offered to listen to it. Shortly afterwards, the abusive calls stopped, but nothing further was ever heard from the local police.

Frank decided to write to the Chief Constable asking whether any progress had been made in identifying and prosecuting the culprits for the serious threats of arson and assault. The Chief Constable replied that he was satisfied that the incident had been fully investigated, but that it had not been possible to trace the offenders.

I couldn't recall the Mixed Race Support Association offering me any help when I was growing up. "What happened to this Association of yours?" I inquired.

"It was active for about five years," Mom replied, "but then, as we pursued other interests, it became just a network of old friends who'd shared the same experiences."

"After that," Dad added, "It lived on for many years as a name and address on official mailing lists."

"We set it up as a group to campaign for the rights of the emerging mixed-race population," Mom explained, "but that wasn't why most of the members joined. They wanted us to provide them with specialist services."

"What services?" I asked, intrigued.

Many of the original members had been white couples, often living in all-white areas in Shropshire and Staffordshire, who had adopted black or mixed-race children. Others were single white mothers struggling to bring up mixed-race children by themselves. The organisation was also asked to give talks to white foster parents caring for black and mixed-race children. Most people just wanted practical help with rearing their families. They hoped to give their children opportunities to play with others of the same appearance and to have black adult role models on hand. They requested lessons on how to comb and plait curly hair. Many needed emotional support and companionship to deal with the rejection they'd experienced at the hands of family members, former friends, or neighbours.

"Most were bent on a social club," Dad said, "that laid on weekend outings, garden parties, and multi-cultural picnics. They didn't want me blackmailing them into attending a rally against the National Front."

"The picnics were all right to begin with," Mom reflected. "We took you all, including Robeson in his carrycot. But we hadn't had picnics in mind when we set up the Association."

Chapter 3

The black man's bar

How were we, as the children of a black mother and white father, regarded by black Caribbean people in Wolverhampton? For most, as in the Caribbean, being racially mixed was not an issue. Reassuringly, the motto below the Jamaican coat of arms reads 'out of many, one people', which is just as well, given the extent of the racial mixing that has taken place on that island over the centuries. Nevertheless, the historic legacy of a stratified slave society in Jamaica still imbues the shade of one's skin with significance, and gives rise to an ever-present but rarely openly-expressed politics of race and colour.

Mom told us once how upset she'd been when she overheard Black Nationalists in Wolverhampton describing mixed-race children as 'the un-dead', and advancing the theory that we were all the product of 'psycho-pathological rape', the logic being that no sane individual would ever agree voluntarily to parent a mixed-race baby. In their view, we were neither white nor black, unwanted by either side of the great racial divide, and entirely bereft of genetic, social and psychological roots. Not only are there white bigots but, as the events described in this chapter demonstrate, there are cruel, obnoxious, discriminatory, and racist black people, too.

When Black Arrow was formed after the 1978 disturbances in Wolverhampton, Mel persuaded the young people in the group to make a list of their grievances and demands. Foremost was the wish to see an end to racial harassment and attack by Far-Right gangs and what the young people saw as complicity by the police in aiding and abetting the perpetrators. But there was also a more general and deeply-felt concern for the prospects of the black community in Wolverhampton and, especially, its black youth.

Mel convinced the group that it should try to express its demands as a series of practical and achievable policies which the local council might be able to act upon, particularly if it saw that they had the backing of the majority of black people in the town. She pointed out that black people themselves could use the limited political power at their disposal to solve their own problems.

The young people complained about the disrespectful way they were treated at school and of being harassed by the police whenever they gathered in the town centre.

"We've nothing to do, nowhere to go, and no job prospects when we leave school," was how they summed up their situation.

When urged to progress from stating their problems to finding solutions to them, they made two practical suggestions. Black Arrow should start a night school for Caribbean children to help them with their education. And it should campaign for a Caribbean youth centre, specifically designed to meet black people's cultural needs.

Shortly afterwards, in the Spring of 1978, the Black Arrow Night School was set up in the New Testament Church of God at Heath Town. Within three weeks, the School had enrolled fifty students aged from 5 to 16 through personal contact and advertisements in the black churches. Mel and Frank also managed to persuade ten people to volunteer as teachers and teaching assistants, of whom about half were qualified teachers, some of them black.

From the outset, the School was set up with three aims. It sought to increase the sense of community purpose and pride among Wolverhampton's black Caribbean families. It wanted to improve their children's educational performance, particularly in the key disciplines of English and Maths. And it set out to provide information about the history, culture, and struggles of the Caribbean people.

At first, classes were held twice a week on Wednesday and Friday evenings. While the Church's support was most welcome at the time, the adults found the pews a demanding teaching environment, while the children had difficulties in adjusting to study in a place where normally they were expected to pray. The following year, the local education authority was persuaded to provide classrooms free of cost at St Stephen's Primary School in Woden Road, close by. Owing to the intensity of the work and the heavy demands on volunteer staff, sessions were reduced in September 1979 to one night per week.

The School was divided on the basis of age into five mixed-ability classes of approximately ten pupils. Older classes were provided with an hour of maths and an hour of English teaching every evening that the school met. Despite the small groups, methods remained somewhat formal. A tuck shop was provided in the short break between sessions. The teachers took it in turn to lead assemblies on topical issues of concern to black people. Pupils were urged to work for their individual success as black people, as well as to devote themselves to the needs of the black community and humanity as a whole.

Toussaint and I both remembered the Night School at Woden Road, which we had to attend regularly, as both our parents taught there and Margaret, our baby-sitter, helped out, too. We still recognise and acknowledge former pupils when we meet them in town.

"You used to take Robeson in his carrycot," Toussaint recalled. "I remember him crawling into the tuck shop and eating all the sweets."

"What I liked best," she added, "were the summer projects, when you took the school away on holiday, and we all had to sleep together in those crowded dormitories!"

For many years, the Black Arrow Youth Group collaborated with the West Midlands Caribbean Association in running a children's summer project, which recruited increasingly from the regular attenders at the night school. This enabled the School to extend its educational work into a residential week, an arrangement that contributed spectacularly to the youngsters' enthusiasm and esprit de corps. The summer project blended sport, leisure and education, with the added discipline of communal living away from home.

The first residential was held in a large cottage on the Brown Clee Hill near Burwarton in Shropshire. Frank remembers taking pupils for a long walk over the hill to Clee St Margaret, where he fell into conversation with the local vicar, curious to discover more about the thirty or so black youngsters traipsing through his village.

Clee St Margaret happened to be holding its village fete and games that day. The vicar, little realising what he was letting himself in for, invited the youngsters to join in, an invitation which they accepted with alacrity. There were three-legged races, sack races, relay races, apple-bobbing, and a great many more games besides. Success was rewarded with prizes, usually of sweets and chocolate.

The Black Arrow children competed with gusto, unashamedly thrashing the white village children in almost every event.

It was here at Clee St Margaret that the youthful Denise Lewis, subsequently awarded gold in the heptathlon at the 2000 Sydney Olympics, first showed her sporting prowess by winning the sack race, although at the time her international potential went unrecognised.

By the time it came to the apple-bobbing, the village children were becoming mutinous, and the organisers of the games desperate to find other winners. When a local child was declared to have won, the black youngsters, who'd seen the true victor with apple in mouth, began arguing with the judges, until the decision was overturned in their favour. At this point, Frank decided it was high time for his party to leave before race relations deteriorated any further. The School pupils marched from the field like true Olympians, giving three resounding cheers for the people of Clee St Margaret.

Other summer projects were held at Hanley Swan near Malvern and at a hostel near Pwllheli on the Lleyn Peninsula. Mel and Frank used to visit the venues beforehand to prepare the field work exercises. The educational aspects of the residentials were refined with the children organised into competing all-age teams with teenage 'leaders' put in charge. One of the most successful and natural of the School's 'leaders' was Pamela Anderson (now Smith) who went on to train as a teacher and has since emigrated to the United States, where she now works as a curriculum manager.

In Wales, the youngsters climbed Snowdon, descended into the Llechwedd slate caverns near Blaenau Ffestiniog, visited Beddgelert, and went from Abersoch on a fishing trip around St Tudwal's islands.

Half way up Snowdon, having already eaten his packed lunch, one boy asked where he could buy crisps. Mel and Frank told him he would have to wait until he reached the top where there was a shop. He assumed they were joking, but just in case, he asked a passer-by coming down the mountain. "Yes, sure!" she replied, "and there's a railway station, too!" which of course, there was.

In the Llechwedd caverns, an old miner employed as a guide was eagerly asked the answers to questions on the work sheets. "Where are you from?" he asked inevitably and was told "Wolverhampton". Later, he approached Frank and complimented him on the children's good manners and enthusiasm. "You must be very proud of them," he remarked. "You wouldn't believe the misbehaviour of some school parties who come down here!"

The Black Arrow youngsters enjoyed the story of Gelert, the faithful hound, so unfairly slain at the hands of Prince Llywelyn, who later experienced intense remorse when he discovered that the dog had, in fact, killed a marauding wolf and his baby son was safe. Naturally, the moral of the story - not to jump to hasty conclusions on the basis of superficial appearances - was drawn out and applied to presumptions based on the colour of a person's skin.

On their fishing trip, the youngsters were lucky to catch plenty of mackerel, sufficient to provide the whole school with a fish and chips supper. To everyone's amusement, all Frank caught was a bony dog fish that had to be thrown back in.

The Night School was put on a more formal footing when it registered as a charity under the name, Afro-Caribbean Education Trust. Mel remained chair of the Trust and de facto Headteacher until 1990 when she left to become Head of Department of Nursing at the University of Central Lancashire.

We had long been aware of the effort involved in keeping the voluntary educational project on track for a decade or more, but not conscious until recently of the specific difficulties our parents encountered in doing so. We'd assumed without question that black people would support any project aimed at improving their children's education. What we hadn't envisaged was that they could disagree so profoundly on how to go about the task.

The Black Arrow project was set up in the belief that schools run by white teachers were failing black children, and that, by making some kind of special provision, those children could be helped to succeed. But in what way did the provision have to be special? The Night School had been faced from the start with a series of questions about its stance towards white people and the organisations controlled by them, such as the local schools and education authority. How was the School to pursue its purpose? How should it select its pupils and volunteer teachers? And what exactly should be taught?

Decisions such as these could not be made without taking into account ideas and practices prevailing at the time among the black community and its leaders. Mel and Frank were steeped in the anti-racist international socialism of the Labour movement which saw education primarily as a class issue. Black people were part of the working class, but faced additional problems of discrimination, stereotyping and neglect. Fundamentally, these were a product of the competition, real or perceived, between ethnic groups for scarce social resources, such as jobs, accommodation, hospital beds, or school places.

Many black leaders and professionals, however, were sympathetic to an alternative set of ideas, best described as 'Black Nationalism', deriving from a variety of political traditions, including Garveyism, Pan-Africanism, Rastafarianism, and the American Black Power movement. All explained black people's problems as a product of their contact with and treatment by white people, and saw the answer in terms of separate racial development, as either a temporary or a permanent solution.

Jamaican-born Marcus Garvey sought deliverance for black people in a new world in which they would no longer be slaves or serfs, but creators of a new black civilisation. Black skin would become a glorious symbol of national greatness in an independent negro nation in Africa. From this point of view, the aim of the Night School was to inculcate pride in being black.

Pan-Africanism is an anti-colonial political movement that seeks to liberate Africa from European domination and to uplift African people for life in a modern industrial state. In the context of the Night School, it could be interpreted as a warning against the uncritical acceptance of white values and the dangers of allowing white teachers to colonise the minds of black children.

The Rastafarians, a Jamaican religious sect distinguished by the wearing of 'locks' and 'tams', and the use of marijuana as a sacrament, reject the worldliness of 'Babylon', the term chosen to describe an evil godless white world and its agents: politicians, police, social workers and, not least, teachers. As a broad generalisation, the movement is distrustful of white teachers' motives and values, and the effect on black children of white-dominated schools.

Black Power comes about when black people recognise the heritage they share in common, and unite to take control of their own destiny. Stokeley Carmichael and Charles Hamilton's overriding message was that schools for black children must be based in and controlled by the black community itself.

In this context, we began to see our parents' relationship in a different light. Far from bridging the gap between the white and black communities, they were seen by white racists as traitors to their respective races, and by Black Nationalists as a threat to the development of a proper black consciousness and racial pride.

In the Night School situation, Black Nationalist ideas translated into questions such as whether Mel with a white husband, could possibly serve as a suitable black role model to head the project. Should white people, like Frank, be accepted as volunteer teachers? If white children were brought along by their black friends and wanted to enrol at the night school, should they be accepted or turned away? And wasn't it just a waste of time cooperating with the inherently racist white teachers who ran the local schools?

These challenges forced the Night School to spell out its position with greater clarity and to point out that it accepted children of all races, and was most willing to make use of the services of suitably-committed white teachers.

There was less agreement among volunteers over the content of the curriculum, which ended up as a compromise between advocates of basic studies, such as English and maths, and those who wanted a syllabus consisting only of black studies, black history, and black consciousness-raising. Should the curriculum aim to provide black children with the basic skills to succeed in mainstream schools, or should it concentrate on developing black self-awareness and an alternative community-reliant approach to the white educational environment?

Most vocal in their support of black consciousness-raising were the volunteer black graduates - ironically, those who had benefited most from the British education system, a point that some of the less well-educated helpers, committed to the grind of teaching literacy and numeracy, were quick to point out.

The black graduates were not always the most successful or popular teachers. The children used to complain that they didn't understand what they were talking about. When it eventually dawned on eager black graduate volunteers that they did not have a special hot line to the soul of the black child simply by sharing the same skin colour, they frequently became disillusioned and left the School.

The underlying tension among the band of volunteers was illustrated by the events that unfolded when Jamaican creole, or 'patois', was used in the classroom. For his English class, my father took one of the Louise Bennett's Jamaican creole poems and wrote a comprehension exercise to accompany it. He persuaded Berti Nedrick, a Jamaican friend and teacher, who gave recitations at local Caribbean evenings, to tape the poem, and he played the recording to his pupils. The pupils were given a photocopy of the poem together with the comprehension questions and asked to write their answers in standard English in their exercise books.

On a subsequent occasion, a black graduate teacher took photocopies of the poem to another group and asked the children to read the verses aloud. Some of his pupils began to sulk and refused his request point blank. Others used the opportunity to demonstrate their proficiency in speaking creole. The teacher then asked them to write down what the poem meant in their exercise books. Some children obliged him by writing in creole.

The consequences were dramatic. Mel received a stream of telephone calls from indignant parents complaining about the teaching of creole, and threatening to remove their children from the school. Three children never returned. A parents' meeting had to be called to reassure the community that the school wasn't teaching 'patois'.

"We send them to school to learn the Queen's English", Mel was told. "Without it, they won't get jobs."

Mel was condemned by the black teacher who had caused the furore and by his friends. They protested that she should have taken a firm line with the parents, emphasising the value of creole as 'nation language'. In their eyes, my mother was as ashamed of her own culture and roots as the ill-informed parents.

The hard-line Black Nationalists walked out, and attempted to set up a rival school, and to take their favourite pupils with them. The children's parents and the established Caribbean organisations and church groups remained solidly behind the head teacher and the Black Arrow School survived.

In 1977, before the disturbances, the Wolverhampton Council for Community Relations had investigated youth facilities for black Caribbeans and found them deficient. Young black people wanted separate provision to accommodate their cultural preferences, to be able to relax in a discrimination-free environment and congregate without being seen as a threat to others. Black Arrow members' demand for 'a place of our own' was now taken up by a Steering Committee made up of representatives from most of the black organisations in the town. It proceeded to endorse proposals to set up an Afro-Caribbean cultural centre.

At first, the Steering Committee envisaged converting an empty Anglican church with the help of the Inner Area Programme and money from charities. However, Wolverhampton's Labour-controlled Council was persuaded to provide a redundant office block in the town centre and make a grant of £150,000 from the Inner Area fund to refurbish it.

The Conservatives objected to the proposed cultural centre on the grounds that it would perpetuate racial difference and amounted to 'racial integration in reverse'. They were supported by an Indian Labour Councillor, Dr B Chakraborty, who said the centre would be communally divisive and set one group against the other. The Ratepayers Association described the grant as a deliberate insult to the ratepayers: white minorities had never received financial aid of this kind.

Mel, as secretary of the Cultural Centre Steering Committee, was expected to defend the Council's decision from these attacks. She wrote to the press to point out that the Centre had no intention of excluding whites and to suggest that it would 'discriminate in reverse' was absurd. As for the ratepayers, black Wulfrunians paid taxes and rates like everyone else and were entitled to their share of council leisure provision. She added that the integration that everybody wanted could only occur in situations of equality and respect, one of the prerequisites for which was that, after years of neglect, black Caribbeans' cultural needs were recognised and catered for. Instead of blaming black people for failing to integrate, white people should do something about the colour bar which still existed in many of Wolverhampton's private clubs.

Soon after the Council had agreed to fund the Cultural Centre, the National Front announced it would hold a protest march to demand the money be spent on 'indigenous' people. The newly-formed Anti-Nazi League planned a massive counter-demonstration. Despite fears of widespread violence, the Chief Constable refused to ban the National Front march. Peace was preserved on the day by scheduling the 25-strong National Front protest for early morning, and the 2,500-strong counter-demonstration at noon.

The Clarence Street building was eventually refurbished and officially opened as the Afro-Caribbean Cultural Centre, by Mel, then a councillor, on 13 March 1983. The Centre was equipped with a large bar, catering facilities, and a function room that could double as a dance hall or conference suite. These premises served as a convenient central meeting place for Wolverhampton's black community for over twenty years.

Two months after the Centre opened, when Mel had stepped down from the Centre's executive committee, Frank went to attend the Annual General Meeting of Wolverhampton's Council for Community Relations which was held in the function room. With the business completed, he made his way with others to the bar. While standing there, waiting to buy a beer, a large black man, Salter Whyteman, who Frank knew to be a friend of an executive committee member, approached him aggressively and said in a loud voice:

"You white trash. What the rass-clate do you tink you're doing in a black man's bar? Fuck off out of here before I fucking throw you out."

Frank, as usual, stood his ground. He replied that he was as entitled to buy a drink there as anyone else, and told Salter Whyteman to stop his swearing. Thereupon, Salter started throwing punches at Dad, which he did his best to parry, before they were pulled apart by the bouncers and ejected from the building.

A month or so later, Dad received a letter from the Executive Committee, informing him that it had decided to expel him from membership of the Cultural Centre and to ban him from the premises until further notice. Dad wrote back pointing out that he had been the innocent victim of an unprovoked and brutal attack, and requesting the reason for the Committee's decision. He added that he happened to be on the premises only because he had been invited to attend a meeting there of the Community Relations Council and, as far as he was aware, he could not be expelled from membership because he wasn't a member.

The Centre responded, asking Frank to state in writing his version of the event to enable the Executive to do justice to both parties involved. Frank replied that he had no intention of participating in a kangaroo court set up by the Executive Committee. What angered him most was that executive members knew him personally, had actually witnessed the unprovoked assault on him, and had previously worked with him on projects of benefit to the black community, including plans to set up the Centre, itself.

The ban was not lifted until some fifteen years later, when one of Mel's friends became Cultural Centre president. Frank had always assumed that the attack and ban were staged on behalf of Black Nationalists on the Executive, in an attempt to undermine Mel's influence on the council and in the community. He believes that he was the only white person ever to have been specifically banned from the Centre during its lifetime, but stands to be corrected. The irony of the exclusion wasn't lost on Mel, who had so publicly gone on record to refute the allegation that the Centre would serve only black people.

Chapter 4

A brick through the window

A picture of Mel's momentous first election victory still hangs on the wall of our parents' house. It shows Mom being given a kiss of congratulation by Labour Leader, Councillor John Bird, with Wolverhampton's mayor, Councillor Ernest Bold, and Dr Len Moore, her agent, grinning like Cheshire cats. Mel is wearing a giant rosette made, we were told, by Aunt Epsi, from red, gold, and green ribbon: the red and gold for Labour, and the extra green to give a Caribbean - even a Rastafarian - character to the campaign. While there were already Asian councillors, Mel was the first black Caribbean to be elected to Wolverhampton Council.

The Graiseley Ward by-election in Wolverhampton, scheduled for 17 September 1981, was one of the first to be contested by the recently-forged alliance between the Liberal Party and the Social Democratic Party, or SDP. The SDP had been formed in March that year by the 'gang of four' - Roy Jenkins, David Owen, Shirley Williams, and William Rodgers - who had resigned from the Labour Party led by Michael Foot on the grounds that it was becoming too Left-wing. As a trickle of Labour MPs continued to defect, the SDP candidate for Graiseley, Roger Steele, was expected to win against an inexperienced black Left-wing extremist.

Mel and Frank had been active in the Labour Party for two years when their local ward Labour Councillor, Mrs Nellie Jones, decided to stand down for personal reasons. Some leading members of the Graiseley Ward Labour Party approached Mel to ask her whether she would allow them to nominate her to stand as a candidate in the by-election caused by Nellie's departure. Mel was short-listed and selected by the Ward, despite attempts by one or two older Party stalwarts in the Labour hierarchy to stop her standing. Some Party members believed that white and Asian voters would be disinclined to vote for a black candidate and that she was at risk of losing the seat for them. Mel asked Dr Len Moore, a fellow member of the Graiseley Ward Labour Party, to be her election agent, and a small committee was set up to plan the campaign.

The election leaflet shows a picture of a serious-looking Mel proclaimed as "Your Labour candidate, a health visitor aged 37, with two children." 'Health visitor' was felt to be more appealing to voters than 'health visitor tutor' and Robeson, our brother, had yet to be born.

In her address, Mel spoke of how she enjoyed living in Graiseley because it was a friendly place which proved working-class people of all ages and races could get on well together. She mentioned what she would do for old people, young people, children, and the electorate as a whole. Children, for example, needed nursery places, safe play areas, and a sound education. Most importantly, they had to learn to be honest citizens who treated the aged, infirm, and poor, with respect. To live in harmony, they needed a multi-cultural education encouraging them to appreciate other people's history and achievements. She warned of the vicious attack being mounted on living standards and public services by a Tory government, whose economic policies were closing factories, creating mass unemployment, and culling the caring services by taking money from local councils.

The local Labour Party conducted a full general canvass of voters, but this was followed by a decision to segment the electorate on an ethnic basis and to allocate to each group of voters a team of canvassers sharing the same national origin, culture, language, or religious affiliation. People of black Caribbean origin were visited by Mel's supporters from the West Midlands Caribbean Association, the Bengalis by Frank's friend, Raj Mitra, the Gujaratis by a Mr Patel, and the Punjabis by comrades from the Indian Workers Association. Sikh Gurdwaras, Hindu temples, the Buddhist Vihara, the Muslim community, and the various black-led churches were all visited and their congregations urged to support their Labour candidate. The campaign was systematic and intense and undoubtedly contributed to the result.

On a turnout of 48 per cent - extremely high for a local election - Mel Chevannes topped the poll with 1,887 votes, the Social Democrat came in second with 1,114, while the Conservative trailed in last with 546. The result left Labour in control of the council by 32 seats to 28. Mel's majority of 773 compared with a Labour majority of 630 in the ward election of 1980. Against the expectation of the media, who were present in unusual numbers at the count, Mel had defeated the Social Democratic Party Alliance in its first joint bid for a seat in a local election in the West Midlands. She was to remain on the council - bar a break of one year - until

1992, that is, from when I was seven months old until just after my eleventh birthday.

We children grew up in the knowledge that our mother was a councillor. From a young age, we referred to councillors, MPs, and other prominent local people, by their first names, as we never heard their surnames used. The downside was that our mother led an inordinately busy life, struggling to balance her domestic, occupational, and council duties, which she just managed to achieve, assisted, as always, by remarkably stable child-care arrangements.

She took her council work very seriously, meticulously recording and chasing her ward case work, attending all ward and group party meetings, serving on the council committees to which she was allocated, and taking her place in the Council chamber. Drawing on her experience as a health visitor, she devised her own case work record sheet, which was later adopted by the Council as a whole and printed in duplicate.

Knowledge of the determined way in which she pursued cases to her clients' benefit soon spread and attracted yet further demands on her time. We were constantly answering the door to distraught constituents seeking help from "that black woman councillor who lives in Oak Street". Mel found time for them there and then, or arranged to meet people at their own homes so they could show her in person the repair to be done or the rubbish to be removed.

As soon as we were able to transcribe figures, we were expected to stand outside local polling stations during the annual May-time council elections, collecting the polling card numbers to be relayed back to the party election office, where they could be crossed off to show who had voted, and who had yet to vote. We became very excited, especially when our mother was standing for re-election, although we were sent off to bed well before the votes were counted and the results declared.

Not only was Mel Wolverhampton's first black councillor, but the first councillor in the town to give birth while in office. When Robeson was born, Dad used to transport him in his carrycot to the Civic Centre, so that Mom could breast feed him during the adjournment between sessions of the council.

As Robeson grew older, Dad would take all three of us to sit in the visitors' gallery to watch the council meeting in full session. The mayor, in his elaborate robes and heavy gold chain, sat in a high chair with a mace on the desk in front, presiding over the chamber, while the councillors sat in their black gowns in the amphitheatre of seats and tables beneath him. Labour councillors were situated to the left and Conservatives to the right of the viewing gallery.

On one occasion, Robeson managed to scramble off Dad's knee, duck under the barrier, and scuttle off to the left in the direction of mom's seat, while at the same time letting out, at full throttle, the cry: "mommee!" John Bird, the Council Leader, seeing the commotion, stood up and, with a twinkle in his eye, proposed a short adjournment, giving Mom time to retrieve Robeson from the arms of the marshals.

Mel got on well with her fellow councillors, in particular John Bird, the Labour Leader, and Dennis Turner, the Deputy Leader, both street-wise and experienced local politicians. Together with Councillor Ken Purchase, they were destined for higher office.

John Bird resigned from the council and was elected in March 1987 to the European Parliament for the Midlands West constituency in the by-election caused by the death of the sitting MEP, Terry Pitt.

Shortly afterwards, in June 1987, Dennis Turner, replaced the kindly Bob Edwards, to become Member of Parliament for Wolverhampton South East, representing that constituency until the May 2005 General Election, after which he was created a life peer: Baron Bilston. He and his wife, Pattie, are still close friends of our parents and, for as far back as we can remember, we have known them as 'Dennis' and 'Pattie.'

Ken Purchase was selected to fight the Wolverhampton North East constituency in 1987, eventually winning it for the Labour (Co-operative) Party in 1992. He went on to serve for six years as Parliamentary Private Secretary to Robin Cook, the Foreign Secretary, who resigned over Tony Blair's decision to take Britain to war in Iraq.

Dennis Turner and Ken Purchase were both members of the Co-operative Party, an integral part of the Labour Movement. While co-operatives are run along business lines, they are based on the values of honesty, openness, social responsibility, and caring for others. My parents, I know, admired the Co-operatives' emphasis on collective self-help and responsibility.

Dennis, himself, was a founder member of the Springvale Co-operative, a social club set up next to the derelict British Steel works in premises purchased with the pooled redundancy money of workers who had lost their jobs when the plant closed in 1980. Dennis had been chair of the Joint Trade Union Action Committee which had aroused the whole of the Bilston community in strident opposition to the closure, an early taste of what was to follow under the Thatcher government for the Black Country's traditional industries. Dad remembers marching down Bilston High Street behind trade union banners in a vain attempt to save the steel works.

Soon after Mel became a councillor, the Labour Group under John Bird, deeply concerned at the effect on the town of mass youth unemployment, commissioned a review of the needs of young people and of the council's youth services. The Youth Review Team was led by Paul Willis, a social anthropologist who lived near to us in Hartley Street. When his grass was high, he'd come round to borrow our motor mower.

Paul's Youth Review described the disastrous effects of unemployment on the young, who were blocked from pursuits and pleasures that were taken for granted by people in work. Discrimination meant that young black Caribbeans suffered from the highest rates of unemployment, an experience that contributed to black consciousness and the sense of an all-pervading racism. The Review recommended that the Council adopt a new dynamic youth policy to reinvigorate its current youth services, involve young people in the decisions that affected them, and draw up plans for an ambitious centrally-located youth facility.

While the report was well received and a new post of youth coordinator was created, Paul's vision for Wolverhampton's youth did not materialise. In fact, the council's youth services deteriorated still further, except in relation to the youth team initiative at Bilston Community College that was led by Adrian O'Connor, who had worked with Paul on the Youth Review.

Paul, who became famous for his book on unruly schoolboys, entitled *Learning to Labour*, became a family friend, helping Mel in her election campaigns. Frank used to discuss sociological theory with him, teasing him for being an 'Hegelian', and not 'a proper Marxist', whatever that might have meant. We merely remember the occasion when Paul came round to the house dressed as Father Christmas. When he rang the bell and said "ho, ho", Robeson, in his eagerness to see Santa, tumbled down stairs with a bump!

After a comparatively short time finding her way on the Council, Mel was nominated by the Appointments Group, led by John Bird, to chair the borough's social services committee, a position she held until her election defeat in 1987. During her time as chair, she pushed through a radical reorganisation of the Social Services Department, despite obstruction from the trade union. She also planned and drove forward a scheme to extend and modernise social services provision, in particular, for Wolverhampton's increasing number of elderly people. Her committee took the bold decision to build a brand-new 40-bed old people's home and, on Mel's insistence, to give it the name, 'Nelson Mandela House'.

Invited to the opening of the home on the 27th March 1986, Mr Solly Smith, from the African National Congress, spoke of his pleasure that the people of Wolverhampton had chosen to honour Nelson Mandela in this way. It was a fitting choice of name, as Mandela was himself now a venerable old man, having spent the last 22 years of his life as a prisoner of the barbaric apartheid regime. He believed that public recognition such as this made an important contribution to the campaign to release Mandela and all the political prisoners in South Africa. In 2010, Nelson Mandela House remained one of only two residential homes for the elderly still run by the Wolverhampton Council.

We dimly remembered the disappointment we'd experienced at the time of Mel's election defeat, and wanted to learn more about the circumstances under which this had occurred, as we knew how vigorously she waged her campaigns.

"How," Robeson asked, "did you come to lose your seat on the council?"

"It was a drama," she replied, "tied up with the events surrounding the death of a young black man at the hands of the police."

At midday, on Friday the 20th February 1987, a 22-year-old black man, Clinton McCurbin, died while being arrested and restrained in the Next clothes shop in Dudley Street, Wolverhampton's main shopping area. On learning of the death, a hostile crowd of young black people gathered outside, chanting and jostling the police, who cordoned off the spot. A Home Office pathologist was called to the scene to examine the body. Some hours later, as the body was taken away wrapped in a green canvas bag, fights broke out between the mass of onlookers, some 200 strong, and the 50 or so police officers surrounding the shop entrance. Police helmets were sent flying, and the enraged crowd went on the rampage through the town centre, leading the police to equip themselves with riot gear. The Mander Shopping Centre was closed and shopkeepers advised to wind down their window shutters.

The violence continued on the Saturday when, after the Wolverhampton Wanderers' match with Northampton at Molineux, hundreds of young people charged along Dudley Street, terrorising shoppers, smashing shop windows, and looting.

By this time, a leaflet had been circulated to the black community, describing how the police had 'murdered Clinton'. He had been 'kicked, punched, and dragged downstairs' while 'pleading for mercy'. He had been held in an arm lock until 'his neck went limp, as if it was broken', and left lying lifeless on the floor of the shop for three hours, until his body was removed. Still not satisfied, the police had then set about 'attacking concerned bystanders... as a result of which around 35 youths were arrested and battered in jail because they protested at injustice. Some were left with broken jaws, fractured bones and bruising'. The leaflet urged its readers to stand firm and organise against 'state terror machine tactics'. Who among the black community would be next? Recalling the deaths at the hands of the police of Cherry Groce and Cynthia Jarret, the leaflet threatened war unless the black community received justice.

An emergency meeting held at the Afro-Caribbean Cultural Centre showed feelings running high. White people and reporters who tried to attend were refused admission. Further disorder seemed likely unless measures were taken to calm the situation.

At first, the press reported the police story that a man had collapsed from a medical condition in the process of being arrested. Other witnesses claimed to have heard the sound of glass breaking, and of a fight, after which the police had been seen sitting on a man's back while holding down his feet. The next day, pathologists confirmed that Clinton McCurbin's death had been caused by asphyxia consistent with being restrained.

The local newspaper informed its readers that the dead man had been trying to obtain property dishonestly by passing a cheque. This detail was later altered to that of using a stolen credit card. Furthermore, McCurbin was said to possess a police record for violence and to have been fined by Walsall magistrate for punching his former boss in the face. Police efforts to discredit McCurbin and excuse their behaviour served only to incense the black community still further.

Aware of the passions raised by the death, and the danger of allowing matters to slip out of control, a delegation, including the Chief Executive, Mick Lyons, and Deputy Council Leader, Pete Bilson, arranged to meet with an official from the Police Complaints Authority. At that time, the Independent Police Complaints Commission did not exist, and complaints against the police were investigated by police from other forces, an inconvenient fact, of which complainants were only too aware. Nevertheless, the council delegation, in the interests of community relations, pressed for a full and open inquiry into the circumstances surrounding the death and suggested that it also involve members of the black community.

Meanwhile, Clinton McCurbin's mother, Mrs Esther McCurbin, flew into Britain from her home in New York. Ostentatiously throwing a wreath of carnations into the Next shop in Dudley Street, she demanded to know why her son had died, vowing to transport his body back to New York to discover the true cause of his death.

The Labour Group met to discuss what it could do to take the heat out of the situation and, after some argument, agreed to give financial assistance to the McCurbin family. Mel spoke and voted against the resolution, in recognition of its questionable legality, and the way in which she foresaw it would be publicly interpreted. Despite the fact that she was the only black councillor in the Group and its chair, her views were ignored. She turned out to be right, but became one of the principal victims of the decision.

The Deputy Leader, Pete Bilson, in charge while John Bird contested the European by-election, declared, amid maximum publicity, that Wolverhampton Council would meet in full the expenses incurred by the McCurbin family, including legal fees, the cost of an independent post-mortem, and Mrs McCurbin's trans-Atlantic air fare.

"We want to ensure that the relatives are looked after," he was reported as saying, "and to make money available to cover her expenses."

The Conservatives immediately denounced the decision and called on the District Auditor to declare the action illegal.

The promise to pay the family's expenses resulted in a storm of protest that raged unabated in the local press for the three months prior to the annual council elections. The proposal was widely and negatively interpreted as a Labour willingness to reward criminal activity with ratepayers' money. The discriminatory aspect of the action caught public attention, too. Would the Labour Party have met the expenses of a white family who had lost a member in similar circumstances? The *Express and Star* described the Council action as provocation, certain to infuriate the vast majority of ratepayers, and far more likely to inflame racial feeling than to allay it.

In the meantime, more leaflets were produced and distributed by black activists under the name of the Black Community Action Group. One handbill called for the black community to boycott Next shops, MacDonalds, and The George Hotel. Next was the place where Clinton McCurbin had died, and MacDonalds and the George Hotel had provided the police with food and refreshment after the action on the previous Friday and Saturday. The police were singled out for their total contempt for black people and their abuse of power, illustrated by the daily instances of 'brutal beating, false arrest and murder throughout the country'.

One night, almost a week after Clinton McCurbin's death, Mel and Frank were asleep in bed at Oak Street when they were woken by a deafening bang, as if the house had been hit by a bomb.

Frank leapt out of bed and ran downstairs to the living room. There was a gaping hole in the front window and the carpet was covered with glass splinters. A large house brick, wrapped round with paper and cling film, lay on the floor. Frank hurried to the front door, but the road was empty.

After dialling 999, Mel and Frank gingerly examined the brick. A message had been typed on the paper wrapper. It read:

'THE BLACK LIBERATION FRONT HATES COLLABORATORS.'

Soon afterwards the police arrived, examined the scene, and took away the brick in a plastic bag.

Minutes after the attack on Oak Street, another brick, with the message: 'THE BLACK LIBERATION FRONT HATES RACIST COUNCILLORS', was hurled through the window of Councillor John Bird's home in Bushbury and the phone wires to his house were cut. John was at home at the time with his wife Gwen and his son and daughter-in-law.

"Where were we when all this was going on?" Robeson inquired.

"It was half term," Mom said. "Luckily, all three of you were away, staying with Aunt Epsi in Birmingham. The brick landed on the exact spot on the floor where we kept your carrycot during the day."

"We heard about the attack on the news," Toussaint recalled. "Aunt Epsi was trying to contact you. We got very anxious."

"We didn't think it would be reported so widely," Dad said, "and didn't want to worry you or Gran."

The headlines declared that the homes of two leading Wolverhampton councillors had been attacked by vandals signing themselves 'The Black Liberation Front'. Councillor John Bird was reported as saying he suspected the attacks were connected with the death of Clinton McCurbin, but Councillor Mel Chevannes declined to comment.

Nothing further was heard from the police about the incident, although an officer came to advise on security and safety precautions. Mel and Frank were told to look under their cars every morning for evidence of explosive devices. Our front window was replaced with a toughened glass pane which, it was sworn, was so strong that it could repel bricks and other missiles. Many years later, this claim was convincingly rubbished when the glass was chipped by boys throwing pebbles at one another in the street.

Who or what was the Black Liberation Front? The name differed from the 'Black Community Action Group' which had called for protests over Clinton McCurbin's death. Nobody in the black community had ever heard of the organisation. As for its choice of targets, both John Bird and Mel Chevannes were widely respected by the local black, Asian, and white communities for their stand against racialism. Even at the time, Mel and Frank smelled a rat. To them, the perpetrators were more likely to be extremists and agents provocateurs from the Far-Right, rather than Black Nationalists.

As the May council elections approached, it became apparent to Labour canvassers that public opinion on the doorsteps was still vehemently opposed to the decision to give money to the family of Clinton McCurbin, even more so in a context in which the controlling Labour Group had chosen to increase the rates by more than 13 per cent. In Graiseley ward, Mel faced the Conservative candidate, John Mellor, who, in the adverse post-McCurbin political climate, was able to capitalise on his reputation as a former senior police officer. Despite a hotly-fought campaign in which Mel managed to pull out more supporters than ever before, she lost her seat. John Mellor polled 2,412 to Mel's 2,096, a Conservative majority of 316 votes. She was not alone in defeat.

At the count, the National Front taunted and gave fascist salutes to the Asian mayor, Bishen Dass, when it was announced that he had lost his Heath Town seat. That night, Labour lost seven seats in all, wiping out its fourteen-strong overall majority, to leave it with thirty of the Council's sixty-seat total, and no party in overall control.

Afterwards, the Conservatives entered into an electoral pact with the Liberal Alliance to take control. As a direct consequence of the decision to fund the McCurbin family, Labour's Deputy Leader, Councillor Pete Bilson, who was expected to take over from John Bird when he became an MEP, lost the ballot for leadership of the Labour Group to Councillor Norman Davies.

Graiseley Ward Labour Party continued to support Mel after her defeat, and selected her as their candidate for the subsequent election in May 1988. She was able to campaign on the appalling record of the Conservative and Liberal coalition, which, in one year, had increased the cost of meals on wheels, introduced charges for home helps, and threatened the closure of residential homes. Hospital wards at the Royal, the Eye Infirmary, and Penn Children's Hospital had been shut down, showing that the local Tories didn't care about sick people, or the Health Service. Under the unpopular Poll Tax, which was set to replace the rates, households with more than two people aged 18 or over - a considerable number in Graiseley - would have to pay more.

As before, Mel was helped in her campaign by an enthusiastic multi-cultural team of supporters. Toussaint and I can remember Ezra Dryden, the town's local black street preacher, dancing in front of the polling station at Norfolk Road and singing hymns to the Labour voters. This time Mel polled 2,627 votes to the Conservative candidate's 1,876, vindicating herself with a majority of 751. She remained on the Council for another four-year term, before standing down to focus on her paid university career.

"Did they catch the Black Liberation Front?" Robeson asked.

"Judge for yourself," Dad said. "We think there was a cover-up, but can't be sure, as we were never privy to the investigation."

The Black Liberation Front continued to make headlines. In July 1987, under the headline 'Big car bomb set to kill at police HQ', the *Express and Star* reported that a massive explosive device had been planted in a yellow Ford Escort parked at the Birmingham Road Police Station. It had taken three hours to diffuse. Another incendiary device had been recovered from Wolverhampton Civic Centre. Both bombs were said to be linked to the death of Clinton McCurbin.

In May 1989, an *Express and Star* reporter, Jon Griffin, broke the story that a West Midland police inspector, who worked in the police press office in Birmingham, had been suspended from duty and was being questioned over a letter allegedly sent to Superintendent Martin Burton, who handled the Force's public relations. The letter was understood 'to refer to the activities of the Black Liberation Front, a terrorist group accused of sending letters to several prominent people including Superintendent Burton'. Burton had been 'named as a potential target for Wolverhampton's

Black Liberation Front in a letter he received supposedly from the group in December'. West Midlands Police refused to comment on the inquiry other than to confirm that the inspector was under investigation for a possible criminal offence, and that a report on the allegations would be submitted to the Crown Prosecution Service.

Soon after the report appeared, an inquiry was launched into the source of the *Express and Star*'s information which 'should have been confined to police circles'. The newspaper received a letter from Birmingham-based solicitors, Glaisyers, representing the police inspector under question, telling it that a formal complaint had been lodged with the West Midlands Police over a breach of the Official Secrets Act.

After this so-called breach, the Black Liberation Front was never heard of again, either in relation to further terrorist threats or attacks, or to bringing the perpetrators of the crimes committed in its name to justice. The police or Crown Prosecution Service have yet to contact Mel or John Bird (who died in 1997) to report on their progress in investigating the offences that took place in the crucial run-up to the 1987 local council elections.

Chapter 5

Rex, rum and research

My birth certificate gives my father's occupation as 'research fellow'.

"What research were you doing when I was born?" I asked him.

"I was researching British ethnic and race relations," he explained. "I worked at the Social Science Research Council's Research Unit on Ethnic Relations on its urban programme. We were based on the Saltley campus at the University of Aston."

"Why did you want to do research into ethnic and race relations?" I inquired. "Was it to do with your relationship with mom?"

"Perhaps," Dad replied, "but for as long as I can remember I've always been fascinated by issues of race and ethnicity. I suppose I ended up in the Research Unit because it offered me an opportunity to pursue what has always preoccupied me practically and theoretically."

"What opportunity was that?" I persisted.

"It all started with John Rex," Dad said. "He was a professor of sociology at Warwick University when I went there for an interview in the summer of 1976. He, more than anyone else, inspired and encouraged me to study, and then to pursue a career in the sociology of ethnic and race relations."

John Rex had interviewed Frank when he applied to take a master's degree in sociology at the University of Warwick. Frank had just completed his MA in education, but had no prior qualification in sociology, despite the fact that he had for many years taught the subject at GCE A level.

John Rex had a personal interest in the sociology of race relations, as he had been brought up in Port Elizabeth, South Africa, a racially-hierarchical society, which the population was conditioned to accept and to rationalise with the help of a battery of racist assumptions. Finding the social and political atmosphere suffocating, John left South Africa to work as an extra-mural teacher in Yorkshire and then as a lecturer at the University of Leeds, where he produced his first book, *Key Problems of Sociological Theory*. It revealed his interest in the dynamics of social conflict, in marked contrast to the predominantly consensual and empirically-driven approaches to sociology adopted by many British sociologists at that time.

Soon afterwards, he turned his attention to the study of race relations and, when Frank first met him, he had established a reputation in that field with his book, *Race, Community, and Conflict*, co-authored with Robert Moore, and published in 1967. It dealt with race relations in the district of Sparkbrook, situated to the south-east of Birmingham City centre. It was here, as it happened, that Mel's mom, Aunt Epsi, and stepfather, Mr Son, owned a small terraced house and provided Frank with a bed while he was studying at the University of Birmingham. Before presenting himself for interview, Frank had read *Race, Community, and Conflict* avidly, appreciative of its realistic account of the social landscape of the Sparkbrook he knew.

After being given an intense grilling over his knowledge of Marx's contribution to sociological theory, Frank managed to convince John Rex that he would be able to cope as a post-graduate sociology student, and was accepted onto the course at Warwick, completing his MA within the year.

John turned out to be an enthusiastic teacher, imbuing his students with a love of sociology and an appreciation of the founding fathers: Marx, Durkheim, and Weber. He described his own theoretical stance as neo-Weberian. Frank succeeded in impressing John with a paper he wrote for the course on 'the Kantian foundations of Weberian sociology'. Fortuitously. Frank had been able to draw on his prior knowledge of philosophy, the subject of his first degree. Frank became a loyal friend and supporter of John Rex, despite John's disputatious and irascible personality.

After Frank completed his MA, John Rex encouraged him to enrol for a PhD in the sociology of race relations, agreeing to be his supervisor, and securing for him a small research grant. For the next two years, Frank worked on his PhD, supplementing his income with a part-time job as an Open University Assistant Senior Counsellor.

Frank made lasting friends and acquaintances during his time at Warwick. He continues even today to contribute articles for journals, and chapters for books on race relations. The period spent as a post-graduate student was the most intellectually stimulating of his life. He remembers with affection his lecturers: John Rex, Margaret Archer, and Meg Stacey, and fellow students, such as Mohammed Bashir, Ivan Henry, Hilary Homans, Phil James, and Paul Rich.

As children, we had met Ivan. He was a black Barbadian friend of Dad's who could drink a bottle of over-proof rum and remain upright. They had studied for their PhDs together at Warwick and would converse amicably for hours about some esoteric aspect of sociological theory, although Frank despaired of Ivan's romantic search for a holy grail of communal love, black diaspora solidarity, and ancestral identity.

Ivan directed the Handsworth Employment Project during the period of mass unemployment under the Thatcher government in the 1980s. Under his leadership, it grew into a multi-million pound enterprise. As unemployment subsided, Ivan took a job with the Commonwealth Youth Secretariat and spent many years in Guyana, before returning to Barbados, the country of his birth. When Frank and Mel visited him there in 2005, he showed them the island and took them to visit his aunt who prepared a typical Bajan dish of black pudding and souce. The black pudding consisted of seasoned sweet potato packed in sausage skins, the souce of pickled pork chopped up small and seasoned. The meal was all very welcome and tasty and they washed it down with a bottle of the finest ESA Field white rum.

"I bet your thesis was on race relations!" I surmised.

"You might say that," Dad acknowledged. "It examined the vocabulary used by people in authority - especially politicians - when they talked about race relations. I called their choice of language 'deracialised discourse', or 'sanitary coding'. Decision-makers carefully select euphemistic expressions to disguise the shabby, racially-discriminatory courses of action that they want to pursue."

"Give an example", I challenged him.

“When I was preparing the thesis,” Dad replied, “politicians were fearful of the often violent public reaction provoked by the presence of black and Asian immigrants. The usual solution was to call for more stringent immigration control. Everyone automatically understood this to mean reducing, or halting, ‘coloured immigration’, even though the word ‘coloured’ was never mentioned.”

‘Immigrant’ soon began to lose its original meaning of a person who had travelled from elsewhere to live and work in Britain. A headline reading ‘immigrant births on the increase’, meant simply ‘more births to non-whites’. It didn’t seem to apply to the children of Polish, Italian, or Hungarian white immigrants. And when journalists wrote of ‘second-generation immigrants’, the word no longer meant ‘immigrant’ in its original sense, either.

“Is this why you object to mixed-race people being labelled ‘dual heritage’?” I probed.

“That’s right,” Dad nodded, “but the matter’s far more serious than that. The worst kinds of racial discrimination and injustice can be justified without the help of explicitly racist arguments. I made a list in my thesis of the kinds of rhetorical techniques politicians of all persuasions use to justify their decisions, particularly in regard to immigration and race relations. They sometimes go so far as to claim that the discrimination they are advocating is for the benefit of all concerned, even the victims of the discrimination.”

“Do you think your research was important?” I asked.

“It’s not for me to say,” he answered, “but I believe I was the first to point out the significance of what I called ‘discursive deracialisation’ and to compare and contrast it with ‘practical deracialisation’.”

“Do you have to use this kind of highfalutin jargon?” I retorted.

“You can read the abbreviated version of the thesis for yourself,” he rejoined, somewhat crestfallen, indicating an austere-looking book published by Cambridge University Press. I glanced at it, but found even the blurb on the dust cover off-putting:

'Traditional class-based ideologies are perfectly capable of supporting racially oppressive institutions... The objective structures of British race relations are obscured by a façade of 'deracialised ideology'.'

Ugh! Why couldn't Dad keep it simple? It put me in mind of the title of a book in his library: *Social Science as Sorcery*. I felt that he was conjuring academic value into being simply by the insertion of complicated incantations incomprehensible to the uninitiated like me.

Shortly before completing his PhD, Dad was encouraged to apply for a full-time research post at the Research Unit on Ethnic Relations which, in 1979, was relocated to the University of Aston under the directorship of John Rex. Dad, by this time, was well versed in the sociology of race relations and particularly attracted to the practical and applied aspects of the research that John was advocating.

John wanted the newly-constituted research unit to explore whether and how ethnic minorities were becoming integrated into British society, favouring the definition of integration used in 1967 by Roy Jenkins, the Home Secretary, who had spoken 'not of a flattening process of uniformity' but of 'equality of opportunity accompanied by cultural diversity in an atmosphere of mutual tolerance'. John had in mind 'the notion of individuals who are free members of society, free to move within it, free to retain distinct languages, religions and cultural patterns, or to abandon them, and who are treated equally and fairly without being subject to any kind of discrimination as a result of their group membership'. Under John's directorship, the unit dealt with the question of the position of the various ethnic minorities relative to the rest of the population in the work situation, in housing, and in education.

"But surely everybody knew black and Asian people suffered discrimination?" I interjected. "Weren't you just restating the obvious?"

"No," Dad said. "The situation was far more complex than that. You couldn't take common-sense assumptions for granted. Besides, we were concerned to examine in detail the way people systematically ended up being treated unequally and unfairly."

He gave the example of the high rate of unemployment among black and Asian youngsters which was generally attributed to their low educational attainment. The Research Unit had shown, on the contrary, that in comparison with their white peers, the more educated and skilled ethnic minority youngsters had greater difficulty gaining work than those with no, or fewer, qualifications. The research exposed once more the ubiquitous tendency to blame victims for the plight in which they found themselves.

"So what if anything," I asked disparagingly, "did you personally contribute to our knowledge of race relations?"

He paused for a moment: "I'll tell you about some of the research I did, and then you can judge for yourself whether you think it was useful."

Frank had worked with a colleague called Robin Ward on a project examining black Caribbean - or, as it was called then, West Indian - business activity. The report was commissioned by the House of Commons Home Affairs Race Relations and Immigration Sub-Committee. Frank and Robin found that in 1978, the heads of black Caribbean households were on average three times less likely to be self-employed than those of the general population. There were Black Caribbeans in business, but mainly in the fields of construction and the service sector, not - as with the Asians - in distribution.

Frank and Robin explained black Caribbean under-representation in small business activity in terms of the practical obstacles they encountered in setting up and developing their enterprises. For example, unlike the Asians, they were residentially less concentrated and found it far more difficult to set up businesses targeting only people from their own ethnic group. They also experienced difficulty in raising business loans from the banks, in relationship to which Frank and Robin uncovered evidence of more stringent conditions being imposed on black business.

Explanations along these lines ran counter to the prevailing wisdom that black people were culturally averse to commerce and lacking in business acumen, a comment sometimes reiterated by blacks themselves. Mel's cousin, Lionel, was a successful black businessman, and had been interviewed for the study. Aunt Epsi, herself, had also shown aptitude in her earlier life as a market trader (or 'higgler') and shopkeeper. Explanations in terms of cultural predisposition, or lack of it, were sheer bunkum. The report concluded with recommendations on measures to encourage black Caribbean business activity, some of which were eventually taken up by the Department of Industry.

In June 1981, the interim report of the Committee of Inquiry into the Education of Children from Ethnic Groups (known as the Rampton Report), which dealt specifically with West Indian children's educational performance, was presented to the Secretary of State for Education and Science. On behalf of the Research Unit, and as teachers in the Black Arrow Night School, Mel and Frank jointly reviewed the report for the journal, *Multi-Racial Education*.

They argued that the data in the form in which they were presented were insufficient to support the assertion that black children were underachieving, or to provide clues as to why this should be happening. They did not pass an opinion on whether black children were in fact underachieving, but pointed out that the report itself provided no evidence to confirm the claim. The data had been broken down by ethnicity, but the figures remained un-standardised for crucial variables, such as parental social class and educational level. Frank and Mel argued that before ethnicity was assumed to be the crucial factor, it was necessary first to rule out the possibility that the poorer performance of black children might largely be explained by differences in their parents' social class and level of schooling.

The review was also highly critical of the Rampton Committee's recommendations, pointing out that most of them could have been made irrespective of whether or not the report was considering the education of black Caribbeans. The unanswered question was whether black children were underachieving because the education service was inadequate for all children, or because it was specifically inadequate for black children.

Frank and Mel's article: 'The Underachievement of Rampton', was regarded at the time as an effective and devastating attack on an official report into black education, and proved in the long run to be the most frequently cited of all their publications.

Arguably, Frank's biggest contribution to the work of the Research Unit's race and inner city programme was his study of local authorities and their various policies towards ethnic minorities. The government's White Paper, *Policy for the Inner Cities*, emphasised that local authorities were 'the natural agencies to tackle inner area problems', but accepted that many people might be 'alienated from or apathetic towards the impersonal workings of local government'. Frank set out to focus his research on ethnic minorities' political relations with local government and its response to their needs. While his project was at first more broadly conceived, he eventually decided to prune it down and to focus on one town: Wolverhampton. The eventual manuscript was published under the title: *Race and Borough Politics*.

The purple-covered book in Avebury's Research in Ethnic Relations Series spans forty years of political relations between the white population of Wolverhampton and the black and Asian people who came to live in the town. It traces the ways in which racial issues affected the Council's policies in regard to employment, housing, education, social services, and community relations. And more optimistically, it shows how people from ethnic minorities have been gradually accepted as full citizens.

The Research Unit invited learned experts to give lectures, lead seminars, and participate in its conferences on race relations. Its staff were invited, in turn, to academic symposia at other universities at home and abroad. In the course of these intellectual exchanges, Frank met scholars and activists in the same line of business as himself from all over the world.

He remembers, in particular, an evening at St Catherine's College, Oxford, in March 1984, spent with the Jamaican anthropologist, Mike (Garfield) Smith, Professor of the Human Environment at Yale University. Together, they consumed a great deal of rum and discussed, into the early hours of the morning, race, ethnicity and pluralism, particularly in regard to the Jamaican context. Frank also discovered that Mike had been a front-line soldier in the Second World War and that they shared an interest in Caribbean poetry. What really impressed Frank was the genuine unpretentiousness and warmth of this great scholar who, in 1965, with his book, *The Plural Society in the British West Indies*, had begun - merely with case studies of Caribbean society - to challenge the then prevailing paradigm of structural functionalism as expounded by Talcott Parsons. Mike had also served as a policy adviser to the Jamaican government of Michael Manley and had amazing anecdotes to relate about the politics of that period. Frank was greatly saddened to learn of his death in 1993, aged 71.

"Dad, you appear to have been good at what you were doing and able to get your books and articles published," I concluded. "Why did you quit the Unit?"

"There were two main reasons," he explained. "The first was that I never felt entirely comfortable in a research role. I wanted to be a participant or doer, as well as an observer or interpreter. Have you come across the word 'praxis'? It really sums up my state of mind. My most relevant and useful ideas come from my practical involvement in efforts to change things around me in a direction of my choosing. For example, through teaching in the Black Arrow Night School, I became better equipped to think and argue about black educational performance. For me, research on its own never feels sufficient."

"And the second reason?" I prompted.

"Researchers' conditions of service were poor," he replied. "Most of us were on fixed-term contracts. Mine was for three years, but there was no guarantee that it would be renewed. Pay and prospects weren't particularly good either and, what with you being born, I had to take my economic responsibilities seriously."

"So that was the real reason, then!" I quipped.

Frank left the Unit for a permanent post as a Senior Lecturer in the Education Department at Wolverhampton Polytechnic, now the University of Wolverhampton. He found the experience stultifying after the intellectual stimulus of the Research Unit. His radical views on ethnicity and racism in education were viewed with horror. Senior staff in the department closed ranks to keep him away from research, particularly that involving direct contact with local education authorities, schools, or colleges.

Chapter 6

Poetry and sweet tea

We knew him as a middle-aged Indian man, bare-headed with a well-trimmed beard and moustache. Dressed always smartly in suit and tie, he spoke with a soft but authoritative voice. His powerful thick-lense spectacles gave his eyes a perpetual twinkle. Whenever Mel stood for election in Graiseley ward, he would appeal in Punjabi over the loudspeaker for people to vote for Labour and, more specifically, for Mel Chevannes. We were told that he didn't do this for anyone else in the Labour Party. Indeed, in previous elections, he'd stood as an Independent against the Labour Party candidate. Mom and Dad cooperated closely with the local branch of the Indian Workers' Association, and came to know and respect Niranjan Singh Noor, its president, who became a lifelong family friend.

Dad first met Niranjan in the early 1970s at meetings of the Community Relations Council, and was invited by him to the various Independence and Martyrs' Day rallies that the Indian Workers' Association (Communist Party of India (Marxist) faction) organised regularly in the Wulfrun Hall. On arrival, Dad would be invited to sit on the platform and, at the end of a queue of more eminent speakers, asked to address the thousand-strong audience. The proceedings were conducted in Punjabi and, although Frank could make out the occasional English-sounding word like 'imperialism', the speeches passed over his head. Being on the platform, he couldn't escape.

Niranjan was born in 1933 in the district of Montgomery in what is now Pakistan. With partition, his family was forced to resettle in the portion of the Punjab that is now India, where he graduated in 1954 from the Punjabi University. He arrived in Wolverhampton in June 1965 and took work immediately as an assistant labourer in Cannon Industries, but later found a job as a postman. He then underwent teacher training and in 1969 was appointed as a primary school teacher.

His real talent and interest, however, lay in writing poetry in Punjabi. His pen-name 'Noor' meant 'enlightenment', a mission to which he dedicated himself with vigour and determination. He achieved fame in the Indian community for his great epic poem on the life of Ho Chi Minh, under whose leadership the Vietnamese people eventually defeated the military might of America.

Niranjan's background as a teacher and interest in education made him intensely critical of the way Indian children were being treated in Wolverhampton schools, and he began to throw the weight of the Indian Workers' Association behind a collective effort to improve the situation, which he described as a campaign for 'multi-racial education'.

In 1975, the Association organised a conference attended by ethnic minority representatives, educationalists and anti-racists at which Niranjan denounced racial discrimination against pupils and teachers, the failure to recognise minority cultures, and the unsuitability of the 'white' curriculum. He urged the Local Education Authority to set up an advisory team to develop a new multi-cultural approach to education in Wolverhampton and a training programme for directors of education, head teachers, teachers, and school inspectors. Local councillors and local education authority officers ignored the campaign and so, in the subsequent two years, the Indian Workers' Association regularly denounced their apathy and 'the programmed murder of Asian and West Indian cultures'.

Niranjan's movement for multi-cultural education elicited support from a wide range of communities, but each of them understood it in their own way. The Indians were concerned to preserve their language, culture and religions, black Caribbeans wanted to improve their children's performance and tackle the unsatisfactory attitude of teachers to their children, while white teachers sought to improve relationships between communities, professionals and pupils to make the atmosphere in schools more conducive to study.

At the 1977 Indian Independence Day Celebration, Niranjan upped the ante by threatening a hunger strike unless more effort was made by the local authority to introduce minority cultures into schools which, as he put it, were busy 'slaughtering them'. He proceeded to stage a day-long hunger strike outside the Wolverhampton town hall, surrounded by placards stating his demands. These included the teaching of community languages, the replacement of imperial history in the curriculum, and a ban on National Front members working in schools. In an effort to forestall the protest, the chair of the Education Committee agreed to set up working parties to study whether more multi-cultural education was needed. Frank and Mel, as active members of the Anti-Racist Committee, joined Niranjan and others on the working parties, which went on to produce a series of reports that were circulated among the schools.

By 1978, just to help matters along, the Indian Workers' Association threatened to stand its own candidates in five Labour-controlled wards with the largest number of Indian electors. In the adverse political climate of the time, the Labour Party knew that it would be hard put to retain control of the council unless it did a deal. The Indian Workers agreed not to put up candidates in return for a Labour pledge to introduce multi-cultural education.

The Labour Party just managed to hang on to power in 1978 with the help of the mayor's vote, but eventually lost control to the Conservatives later in the municipal year. The Conservatives were largely hostile to Niranjan's multi-cultural education demands.

Discontentment over the treatment of Indian pupils in Wolverhampton schools came to a climax in 1979 when Ernest Rhoden, the head teacher of the Grove Primary School sent home an eleven-year-old boy, Kulbinder Bhamra, for wearing a turban. The boy's father, Prem Singh Bhamra, complained angrily to the Education Department, the Community Relations Council, and the Indian Workers' Association. The Community Relations Council attempted to mediate, but the head teacher was adamant that the turban was not part of the school uniform and might adversely affect the boy's school work. He was supported in his decision by the Conservative Chair of the Education Committee. A transfer to another school without a uniform policy was the only offer the Local Authority was prepared to make.

The Indian Workers' Association and the Anti-Racist Committee organised a picket of the school. Meanwhile, the Conservatives lost control of the Council in the May 1979 election. Shortly afterwards, the head teacher suddenly announced that he would take the boy back with turban, but insisted the boy's father sign a compromise agreement, one clause of which stated that the relaxation of the school rule in this case would not create a precedent. Bhamra refused to sign until this condition was removed, which eventually it was.

The head teacher subsequently issued a libel writ against Niranjan for calling him a racist and suggesting his refusal to allow the boy to wear a turban rendered him unfit to be either a Justice of the Peace or a head teacher. The action was eventually tried and the jury found for the plaintiff. Noor appealed against the decision and began to gather expert and character witness statements.

Frank wrote a letter from the Research Unit on Ethnic Relations where he worked, to urge the court to see Niranjan's actions in the light of the importance Sikhs attached to their cultural and religious symbols. He was due to appear on Niranjan's behalf in court, but was stood down at the last minute. Noor lost the appeal, leaving him to pay damages and full legal costs for both parties, a sum well in excess of £50,000.

Amazingly, this did not deter Niranjan one jot from his ongoing campaign for multi-cultural education. The Indian Workers' Association afterwards published a survey of the opinions on multi-cultural education of a thousand Indian parents, showing dissatisfaction with the schooling their children were receiving and with the ethnocentric nature of the curriculum.

In 1980, Wolverhampton Education Committee had a change of chair and in 1981, the old Director of Education retired, heralding a sea change in policy. The new Director declared that the biggest task facing Wolverhampton schools was the need to meet the demands of a multi-racial community and that it was important "to allow each child to develop personal pride in his origins and culture."

Not long after, plans were unveiled for supporting existing language tuition in the gurdwaras and for teaching Punjabi and other Asian languages in selected primary schools on Saturday mornings.

The new chair of the Education Committee, Norman Davies, who had discussed the issues involved with Frank and Mel (who was by then a borough councillor), announced that "the Asian community feels mother-tongue should be maintained and we feel we should encourage it".

In the late 1980s, our parents, in the knowledge that Gurbax, our carer, spoke only Punjabi, decided to enrol us for the Saturday morning Punjabi classes that were now being held at our primary school. We went along with Jagwinder, Gurbax's son, and quite enjoyed meeting our Indian school friends there. After a few weeks, Dad wanted to know whether we could speak any Punjabi words or phrases.

"That's not what we learn," we told him.

"So what do you learn?" he asked.

"We copy out the Punjabi alphabet," we explained, "and we do one letter a week."

The next Saturday, Dad came in at the tail-end of the class and stood at the back with some of the Asian parents. The beginners' class was large, with children seated in rows at the tables. The Indian teacher - an elderly woman - stood at the front speaking Punjabi in a loud voice. Dad could see the black board with some Punjabi script chalked on it and, on the tables in front of us, our attempts at copying it into our exercise books. The children weren't listening to the teacher but whispering loudly to one another - in English.

Dad asked us afterwards if the Indian children could all speak Punjabi.

"Not all of them," Toussaint said. "They have to ask the other children what the teacher is telling them to do."

After that, Dad decided we could attend Punjabi Saturday School only if we wanted to, but that he personally couldn't see much point in us doing so.

"What happened to the Indian Workers' Association?" Toussaint asked, conscious that she hadn't heard her parents mentioning it in recent years.

"I believe it still exists in a much-reduced state," Dad replied. "But it seemed to disintegrate with the rise of the Khalistan movement after 1984."

"What was the Khalistan movement?" I asked.

"It was a movement of radical Sikhs who wanted an independent homeland for the Sikh people in the Punjab," Dad explained.

In the summer of 1984, Jarnail Singh Bhindranwale, a devout Sikh nationalist, together with a group of his followers, armed with guns, set up a base in the Akal Takht complex near the Golden Temple at Amritsar in the Punjab. The Indian Prime Minister, Mrs Indira Ghandi, sent in the Indian Army to deal with the insurrection. In the ensuing battle, Bhindranwale, his supporters, and many innocent bystanders were killed, and much of the temple precinct was reduced to ruins.

Sikhs living in Britain, shocked and stirred into action by the desecration of their holy temple, staged a huge national demonstration in Hyde Park. These events resulted in a massive revival of Sikh religious fervour and renewed interest in a homeland for the Sikhs, independent of India.

Later that year, in revenge for the attack on the Golden Temple, two Sikh security guards assassinated Indira Ghandi with their service weapons in the garden of the Prime Minister's Residence in Safdarjung Road. Mel and Frank visited the site of her killing, marked out on the ground, when they stayed in New Delhi. They also described the burnt-out houses of Sikh families, attacked in the extensive communal rioting that followed the assassination.

After 1984, Sikhs became preoccupied with issues of ethnic and religious identity. The supporters of Bhindranwale and Khalistan took control of many of the gurdwaras and other Sikh institutions in Britain and shook out the people they considered less devout and less committed than themselves. Support for the leaders of the Indian Workers' Association, like Niranjan, fell away because of their class-based politics and their lack of enthusiasm for the resurgent, religiously-based, Sikh nationalism.

Niranjan, however, had many strings to his bow. He was able to devote more time to his literary endeavours, and to make use of other Sikh organisations as outlets for his ideas. Frank was now invited to symposiums of poetry reading arranged by the Progressive Writers' Association (GB), a group of literary-minded Punjabi authors, many of them former members of the Indian Workers'. The Progressive Writers demonstrated their support for Punjabi identity, culture, and language by producing Punjabi literature and poetry.

Firmly committed to internationalism and communication across linguistic boundaries, Niranjan chose not only to write in his Punjabi mother-tongue but to compose in English, too. One of his first poems written in English in 1986 was called 'Mammon's Malvinas: Maggie's Monologue', a vitriolic denunciation of the Falklands War. He gave Frank the formidable task of editing the manuscript to make it more acceptable to an English audience, an impossible exercise given the entire content consisted of a venomous attack on Margaret Thatcher's integrity.

Niranjan and Frank also cooperated on anthologies containing poems written or translated into both Punjabi and English, namely *Candles in the Storm,* and *The Best Friday*. Frank has retained contact with the Progressive Writers' Association and was recently asked to review the English translation of a novel written by Darshan Dhir, one of its internationally-recognised authors. Frank's own book of poetry, *Black Woman in the Night Sky,* was published in collaboration with the Progressive Writers.

Frank shared a great deal in common with Niranjan: a faith in humanity, an interest in Marxist philosophy, a belief in mass education, a love of poetry and literature, and a profound hatred of racism, xenophobia, and 'the colonial mentality'. Frank believes that it was Niranjan who convinced him of the feasibility of writing committed multi-cultural, anti-racist and progressive poetry, rather than the usual pap of descriptive emotional and relational verse.

Like Mel, Niranjan was forced to leave the West Midlands to win promotion. Realising the political vacuum left in Wolverhampton by Niranjan's absence, Frank eventually persuaded him to accept a post at the Community College, and return to the area from Southall. An inveterate student, Niranjan enrolled at the age of 53 on an MSc course in ethnic relations at the University of Warwick (Frank had studied there, too), and was awarded his degree in 1986.

As director of the Centre for Asian Continuing Education and later the Community Education Division at Bilston Community College, Niranjan rapidly expanded the number of enrolled students - especially those from the Asian community - thus extending educational opportunities to many thousands of older people who had previously believed that only their children could benefit from the British education system. He was assisted in this ambitious project by his loyal friend Niranjan Dhillon, who, even in retirement, still runs educational projects at the local gurdwara.

Niranjan Singh Noor died suddenly of an asthma attack in 1999. Frank went to his funeral at Bushbury Crematorium and to a memorial ceremony held afterwards at the Sedgley Street Gurdwara. There, Frank was invited to recite a commemorative poem that he'd written in honour of his friend. The last verse brings a lump to my throat even now, and reads:

> 'Somewhere deep in a Midland town,
> Beneath a sky of purest red,
> Together, we shall drink sweet tea,
> And you and I will plot once more
> That last illusive victory.'

Chapter 7

Not a scintilla of evidence

My Dad, a racist? In 1989, when I was eight, my Dad was accused before an Industrial Tribunal of being a racist. Even at that age, I understood that a racist was someone who believed in mistreating people like my Mom. The lawyer claimed that Dad, in his position as a college vice-principal, had discriminated against an Asian lecturer. The lecturer in question was his old friend and best man, Sadun Perera, the very same person who talked politics endlessly with Dad, drank off his beer and wine, and stayed over in the spare room, often for weeks on end. My father was appalled and upset: in his mind he had dedicated the whole of his adult and working life to the struggle for racial justice and equality. The shame and humiliation arising merely from the publicity given to the allegation caused tears to well in his eyes. During the hearing that went on for many weeks, the whole of the family remained anxious, subdued, and on tenterhooks. We were left in no doubt that the world as we knew it would come to an end if the Tribunal decided in Sadun's favour. Dad might have to resign his job. How could he live with the label 'racist' officially attached to his reputation? Only recently have I begun fully to appreciate why this case was so pivotal to my father's sense of worth. He did, after all, have a black wife and three mixed-race children.

In 1984, when I was three, my father was appointed to one of three vice-principal posts at Bilston Community College, a new educational institution formed from the merger of Bilston Sixth-Form Centre and Bilston College of Further Education. The Principal happened to be Frank's old friend and best man, Ryman Reece Roper, who had been head of the Sixth-Form Centre since leaving the Further Education College in 1975. Frank was given responsibility for staffing, staff development, and equal opportunity, with a special brief for developing an equal opportunity policy and translating it into practice.

Ryman Reece Roper – commonly referred to simply as 'Reece' - made it clear that he was relying on Frank's expertise to sort out the new college's racial politics, which they both recognised as deficient and in need of urgent attention. With his experience as a lecturer in further education, master's degree in education, two years of training teachers, local community involvement, and time spent in researching race relations, Dad came ideally prepared for his new job. His two fellow vice principals were responsible respectively for students and curriculum, and resources and accommodation.

Frank was to remain at the Community College until my eighteenth birthday in 1999. My formative years were spent in the knowledge of my father's contribution to the local education service and the considerable demands it made on his time and energy.

While the vice-principal post was comparatively well paid, Dad has never been motivated by money. He has only ever taken on work in the belief that what he did would make the world a better place and contribute in small measure to the sum-total of human happiness. The job at the new Community College was no exception. He believed fervently in the College's objectives and gave himself wholeheartedly to their realisation, working impossibly long hours, including week ends, irrespective of the cost to personal and family life. My mother shared this attitude to work with him and we reluctantly had to accept that both our parents were 'workaholics'. On most evenings, they arrived back home late, many hours after us.

When we were still at Primary school, Toussaint and I were given a door key, which we wore on a string around our necks. A surviving Merridale school photograph provides lasting proof of our key strings.

On one occasion while at home by myself, I watched a report on Newsround, a children's news programme on BBC 1. It was about 'latch-key kids' feeling abandoned and getting into trouble after school. I imagined at first that we were latch-key kids until I realised we didn't qualify, as we were far too well-behaved! Even at a young age, however, I recognised the irony of a situation in which our parents' commitment to the education of others left us for long periods to learn by ourselves.

Nevertheless, for fifteen years, the Community College became the embodiment of my father's socialist ideals and his life project. It was conceived from the start as 'an equal opportunity, open access, tertiary, community college'. From then on, Ryman Reece Roper, the College Principal, members of the local Labour Party, the

Bilston community, and the College's staff, including Frank, worked ceaselessly to convert that vision into a reality.

The College's community objective was its main distinguishing feature. Frank argued that the education on offer had to be personally meaningful and life-enhancing, founded on popular culture, and developed with the advantage and convenience of students, rather than of professional educators, in mind. The community objective was seen as the means by which a mass educational experience could be achieved. The College had to focus on the needs and aspirations of the population it served, using day-to-day knowledge of the locality and demographic information to inform decisions about the curriculum and programmes on offer. In this respect, Frank made good use of his social research background.

He soon developed a Bilston model for encouraging participation by individuals and groups by 'reaching out'. Community liaison would lead on to community activity, followed by the development of community projects, then community education arrangements and, finally, further education programmes. He argued that much community learning thrived outside, and despite, the education system. This spontaneity needed to be supported and extended by giving help to voluntary and community groups.

The siting of educational activities was given careful thought with programmes offered both off and on campus. 'Out-reach' described programmes provided in, for example, community centres, day centres, church halls, gurdwaras, and homes for older people. 'In-reach' referred to arrangements for groups to be transported from outlying areas to make use of specialist college facilities, such as computer suites, the library, or sports hall. Simultaneously, close attention was paid to the timing of courses and supporting facilities such as child care. The College began to arrange courses at weekends and traditional holiday times.

Bilston Community College in the impoverished south-east sector of Wolverhampton was originally conceived as a precursor of a borough-wide system of tertiary education. Tertiary (or 'third stage') education would come into being when young people who wished to continue in post-compulsory education transferred at the age of 16 to local colleges providing the choice of a full range of academic and vocational courses, offered on a full, part-time, or evening basis. The tertiary system was seen as a means of improving staying-on rates, of raising educational standards for the 16-to-19 age group as a whole, and of increasing the numbers progressing to higher education. Frank saw it as an alternative to a wasteful 'tripartite' system of 16-to-19 education provided separately in 11-to-18 school sixth forms, 16-to-19 sixth-form colleges, and colleges of further education. Politicians, parents and school authorities committed to traditional sixth forms, opposed the proposal, however, and the borough tertiary reorganisation was never implemented. Bilston remained the Borough's only tertiary college, although this claim was undermined by the growing number of schools in the area each attempting to set up its own sixth form.

'Open access' referred to the intention of making provision for anyone of any age or social class background who could benefit from the college's education programmes and facilities. The aim was to gear courses to individual need, rather than to exclude students who had so far failed to make the grade at secondary school. Traditional education had been selective and elitist, not only erecting barriers to study, but inculcating the belief among large sections of the population that they were not sufficiently worthy or able to study. Open-access education also implied the redistribution of resources in favour of those who had gained least from education in the past. The College developed a range of so-called 'access courses' to help students enter higher education or specialist occupational areas.

The essence of the College's equal opportunity policy lay in accepting the inherent worth and educability of all human beings, irrespective of differences of social class, gender, disability, age, and race. The widespread disadvantage and discrimination in the education system as a whole and the wider society posed a major challenge of converting this principle into routine college practice. The College approached equality of opportunity by expanding student numbers, and ensuring unemployed people, people from working-class backgrounds, women, ethnic minorities, and those with disabilities, obtained their fair share of the facilities on offer.

Frank was in overall charge of the College's equal opportunity initiatives and pursued this aspect of the college's work with vigour in the four fields of access improvement, specially-customised programmes for disadvantaged target groups, the recruitment of staff and staff development, and community relations.

He was assisted in his efforts by the Equal Rights and Opportunities Development Unit which, in collaboration with the Special Needs Directorate, was set up to make sure that the College treated its students, lecturers and support staff fairly, and to develop courses for people who had not previously benefited from education. To paraphrase the famous Heineken advertisement, the College had a mission to reach those parts of the community which traditional education didn't reach.

The Development Unit - later renamed Management Unit - was fortunate to be led throughout the life of the college by outstanding, intelligent, and capable managers. The first, Paul Goddard-Patel, who oversaw its initial development, went on to become the College's Finance Director. His successor, Dr Anna Frankel, was an expert on the quality assurance of college equal opportunity programmes, and helped the College achieve national pre-eminence in equal opportunity community education. Anna and Frank became close friends and cooperated on writing various books and articles about their experiences at Bilston, among them *The Further Education Curriculum* and *Basic Skills and Further Education*.

To improve gender equality in education, the College experimented in setting up a separate department to offer courses just for women. The aims were to help women to return to and remain in study, and to encourage their entry into non-traditional occupational areas, such as construction, engineering and science, where they were very poorly represented. By the end of the 1980s, women made up over 50 per cent of the College's student population and held lecturing and senior management posts in similar proportions. The College provided excellent on-site child-care facilities which included a nursery and subsidised child minding for students and staff.

The College was also committed to expanding facilities for disabled students. By 1992, approximately 10 per cent of students were indicating at enrolment that they were disabled, a large majority having special educational needs, most with learning difficulties of varying degrees. Depending on their individually-assessed needs, some were integrated into the mainstream, some allocated to specially-designed programmes, and some provided with outreach classes in, for example, hospitals, day centres, and the Institute for the Blind.

As expected, Frank used his knowledge of race and ethnic relations to increase the participation of the Asian and black Caribbean populations in education and training, and to recruit more teachers and support staff from ethnic minority communities.

Specially-dedicated centres for Asian and black Caribbean education were set up and suitably-qualified leaders were appointed from the ethnic minorities to manage them. Frank was fortunate to recruit Pasvil Plummer, a black Caribbean ex-student of the Further Education College and former community relations officer, to lead the black Caribbean 'Consortium', while Niranjan Singh Noor (see Chapter 6) and Niranjan Singh Dhillon took charge of Asian initiatives. Vast numbers of new students were brought into part-time education for the first time, through the organisation of out-reach classes in numerous community locations, including the Afro-Caribbean Cultural Centre, the Rastafarian Progressive Association's premises, gurdwaras, mandirs and viharas, and Asian day and community centres. The College encouraged community activity as a prelude to more formal participation in education in a variety of different ways.

For example, the basement at the old Mount Pleasant annexe was turned over to an enthusiastic group of Asian weightlifters who had previously had nowhere permanent to keep their cumbersome equipment, or to exercise in the evening and at weekends. Dharam Paul always acknowledged the College's contribution, as the weightlifters went on to win ever-more prestigious trophies.

After Mel transferred the running of the Black Arrow Night School to a younger generation of teachers and helpers, the College provided assistance in the form of books, equipment, and payment for specialist tuition for children with learning difficulties.

Student numbers increased rapidly and, by the early 1990s, one third (33 per cent) of college enrolments and two fifths (40 per cent) of full-time students came from ethnic minority backgrounds - as compared with one quarter (25 per cent) of Wolverhampton school leavers.

Progress was also made in transforming the almost entirely white workforce, inherited from the further education college and the sixth-form centre, into a truly multi-racial team that was matched more evenly to the ethnic composition of the student population. By the early 1990s, Asians made up 13 per cent, and black Caribbeans 10 per cent, of the college staff. By the time the Community College was closed and its assets absorbed into Wolverhampton College in 1999, more than a third of all staff were from an ethnic minority background.

Frank devised the arrangements for achieving these considerable changes. Ethnic minority staff were often brought in on part-time contracts and offered in-house teacher training. This was essential, as university departments for education were not recruiting or supplying sufficient numbers of teachers from ethnic minority backgrounds. The College set itself the ambitious target of achieving qualified teacher status for all its staff, full time and fixed-term part-time. Routes into teaching were established for community leaders working on outreach projects and for support staff, for example, those working in finance, personnel, student advice, and security.

Frank saw the development of a truly comprehensive community education at Bilston as his life's work, to the extent that he never aspired to become principal of his own college elsewhere. But his time at the Community College was to include its share of disappointments, too. Two of the most upsetting incidents involved Frank's former 'best men', Sadun Perera and Ryman Reece Roper.

When Frank was appointed to the Community College, Sadun was the first to congratulate him and to discuss the radical changes needed to bring about a greater degree of racial equality in the place. Sadun was still teaching sociology in the old College of Further Education, but his position there had never been made permanent. Under the new management, Reece and Frank appointed Sadun as a permanent lecturer in the Social, Community and Health Section, and he was rapidly promoted to Grade II. Shortly afterwards, Bill Toller, Sadun's friend and former fellow-student at Fircroft College, was brought in to head up the Section, a decision that Sadun welcomed at the time.

As was customary in further education, Bill Toller expected all staff in his section to produce schemes of work for their classes. A scheme of work is a session-by session outline of the course the teacher proposes to teach. It enables continuity of theme to be maintained if teachers are absent or changed.

Bill asked Sadun to submit his schemes like other staff, but despite numerous requests, at first verbal, and then in writing, Sadun failed to respond. Sadun apparently believed that he was being picked upon and that management was asking him to produce schemes as a stick to beat him with. The breakdown in the relationship between Sadun and Bill became so severe that Sadun refused to speak to him and communication was reduced to a spasmodic exchange of formal memoranda.

Bill Toller turned to Frank for help. Frank wrote to Sadun, asking him to attend a meeting to discuss his conduct, but Frank found himself faced with the same problem as Bill. Sadun steadfastly refused to come to any of his meetings. The matter was finally referred to Reece Roper, the Principal, who also tried to arrange a meeting, but was initially ignored in the same way. Eventually, after being threatened with suspension, Sadun, accompanied by his trade union representative, went to see Reece Roper and agreed verbally to comply with college procedures, including those of submitting schemes of work and an up-to-date teaching timetable.

Meanwhile, Sadun began to campaign frenetically on behalf of staff and students whom he believed had been unjustly treated by college management. Three female members of staff complained to Sadun that they had been sexually harassed by a college manager who was in the process of applying for promotion.

Sadun wrote to Dr Anna Frankel, the head of the Equal Rights and Opportunities Development Unit, saying that he had received complaints from staff and wanted to know what procedure should be followed to deal properly with their concerns. He declined to give any further information about the complainants. Anna Frankel referred him to the grievance procedure.

He decided instead to write to Wolverhampton Council to ask for copies of their recently-published procedure for dealing with allegations of sexual harassment. He also inquired if it were possible for a woman to complain directly to the Council, if she wasn't confident in the college management's ability to deal with her case. The Council's chief executive wrote back to Sadun advising him that the women should follow College grievance procedure but, if they were unwilling to do so, he was prepared to set up an ad hoc arrangement with the Council acting as an adjudicating body. Inexplicably, Sadun never followed up the matter, either through the grievance procedure, or through the ad-hoc arrangement proposed by the chief executive.

Sadun next took up the case of three black nursery nursing students who claimed that they had been excluded from their course on the grounds of poor performance. The matter also came to the notice of Wolverhampton Council for Community Relations who contacted the College and arranged to meet Frank in his office. In the knowledge that only the Principal could exclude students, Frank had checked out the story in advance and discovered from the nursery nursing course leader that the students had been told by their tutors that on their present performance they were unlikely to pass the examination and would be well advised to switch to a less demanding course. They were free to ignore the advice and continue with the course if they so wished. Sadun turned up unexpectedly at the meeting, apparently as part of the Community Relations delegation. Afterwards, he went around claiming that his intervention had resulted in the students being reinstated.

Following the death of Clinton McCurbin during his arrest by police in Wolverhampton, Sadun, along with others in the local community, called for a public inquiry. He drew attention to the situation by plastering the College with posters with headlines reading 'police crime' and 'licence to kill'. In the aftermath of the death, it was feared that anger in the black community might lead to racial disturbances, not least in the College itself. Some of the lecturers, concerned at the possible inflammatory effect of the campaign, followed Sadun around, taking down the posters that he had put up. Sadun complained about this in a memorandum to Frank, asking him to discipline the members of staff concerned. Frank wrote back sarcastically saying that he didn't know that fly posting was part of Sadun's duties.

Sadun had friends on the Council and in the Civic Centre. Aware of his knowledge of race relations, they asked him to teach on programmes of race and gender awareness training they were organising for council staff, a request to which he willingly acquiesced. While the College Principal's agreement was sought and given, the practical arrangements were left for Sadun to make. Normally, these would have involved him ensuring that his Council commitments did not clash with his regular teaching timetable and informing his section leader of his whereabouts, either directly, or by making an entry in the section diary. As Sadun was no longer on speaking terms with Bill Toller, none of these practical arrangements was ever made. As a result, Sadun failed to attend classes he was supposed to teach, not only at the College, but on an out-reach basis at local schools. Things came to a head when he took it upon himself to telephone one school to cancel his class at impossibly short notice.

On 22 January 1988, Ryman Reece Roper suspended Sadun from his duties at the College for a period of one month. Despite his previous undertakings, he had still not observed normal professional procedures, produced work schemes or records, or submitted a timetable, and had cancelled and refused to teach timetabled classes. Shortly afterwards, College governors endorsed the suspension, a decision that Sadun did not at the time appeal. However, matters were not to end there.

On his return to the College, Sadun decided to lodge a complaint with the Industrial Tribunal of racial discrimination against him by the Council, the College Principal, and the Board of Governors. The case was eventually heard over eight days in February and March 1989. Sadun was given legal support by the Commission for Racial Equality, who hired a barrister, Mr Coke, on his behalf. The College was represented by Mr Prat of Counsel. Ryman Reece Roper, Frank, Bill Toller, Alan Whitaker (Bill's deputy), and John Keat (the chair of governors) were called as witnesses for the respondents.

"Was Sadun accusing you personally of racial discrimination?" Toussaint asked Dad disbelievingly.

"Yes," Dad replied, "and if he'd succeeded, he would have destroyed my reputation and totally discredited me in my job as the person in charge of equal opportunities at the College. How could my former bosom friend and a best man at my wedding accuse me of racial discrimination? He knew that I'd devoted my whole adult life to working for racial equality. His accusation cut me to the core."

Mr Coke, Sadun's barrister, argued that it was easy for individuals and institutions to hide behind a curtain of respectability - the Boy Scout badge of past achievement. According to him, Frank and Bill Toller's former friendship with Sadun had occurred before they achieved their current status in the academic hierarchy, and they had since been exposed to the corrupting influence of power. Mr Coke suggested that they had shown an instinctive white reaction to their former black friend who had overstepped the unstated boundary of tolerance that existed subconsciously in the minds of even the most committed anti-racists, and who was now seen merely as an upstart black who must be put in his place. They had picked on Sadun because he had exposed them for the racists they were in relation to their handling of the three female members of staff complaining of sexual harassment, the three black nursery nursing students, and the McCurbin protest at the college.

With his responsibility for staffing, Frank was expected to attend the Tribunal on behalf of the College for the full eight days of the hearing. He spent one whole day on the witness stand being questioned in turn by Mr Coke and Mr Prat.

Recognising that he needed moral support, Mel and her mother, Aunt Epsi, did their best to attend the Tribunal hearing. Frank has fond memories of Aunt Epsi sitting with her crochet needles at the back of the room, like a tricotier next to the guillotine. She knew Sadun well, having cooked and fed him on a number of occasions at her house in Sparkbrook. Whenever he entered the Tribunal chamber, she would remark in a loud and audible whisper:

"Judas, Judas, Judas Iscariot!"

The Tribunal published its findings in full in April 1989, dismissing Sadun's complaint of discrimination and ordering the applicant - Sadun and the CRE - to pay costs, on the grounds that the claim had been thoroughly unreasonable. It concluded:

'There is not a scintilla of evidence to support Sadun Perera's complaint that there is some species of conspiracy against him or that his suspension and the subsequent issuing of a written warning had anything to do with his race. His suspension and the warning were no more than the richly-deserved rewards for a campaign of wilfully and wholly unreasonably refusing to observe the normal courtesies of a manager/subordinate relationship; breach of undertakings; and generally going his own way regardless of the damage that might do …'

'Racial discrimination is a cancer in our society. It is abnormal that in a society with any pretence at civilisation a man should be discriminated against because of his colour. It is, therefore, particularly distressing that such an able teacher and astute fighter against racism as Sadun Perera should purport to see racial motives in the actions of others where, to any dispassionate analyst, non exist, or worse by far, if it be the case, to use unfounded allegations of racism as a smokescreen for his own manifest shortcomings. Either way, he has done the cause to which he has devoted so much of his energy, a grave disservice.'

On being told of the verdict, we children clapped, more out of relief, than for joy. For the first time in months, Dad had a smile on his face.

Many years later, we revisited the Sadun Perera affair.

"What happened to Sadun?" Toussaint asked.

"The governors resolved to take no further action," Dad replied, "and he went on working at the College until after I left. We haven't spoken since. He looks through me on the rare occasion we pass on the street. I am still unable to explain why he fell out so suddenly and irredeemably with me and Reece Roper when, up to then, we had been such close friends with him. He was, after all, my best man! I found this affair the most emotionally bruising of my entire life. But I can see no point in air-brushing him out of our wedding photographs!"

Chapter 8

Commanding the Empire

Dressed in our finest clothes, Aunt Epsi, Toussaint and I show our passes and are waved through the gates at Buckingham Palace. We are now seated with hundreds of other proud guests in the Ballroom, a magnificent airy room with ornamented ceiling, chandeliers, and a proscenium arch. It is the 30th November 1999 and the orchestra of the Welsh Guards is playing a selection of music that, if I remember correctly, includes 'Moon River' and 'Greensleeves'. Prince Charles enters, escorted by the Lord Steward, and we stand for the National Anthem. Those about to be honoured have their name and achievement read out and are presented in turn to the Prince, who lifts the appropriate award from a velvet cushion to bestow on the recipient. One of the first to kneel on the investiture stool is Trevor McDonald, the black newsreader, who is made a knight for his services to broadcasting. Prince Charles really does tap him on the shoulder with a sword. Some seven names later, in the wake of an admiral and a brigadier, we witness what we have come here for. My mother appears - Professor Melhado Chevannes. She curtsies and is presented with the breast badge of a Commander of the British Empire for services to multi-cultural nursing. Prince Charles stoops to look under her gigantic hat, shakes her hand, and engages her in conversation for a few moments, before turning to the next recipient.

For fourteen years from 1976 to 1990, Mel worked as a tutor on the Health Visiting Course at Birmingham Polytechnic, later to become the University of Central England and now known as Birmingham City University. It was the largest course of its kind in the country, with four full-time tutors and an annual intake of 45 students, overwhelmingly female, although a handful of male students was recruited in the late 1980s. The Polytechnic's Health Visiting was run by the kindly, supportive and motherly figure of Pat Rowe, with whom Mel remained in contact long after she retired.

During the time Mel lectured on the course, it was located first at Bournville on the Bristol Road, then at Camp Hill, and finally at the institution's new site at Perry Barr. Mel became a principal lecturer and, on the retirement of Pat Rowe and her successor, Barbara

Steventon, the acting head of a new department of nursing. This was created in 1989 when pre-registration nursing education was absorbed into the university, necessitating major restructuring of existing facilities and the redevelopment of the nursing curriculum, a process over which Mel was given charge and accomplished successfully.

When the substantive post of Departmental Head was advertised, the woman Dean of Faculty made clear to Mel that she would prefer to appoint an external candidate and, if possible, a man, to balance the management ticket. Despite having completed all the preparatory curriculum and development for a smooth transition, and being eminently well qualified and experienced, Mel wasn't even short-listed for the post. It was made clear that there would be no opportunity for further promotion in that setting. An external male candidate was duly appointed.

Our parents agreed that this refusal to give Mel's application and ability proper consideration could not be ignored, and that the time had come for Mel to move on to make better use of her expertise. She began to apply for senior positions elsewhere, eventually being offered the post of Head of Health and Nursing Studies at the University of Central Lancashire in Preston, where she worked from 1990 to 1994. As at Birmingham, she was required to play a leading role in integrating three local nursing colleges into the university, and to develop a comprehensive new portfolio of professional and academic accredited courses, a task she embraced with vigour.

Mel took up her post at Preston just as the University was holding an in-service conference for its senior staff at Montpellier in the South of France. One of the aims of the week was to forge academic links with the universities there. It was Mel's first visit to France and she was impressed with the beauty of the historic town and the wonderful seafood meals and wine she was treated to. This initial induction contrasted markedly with the work and weather in Preston when she got back. The snag of the new job, however, lay in its distance from home and family in Wolverhampton. One obvious consequence was that she was obliged to give up her seat on Wolverhampton Borough Council.

"You abandoned us," we remind our mother periodically, "and chose to live by yourself in Lancashire."

The three of us were respectively aged 11, 9, and 7 when she left. We are all aware that she still regrets her absence and can thus be manipulated into agreeing to most of our mad-cap schemes to compensate for her deep-felt and lasting guilt. In fact, she stayed in Preston only during the week and returned to Wolverhampton every weekend to do most of the household chores. We did our best to help out, and the three of us began to take responsibility for cooking our evening meals, putting the laundry into the wash, vacuuming the house, and doing the ironing. Regular child-care arrangements remained in place, with Gurbax available during the day, and Margaret in the evening.

Nevertheless, we missed our mother, and Robeson, as the youngest, missed her most. Of course, we still had Dad but, being a workaholic, he often came in late, only to doze off in front of the television. Not until we were much older was it explained to us that Mom and Dad had consciously taken the decision to provide us with a stable living and learning environment by retaining their home in Wolverhampton, rather than following the path of each other's promotion around the country. Dad had also agreed to confine his career ambitions to the West Midlands, preferably locally to Wolverhampton, in order to guarantee the geographical continuity that both of them considered so important to our social and psychological maturation. They had concluded that our roots could best be nurtured in the multi-racial, predominantly working-class, urban environment of Wolverhampton.

In her new job at the University of Central Lancashire, Mel found herself increasingly propelled onto the national stage, becoming a non-executive Director of the English National Board for Nursing, Midwifery and Health Visiting and, later, its Deputy Chair. This prestigious body was responsible for the regulation of the training for the three named groups of health professions in England. Mel also chaired the Royal College of Nursing's Committee on Race and Ethnicity, and was made a Governor of its Institute of Nursing.

In the 1980s and 1990s, black women senior managers were uncommon in academic circles. Obtaining a chair in nursing in 1990, Mel believes that she may have been the United Kingdom's first black woman professor, but stands to be corrected. Most senior positions carry substantial responsibilities and, on occasion, can be very demanding, especially when they involve the management of change, as during merger and reorganisation. Mel's jobs at

Birmingham and Lancashire both involved the melding of organisations with different traditions into new entities, with all the political intrigue attendant on that process. It is to Mel's credit that she was able to create two brand-new schools of nursing with so little friction and falling out.

Yet being a black woman manager comes with its own set of problems. While the majority of staff is prepared to accept the authority of a black manager on its self-evident sufficiency or merit, there are a few individuals - white, black and Asian - who will never acknowledge or accept that a black person is competent, has the necessary knowledge, or possesses the authority, to make decisions on their behalf. These people usually persist in going their own way, irrespective of official guidance or accepted procedure, or try to bypass their line manager by appealing to another authority figure at a parallel or superior level in the hierarchy. The problem for many black managers is that senior figures in the organisation are often flattered by the illicit contact from people outside of their jurisdiction and are sometimes prepared to intervene on their behalf, thus further undermining the black manager's role and position. The racism and sexism implicit in such circumvention of a black managers' authority generally goes unrecognised.

In all her senior positions, Mel has experienced this kind of insubordination and has been forced to develop strategies for coping with it. No one likes to admit that the real reason for ignoring a black manager's decision, or going behind her back, amounts to no more than a deep-seated conviction that all black people are inferior or incapable of making sensible decisions. Incredibly, this kind of attitude is sometimes adopted by black colleagues, too.

Just as Frank was subjected to absurd accusations of discriminatory behaviour by his erstwhile friend, Sadun Perera, Mel, as Head of Department at Lancashire, also found herself on the receiving end of a complaint that she had sexually and racially harassed a member of her staff. She arranged to meet one of the district nursing tutors to discuss her work. During the encounter, the woman became distressed and ran out of the room in tears. Anxious to reassure her colleague and concerned that she had become upset, Mel went after her, only to find she had retreated to her room. Mel knocked and called out the woman's name but received no reply, although she could hear the woman sobbing inside. She tried the door but found it locked. Realising she could do no more, she left the scene.

Subsequently, the nurse tutor submitted a written complaint claiming that Mel had harassed her to the point of pursuing her and trying to enter her room.

The University had recently adopted a harassment policy with the primary intention of ensuring female staff and students were protected from the unwanted attention of men. The human resource unit had designated an equal opportunity officer to investigate and deal with all complaints made under the new procedure. The newly-appointed officer began to work enthusiastically on a detailed investigation of the complaint against Mel, following the procedure to the letter, irrespective of the fact that Mel was the district nurse's line manager. Mel also suspected that the woman's reaction and subsequent complaint were related to her inability to take advice and instruction from a black woman manager. The protracted nature of the proceedings, and the draconian sanctions threatened were the case to go against her, convinced Mel she needed to look for another job, preferably nearer to home in Wolverhampton.

In 1994, she was appointed Head of the School of Nursing and Midwifery at De Montfort University in Leicester, and based initially at its Scraptoft Campus. The scope of the post was more extensive than at Lancashire, and it carried with it responsibility for managing 90 full-time staff and approximately 2000 students. The demands of the job and the distance from Wolverhampton once again meant that Mel had to stay in Leicester during the week, and could only return to see the family at weekends.

While missing us, Mel was able to devote her undivided attention from Monday to Friday to her managerial responsibilities, her research interests, and the completion of her thesis. In 1996, she obtained a PhD from the University of Keele for her research into the policy and practice of community care.

Mel's move to De Montfort provided her with further opportunities at county, regional and national levels. She became a non-executive Director of the Leicester Health Authority and member of the NHS Trent Research and Development Council. In 1998, she was appointed to the Standing Nursing and Midwifery Advisory Committee at the Department of Health where she came to know Yvonne Moores, the Chief Nursing Officer, and the Right Honourable Frank Dobson, then Secretary of State in the new Labour Government.

In 1996, Mel was selected as one of four academics appointed by the Scottish Higher Education and Funding Council to make an assessment of teaching quality in nursing. She travelled to the universities of Glasgow, Abertay, and Dundee, and contributed to the subsequent report and recommendations on nursing education in Scotland.

One of Mel's major achievements at De Montfort was to develop the Mary Seacole Research Centre - a separate research unit focussing specifically on investigating the relationship between health and ethnicity.

Mel chose to name the Centre, situated on the University's Charles Frears Campus, after the Jamaican nurse, Mary Seacole, who travelled to the Crimea in 1855 to treat soldiers wounded on the battlefield, succeeding in her efforts, despite the racial prejudice and rejection she encountered. Mary Seacole's book, *Wonderful Adventures*, is possibly the first autobiography of a mixed-race woman, and a good read besides. At her hospital in Scutari in Turkey, Florence Nightingale, the nurse who everybody has heard of, refused Mary's offer of help. Undeterred, Mary pursued her mission, single-mindedly journeying on to Balaclava near to the front line where she set up the British Hotel to provide medical care, provisions and meals for the soldiers.

Mel admired Mary as a fellow Jamaican, a dedicated nurse, and a person who succeeded despite the prejudice of Victorian society. The Mary Seacole Research Centre was opened by the kindly Frank Dobson, the Secretary of State for Health, who went out of his way to accept Mel's invitation and include the occasion in his busy itinerary.

As Centre Director, Mel assembled a team of able researchers, devised a research programme, and succeeded in winning some well-funded research contracts. The Centre embarked on a series of research exercises, among them an evaluation of multi-cultural nursing in Leicestershire, the development of a curriculum model to help health professional meet the health needs of minority ethnic groups, and a study of accommodation and support for people in Asian communities with mental health problems and learning disabilities.

Despite her self-evident success and value to the university, Mel still encountered barriers relating to her race and gender. Towards the end of her employment there, she discovered she was being paid far less than white male colleagues with not as much managerial responsibility. When the issue was raised, the university defended its stance on the grounds that it was necessary to pay the going rate to attract and retain persons of calibre. Mel wasn't judged of sufficient market value to justify paying her any more and, even after the intervention on her behalf of the Royal College of Nursing, the discrepancy in her pay was never addressed.

Nevertheless, Mel's national reputation was such that, in 1999, she was made a CBE. When her name appeared on the Queen's Birthday Honours List, our home was bombarded with congratulatory messages and bouquets of flowers from friends as well as people we barely knew. In November, she was invited to Buckingham Palace to have the award conferred. She was limited, however, to a guest list of three to witness the ceremony.

After discussion with Frank, she decided that the whole family would travel to London to stay in a West End hotel, and that her mother - Aunt Epsi - and her two daughters - Toussaint and I - would accompany her to the palace.

As we knew Dad was a staunch republican, we were interested in his views on the award and arrangements.

"Don't you want to see Mom receiving her award?" Toussaint asked him.

"Of course I'm pleased that her contribution's been recognised," he replied. "She certainly deserves a medal. But I'd prefer it, if it was called something other than 'The Order of the British Empire'. 'Empire', after all, is just another word for 'dictatorship'."

"That's a bit extreme!" Toussaint remarked.

"The people in the American colonies thought like me" he said, "and fought against monarchy for their independence. Was that extreme?"

"But why don't you want to go to the palace?" Toussaint persisted.

"I've no objection to a system of national honours conferred by the head of state," he explained, "but given the choice, I'll always do my best to avoid situations which appear to show approval for an unelected, hereditary royal family, however popular it might be. Besides, I'm sure Mel's mom and you girls will appreciate the occasion more than I ever would."

"So you wouldn't accept an honour yourself?" Toussaint quipped.

He laughed. "With my track record, I don't think I'd ever be offered one," he retorted, "but in any case I think it can be conferred locally by the Lord Lieutenant of the County without any of the royal razzmatazz."

We travelled by train to London and, in the morning, dressed in our finery, made our way to the palace. Dad, Robeson and Mr Son waited outside for us, while we showed our passes, walked past the guards, and entered the building. Aunt Epsi, resplendent in her specially-made costume and enormous hat was mistaken by an attendant for Trevor McDonald's wife. (Mr McDonald, the black news presenter, was receiving a knighthood on the same day, but his wife happened to be white.) Aunt Epsi, who always enjoys being the centre of attention, made no effort to correct the misidentification, and readily agreed to the proposal that she might wish to use the lift. She was whisked away only to join us later in the Palace Ballroom where the ceremony was to take place.

We then witnessed Prince Charles presenting Mom with her badge. The investiture was filmed. Afterwards Mel received a DVD of her appearance, entitled 'Path of Honour'. A light buffet and photographs followed the presentation of the medals.

After about two hours, we rejoined a cold and miserable Dad, Robeson, and Mr Son, on the other side of the railings, and walked down Birdcage Walk to parliament to meet Mom and Dad's friend, Dennis Turner, MP for Wolverhampton South East. To celebrate the occasion, he had arranged a sumptuous lunch for us all in one of the restaurants in the Houses of Parliament.

At around this time, Mel received three other awards for her services, all of which she values as highly as her CBE.

As part of the celebrations to commemorate the fiftieth anniversary of the arrival on the 22 June 1948 at Tilbury Docks of the ex-troopship Empire Windrush carrying 482 Jamaican immigrants to Britain, the black community set up the 'Windrush awards'. In Wolverhampton, Mel was presented with a certificate for 'services rendered within the community'. This was followed by a joint BBC/Wolverhampton Borough Council award for her contribution to community development.

Mel was also made a fellow of the Royal College of Nursing in recognition of her 'exceptional contribution to the advancement of the science and art of nursing', making her one of a select band of nurses to have her services recognised in this way.

Chapter 9

A whistleblower

Early in July 1998, Professor Melville, the Chief Executive of the Further Education Funding Council, received an anonymous letter headed 'The Unacceptable Face of Socialism'. Copies had also been sent to the Prime Minister's Office, the media, and the local branch of Barclays Bank. The letter posed the question:

"If you were a bank manager, or the Chief of the Further Education Funding Council, on what basis would you be prepared to risk shareholders' or taxpayers' money to offer an enormous monthly overdraft to the Chief Executive and Senior Executive Management Team of a profligate public sector organisation?"

The letter claimed that Bilston Community College – where Dad worked as a vice-principal - had misused tax payers' money. It had squandered tens of thousands of pounds on a film company, an expensive short-lived mail-order catalogue (which recovered only a fraction of its production costs), an expensive conference centre draining £750,000 a year from its budget, a school of banking in Moscow, and a host of other hair-brained schemes.

It went on to accuse the Chief Executive and other senior managers of preferring the life of diplomats, jetting off around the world to South Africa, the USA, Eastern Europe, India, and the former countries of the Soviet Union, at the organisation's expense, and of failing to shoulder their responsibilities to the local community.

Early in 1999, in my last year in the sixth form at Smestow School, my father lost his college job. This occurrence was referred to euphemistically as 'taking garden leave', followed by 'voluntary redundancy'. Now aged 54, Dad believed that he would never be employed again in a senior management position in further education. For six months, he suffered the humiliation of signing on as unemployed, before eventually finding work as a race equality officer. He was unnaturally subdued and spent most of his time filling in application forms, though none for college jobs.

I was aware that, as recently as the autumn of 1998, he had been issued with a new contract as an assistant principal at the College, which had been extensively reorganised under the leadership of Alan Birks, the acting Chief Executive. Why, so soon afterwards, had he been asked to leave?

"The Further Education Funding Council wouldn't accept the Governors' decision to appoint me or Paul Goddard-Patel to such senior positions," he explained. "We were seen as being too close to Ryman Reece Roper, the previous Chief Executive, and to the old regime. Besides, unbeknown to us, the FEFC had already taken the decision to shut down the Community College in favour of a single college to serve all of the Wolverhampton area."

"What went wrong?" I asked. "I thought that the Community College was going from strength to strength."

"That was an illusion we managed to sustain," Dad observed, "but, in reality, matters had been going badly wrong for a while. You must have noticed my relationship with Reece Roper had become increasingly strained."

None of us had noticed.

For the first ten years of its existence, Bilston Community College more than fulfilled the expectations of those Labour councillors, such as Dennis Turner and John Bird who took the momentous decision to set it up. The College continued to expand its student numbers and to increase local community participation on a grand scale, taking full advantage of the independence from local authority control granted to it by the Education Reform Act 1988 and, later, the 'formula funding' introduced by the Further Education Funding Council after 1992.

While under local authority control, the College had only been able to grow in size within the Wolverhampton area and in accordance with the budget it was allocated, thus encouraging it to focus on local people previously uninvolved in education and training. For example, such was the scope and range of the College's provision in the locality that, in the short time when no lower age limit was in place and 'family learning' was in vogue, Toussaint and I attended college classes in keyboard skills, I studied for a qualification in

British sign language, and Dad learned bricklaying while waiting for our sessions to finish.

With formula funding, however, the College received money for every new enrolment and was able to recruit students from outside of the borough. Imperceptibly, the College switched from being politically driven by its equal opportunity and open access objectives, to being financially driven, for ever increasing its income by enrolling larger and larger numbers of students, whatever they chose to study and wherever they lived. The rapidly expanding enrolments fooled most people into believing that the College was fulfilling its mission of extending educational opportunity but, in many cases, it was probably cross-subsidising activities that would have taken place anyway without the College's intervention.

A clue to the change taking place could be found in the three-year strategic plan that the Further Education Funding Council now expected colleges to prepare. An integral part of the plan was the vision statement which in Bilston's case read:

"We aim to be the best college for open access and equal opportunities through meeting individual education and training needs and aspirations largely through partnerships with other providers, employers and the community."

The College relied increasingly on reaching its ambitious enrolment targets by entering into partnerships with other providers through a system of 'franchising.' In essence, this meant enrolling members or clients of other organisations and paying in return those agencies an element of the money received by the College from the Funding Council. In this way, between 1994 and 1997, the College expanded from having 11,000 students to 55,000. The Further Education Funding Council encouraged franchising at that time as the principal means of achieving the ambitious targets it had agreed with the Conservative government.

In the name of community education, people engaging in all kinds of activity, such as bible reading, horse riding, judo and marching bands, were enrolled as students. Later, efforts were made to put in place formal syllabuses and qualifications to give the process a greater semblance of legitimacy.

On one occasion it emerged that the College was running a class in 'exorcism'. My Dad, the ultimate rationalist, was expected to justify this nonsense to the press on the grounds that it might eventually result in the exorcists entering mainstream education.

No longer simply 'Principal', but restyled 'Chief Executive', with increased salary to match, Ryman Reece Roper had far greater ambitions for the College. He envisaged it freed from its parochial past to provide education not only regionally and nationally, but globally, too. Frank teased him about his aspiration of becoming educational ruler of the universe, but Reece was not in the least amused! The planned international expansion was to be achieved by setting up a series of quasi-independent college companies, known collectively as the Bilston Consortium, to do business on a cost-recovery basis anywhere in the world. (The Further Education Funding Council had mistakenly allowed colleges to recruit nationally, but it was not permitted to fund courses abroad.)

Bilston College companies began to sprout like mushrooms: for example, Stowlawn Ltd, Semoon Ltd, and Bilston EO & C Ltd. There were eventually nine in all with a further seven joint ventures. Partnerships were initially sought and ventures embarked upon in Russia, where a business college was set up, and in Eastern Europe. Keith saw the College as playing a key role in economic development, not just in the United Kingdom, but abroad in developing countries. Staff were despatched to make contact with colleagues in the Caribbean, Africa, and India.

Some of the early international projects were very successful. In the aftermath of Hurricane Hugo in 1989, Wolverhampton Polytechnic and Bilston Community College made contact with the Monserrat Department of Education, and submitted a proposal to the government's Overseas Development Administration (ODA) to rebuild six of the schools on the Caribbean island. The resulting project provided on-site work and experience for Bilston's construction students and the redesign and reconstruction of the Monserrat schools. It also fitted neatly with the equal opportunity aims and ethos of the College. While the new schools were designed to be hurricane-proof, they weren't unfortunately able to cope with the eruption of the Monserrat volcano in 1995.

Without international aid money, however, it was difficult to see how activities of this kind could be sustained. There was no way the

College could recover the full costs from the countries most in need of education and development, as they weren't in a position to pay. Nevertheless, a great deal of College money was spent on foreign trips, culminating in a large party of twenty people being despatched to the South African townships to play football.

Dad himself was sent to Chennai (Madras) in Southern India to support Fr Xavier Alphonse's nascent community college movement, but was so impressed with what he saw there that he found it difficult to imagine what more Bilston could contribute. In any case, apart from an initial pump-priming grant from the DfID, no further British funding was made available for developing community colleges in India.

To allow managers greater freedom to develop provision in any way they thought best, and to circumvent those sceptical of, or hostile to, the financially-driven rush for expansion, the College was divided into five sections, each now labelled a 'college' in itself, and referred to by a number 1 to 5.

A College Foundation was also set up to access money from charitable sources. In addition, an 'Open College of the Black Country' was created. This unit was intended at first to manage courses at weekends and non-traditional times, such as Friday evenings, but when this didn't prove sufficiently attractive or popular, its activities switched to negotiating massive nation-wide franchising contracts.

Another initiative, dear to Ryman Reece Roper's heart, was the Ryton Hall Management Centre, set in the Shropshire countryside eight miles from Wolverhampton. This residential facility was rented from the owner and used to stage training days for college staff and company cost-recovery conferences. It was a pleasant venue, but well off the beaten track and difficult to access. Few people, other than Reece Roper, believed that such an expensive venture could ever be sustained by cost-recovery activity alone.

To bring about the changes he desired at the speed he insisted on, Reece Roper continually embarked on large-scale reorganisations of the College, and made elaborate management arrangement to bypass anyone who questioned his judgement, or who was thought to be obstructing the College's expansion. Inevitably, the new structures had to be managed and serviced, which required the willing redeployment of the work force. As a result, Reece Roper was for ever offering escalating financial incentives and promotion to staff. By the time he retired, the College had 240 managers, but fewer than 80 teaching staff.

Frank had been unhappy for some time with the direction in which the College was being taken, and sensed Reece had deliberately phased out his regular meetings with him in the local pub to talk tactics and put the world to rights. He made an appointment to see Reece and explain his doubts about the College plan and strategy, pointing out that it was leading to the neglect and under-funding of the College's traditional work, and of the local Bilston community. The franchising and the cost-recovery activity were having a 'doughnut' effect, with a dearth or 'hole' in provision occurring in Bilston itself. What was worse, the increased student numbers did not automatically imply greater opportunities for the disadvantaged groups the College claimed to be serving. Franchised horse-riding courses weren't of much use to the young people of de-industrialised Bilston.

Ryman Reece Roper dismissed Frank's fears as baseless and made it abundantly plain that he could not afford to have a vice principal who wasn't personally committed to a strategy that the Governors had already signed up to. Paul Goddard Patel, who was experiencing similar difficulties with Reece's approach to the College's finances, encapsulated the Chief Executive's attitude towards them both.

"Despite relying on us to deliver his ideas in practice," Paul remarked, "he sees us as pigmies."

"More like family pets," Frank thought to himself.

After Frank had made Reece aware of his misgivings, Reece began to distrust Frank, and to sideline him in the decision-making progress, gradually removing him from his leading role in human resources and staff development. One by one, Frank's closest friends and colleagues: Anna Frankel, Niranjan Singh Noor, Pasvil Plummer, and Peter Wilson were sidelined, too, and regularly singled out to be dressed down for failing to meet their increasingly unrealistic cost-recovery targets.

In a further attempt to persuade staff to put their backs to the dual tasks of expanding student numbers and raising income from sources other than the FEFC, Reece adopted the doctrine of 'action learning', by which he meant taking immediate, effective and uncritical steps to meet college targets. He brought the originator of the idea, the ninety-year-old Reg Revans, to Ryton to explain its principles.

Frank found the 'don't think about it - just do it' message that Reece was seeking to impose as an alternative to a proper staff development programme, facile, irrational and politically unsound – indeed Right-wing - and told him so, but did not anticipate the violence of his reaction. Reece turned red with fury.

"You're challenging my judgement and undermining my authority," he declared angrily. "You know nothing of management and even less about the college finances. At times like this, I expect nothing less than total loyalty from you."

"I'm talking to you as a friend in confidence," Frank reassured him.

"That's not good enough," Reece fumed. "As Vice Principal, you must support my position. I'm coming to think that I made a serious mistake when I made you a senior manager at this College."

It was Reece's cutting comments, indelibly marked on his memory, which drove Dad to take a master's degree in business administration and to pass it with distinction when he left Bilston.

Thereafter, Reece ensured Frank was thoroughly soiled in the College's dirty business, instructing him to sign letters of complaint to the Funding Council, which was becoming increasingly concerned with what was going on at Bilston, particularly in regard to franchising, and was starting to ask questions about the legal status of the economic regeneration projects. Frank insists that he never expressed publicly his differences of opinion with Reece, nor behaved in a way that wavered from the course Reece had set. This was not enough. Reece seemed increasingly paranoid and convinced that a plot was afoot to oust him and his policies. He turned out to be right about the plot, but not about those he assumed to be the plotters.

"I suppose that explains why you fell out with Reece Roper, the other best man at your wedding," I remarked. I accepted Dad's explanation and felt some sympathy for his position, but was irritated by the effect the rift had had on our friendship with Reece's two daughters, Anita and Christine.

"If he'd valued our friendship, he could have contacted me at any time," Frank said. "After I took the personal belongings he'd left at the College around to his house, he never spoke to me again. He didn't even phone me to express his sympathy when I was made redundant."

Dad wrote a poem summing up the complexity of his feelings at the time. Here are three verses:

> 'I could
> Never again
> Allow myself to be
> Persuaded by his rhetoric
> As it kicked out, like a hot-tempered horse,
>
> Against
> The flimsy fence
> Of my troubled logic,
> Impaired, as always, by a deep
> Appreciation of his achievements.
>
> His part
> I can excuse.
> But my complicity
> Was unforgivable: I did
> As he asked, when I thought it ill-advised.'

The College was now in serious financial trouble, triggered by the retrospective attempt by the Funding Council to tighten up the rules relating to franchising and to terminate the so called 'demand-led element', paid as an incentive to colleges to expand their provision. The situation deteriorated still further in 1997 when Bilston found its unit allocation cut by more than a fifth.

Ryman Reece Roper persuaded the governors to challenge the Funding Council's funding arrangements by asking for a judicial review of its policies. The legal challenge led to a further deterioration of relations with the funding body and a hardening of its attitude towards Bilston.

It was at that point that the anonymous 'whistleblower' letter, 'The Unacceptable Face of Socialism' landed on Professor Melville's desk. Apart from the allegation made earlier in the chapter, it pointed out that the Chief Executive had restructured the organisation a dozen times in as many years and, although the organisation was top heavy with management, it had chosen to carry on recruiting staff, increasing its departments from 9 to 22, each with a well-paid director and deputy.

The Chief Executive was said to top-slice every £14.75 paid by the FEFC per student unit, by a massive £11.00, so that front-line staff struggled to maintain high quality standards of teaching on just £3.75 a unit.

The letter mentioned Ryman Reece Roper's friendship with Dennis Turner, the local MP and member of the Springvale Co-op, from which the College rented accommodation, drawing attention to the fact that Dennis was Chair of the Parliamentary Sub-Committee on Further Education, besides being a governor of the College. It claimed Reece Roper counted Minister Claire Short as one of his friends, attended Labour Party conferences, and believed that his political connections made him invulnerable.

The letter finished by predicting the College would soon be wrecked but that 'the captain would not allow himself to go down with the ship'.

"Who wrote the letter?" I inquired.

"It was anonymous," Dad said, "but signed 'Yours ethically, A.W.' - meaning 'A Whistleblower'."

"But you must have had some idea!" I protested.

"Yes, a name came to mind," he replied. "The letter was intelligently drafted and contained a great deal of detailed information that could only have been known to someone on the inside at a fairly senior management level. It also contained a mistake that would never have been made by someone familiar with the area. It claimed that Dennis Turner and other senior shop stewards had been employed at the Round Oak Steel Works. A local person would never have confused the Bilston Steel Works with Round Oak, now the site of the Merry Hill Centre. From this, I guessed who'd written it and why, but nothing could be proved, and the damage had already been done."

Even before the letter's circulation, the Further Education Funding Council had begun to take an intense interest in the finances of the College. It had already conducted audits into franchising arrangements and financial forecasts. But the whistleblower succeeded in intensifying the pressure on the College.

To Reece Roper's annoyance, Paul Goddard-Patel, the College's finance director, managed to persuade the Governors to reconsider the budget proposals. Shortly afterwards, the Governors agreed to withdraw their demand for a judicial review of the funding methodology, and attempted instead to achieve a reconciliation with the Funding Council. The College remained in dire financial straits. At this juncture, Ryman Reece Roper announced his decision to stand down as Chief Executive, and to take a back seat until his retirement at the end of 1998.

Alan Birks, Frank's former colleague, and Principal of South Birmingham College, was asked by Bilston Governors to help them deal with the deteriorating financial situation. With Funding Council approval, he was made Acting Chief Executive.

Alan immediately embarked on a cost-cutting restructuring programme, deleting four tiers of management and reducing the number of managers from 240 to 104. Following a previous wave of 70 voluntary redundancies, he attempted to shed a further 80 staff. Frank, along with most senior managers in the College, was forced to apply for one of the second-tier posts in the new slim-line structure and, along with Paul Goddard-Patel, was reappointed.

The announcement that Frank and Paul had once again been given senior jobs set in motion another barrage of anonymous letters, the gist of which was that Frank and Paul had been members of the former senior management team responsible for the financial crisis, must accept their share of the blame, and could not possibly continue to perform the same or similar functions in the restructured College.

Alan, as Acting Chief Executive, was summoned to the offices of the FEFC and told he had to give Paul and Frank their marching orders. It availed them not one jot that they had disagreed with Ryman Reece Roper, the Funding Council's main target, who viewed them both as having stabbed him in the back. They were both put on garden leave shortly afterwards while their severance contracts were drawn up.

While the restructuring and redundancies were taking place, the FEFC College Inspectorate embarked on a full inspection of all aspects of the College's work. Unsurprisingly, it found 'serious weaknesses' and the quality of provision to be 'mostly poor' and, significantly, much worse than at the last inspection. The press claimed it was the worst report ever made about a college's performance by government inspectors.

The report followed an announcement by George Mudie, the Education Minister, that failing colleges should be closed, or their governors sacked. The golden age of further education at Bilston, which Ryman Reece Roper had predicted would occur under New Labour, had not materialised.

The Funding Council set up a four-strong panel headed by their chief inspector, Terry Melia, to decide on the College's future. Estimates of the amount of money the College owed rose recurrently from three, to five, to nine, and finally, eleven million pounds, as the Funding Council disallowed and reclaimed funding for franchising, year upon year, back into the distant past - despite the fact that the annual accounts had been signed off each year by Deloitte and Touche, the College's external auditors. Later in 1999, parliament gave the Funding Council powers to wind up Bilston College and hand over its assets to the neighbouring Wulfrun College, from which was created the current Wolverhampton College.

A few die-hards, led by George Barnsby, the veteran Wolverhampton communist, historian and campaigner, set up 'The Friends of Bilston Community College', which waged a rear-guard action in defence of the College's legacy, denouncing the Funding Council's decision as 'institutional racism', and those associated with the Interim Board and College dissolution as 'racists'.

Frank was annoyed by the Barnsby campaign and refused to have anything to do with it on the grounds that, under Reece Roper's increasingly despotic leadership, the College had long since abandoned its original equal opportunity mission and had treated people such as Niranjan Singh Noor and Pasvil Plummer despicably. He felt that by describing the closure of Bilston Community College as 'institutional racism', Barnsby was debasing and devaluing a concept that should have been reserved for use in more appropriate circumstances, as in the case of the Stephen Lawrence Inquiry into the Metropolitan Police. He has since come to accept, however, that the Friends of Bilston College may have made the new college management conscious of the need to counter criticism by retaining the high proportion of black staff that it had inherited from Bilston.

Chapter 10

Gobby Wulfrunians

While working at the Oxfam Office in Cowley, I noticed a greeting card carrying the picture of a haughty old fellow with Victorian sideboards. It was headed: 'Everyone is entitled to my opinions'. By way of a joke, I bought and sent it to my father for his birthday. Some months later, I was surprised to see the card proudly displayed on his mantelpiece.

"I was delighted that you remembered my birthday," Dad said, "and I loved the card. Praise indeed! Enthusiasm and commitment to ideas are the hallmark of a good father and teacher!"

"But another much neglected quality," I replied, "is the ability to listen and learn from others."

"Could that have been why you all did so well at school?" he quipped.

Toussaint was already in the Infants' when, at the age of three, I started in the nursery class at Merridale Primary School. It was 1984. We used to walk with Jaggy, our next-door neighbours' son and other friends across the playing field to the modern classroom block on Aspen Way. The building was situated on a wooded site next to the Victorian Jeffcock Road Cemetery, and had a pleasant rural feel to it in spite of its proximity to the densely-packed terraced houses on Owen Road.

The school catered for approximately 230 nursery, infant and junior pupils, spanning an age range from 3 to 11. Serving a neighbourhood close to the town centre, the intake was ethnically very mixed, although children of Indian background were present in large numbers and there was only a handful of black and mixed-race pupils.

As determined supporters of locally-provided state education, Mom and Dad wanted us to attend the nearest neighbourhood school, but were particularly fortunate that this turned out to be Merridale. Mr Milton, the headteacher, played the guitar and did his best to put into practice his progressive educational ideals, of which a commitment to a genuine multi-cultural curriculum came high on the list, followed by enthusiasm for protecting the natural environment, and a downright hatred of school uniform.

Mr Milton and the governors were repeatedly pressured by parents to introduce a school uniform but, much to Mom and Dad's satisfaction, kept Merridale as one of the few uniform-free zones in Wolverhampton. On reflection, I realise our Mr Milton must have been a former hippy, subtly subverting many of the school's traditional educational practices to reflect his own relaxed life style.

While by law the school had to hold a religious assembly and teach religious education, Mr Milton would add in stories about the lives of exemplary men and women such as Emmeline Pankhurst, Martin Luther King, and Mahatma Ghandi, and increase the repertoire of hymns by singing songs by the Beatles, or about poverty, for example, 'All you need is love' and 'The Streets of London', accompanied by loud strumming of his guitar or banjo. In any case, he had to accommodate the fact that a large proportion of his pupils came from Hindu, Sikh, and Buddhist households.

The school went to great lengths to welcome children and parents from all ethnic groups and income brackets. Our classmates were from Indian, British, Irish, Caribbean, Pakistani, and Traveller backgrounds. Their respective cultures were recognised and appreciated in the everyday life of the school, which seemed to make a point of celebrating as many different religious festivals as possible. Considerable effort went into synthesising and combining myths and stories, and extending participation beyond the adherents of any one faith. The school was fortunate in having two Indian teachers, Jag Atwal and Pinky Sharma, to contribute to this multi-cultural mosaic.

At Christmas, nativity plays would be cast with Asian or black Marys and Josephs, and white Balthazars. The Hindu and Sikh festival of light, Diwali, was given an equal, if not greater, recognition in the life of the school. Diwali is still my favourite festival, probably because I love diva lamps. (Dad would say that I'd always had an obsession with candles and other fire hazards.) Dressed up in a purple Sari, I played one of Sita's three step-mothers, and can remember feeling very spectacular. I had only a few lines to repeat but at least one was in Hindi. I also learned to dance with sticks to Bhangra music, and to perform a diva dance routine. A group of us children went on tour locally, giving exhibitions in the Civic Hall and Mander Centre to rapturous applause.

Parental participation in the catering arrangements on these occasions meant that the meals were supplied from a range of culinary traditions, thus laying the foundation for our appreciation and acceptance of most of the world's foodstuffs, from chick peas, chips, chipolatas and chapattis to escovitch fish, faggots and fromage de chévre. Indian culture, suitably modified within the English school setting, tended to permeate our lives, but we were unable to recognise its influence at the time, as we were cared for after school by Gurbax, our Sikh next-door neighbour. We thus came to take our everyday experiences for granted, assuming our synthesised Anglo-Asian-Caribbean cultural submersion to be main-stream.

In Year 5 we were set a project about the human body in which we had to complete a booklet containing our personal details, such as our date of birth, height, nationality, and religion. The class began to debate what they should write down. Ranvir, one of the Indian girls, decided she was British and that this meant she must be a Christian, too. I disagreed, saying that I was British but that I didn't believe in God. She insisted that I had to be Christian like her, although I suspected all along that her family was Hindu.

This story illustrates how the ethnic mix of the school constantly stimulated questions about our respective identities, cultures and religions, and developed in us a lasting curiosity about, and tolerance towards, other people's practices.

During the time we spent at Merridale, the school embarked on an ambitious environmental project, involving the creation of a nature reserve on waste land to the side of the school. A peat bog was specially constructed and planted to attract insects, amphibians, and birds. The venture was developed around us pupils and conceived from the start as a lesson in nature study and conservation principles. The lessons I learned have given me a passion ever since for human ecology: the relationship between us human beings and our physical environment, nowhere more obvious than here in Kenya where I am now living.

Toussaint, Robeson and I have fond memories of our primary school, although it did have a darker side. Bullies were firmly dealt with if reported, but this didn't stop a gang of boys knocking over Toussaint, kicking her, and breaking her collar bone without it ever being medically diagnosed. There wasn't much racist name-calling, but it did occur, because I came home one day and asked mom the meaning of 'nigger'. She angrily demanded to know where I had heard the word and was at the point of complaining to the school, until I managed to calm her down. It was the black children who called each other 'nigger'. The main term of racial abuse at Merridale was 'Paki'.

Mom and Dad explained to Mr Milton that they wanted us to be stimulated and excited by ideas and not just drilled to pass examinations. Intensely hostile to selective education, and the eleven plus, they wanted us to transfer on completion of Year 6 to the nearest state comprehensive school. They made it very clear that they did not approve of grammar school elitism or faith school irrationality.

While most of the 11-to-18 secondary schools in the borough were by that time non-selective, the independent Wolverhampton Grammar School, Girls' High School, and a couple of faith schools had managed to survive the drive for comprehensive state education, thus generating an intense competition to gain entry to them.

My best friend at Merridale was Neesha Patel, a petite Gujarati girl, who introduced me to Hinduism. Neesha's parents were well off and she always wore stylish matching outfits, quite unlike my clothes, which were mostly my sister's hand-me-downs. Neesha attended Saturday music classes and played a musical instrument. In Year 6, she wasn't allowed to come out to play because she had to prepare for an entrance examination.

"What for?" I asked her.

"My parents want me to go to a good school," she explained.

"So do mine," I responded, but the seeds of doubt were sown, and I returned home to seek an explanation. I was told merely that my parents believed in the merits of comprehensive schooling for all.

Subsequently, Neesha went off to study at the Girls' High School and I followed in Toussaint's footsteps to Smestow Secondary School in Castlecroft. Most of the children leaving Merridale attended Highfields, another of the borough's secondary schools, but a trickle was entered for entrance examinations to selective institutions.

Merridale Primary School succeeded in its main purpose of teaching all three of us to read, write, and do elementary sums and, by the age of eleven, when we transferred to secondary school, we were proficient in the 3 Rs.

Just as importantly, we had been introduced to the rudiments of history, geography, nature study, science, art and literature, and had developed an interest in learning and knowledge for its own sake. In hindsight, however, Merridale's most important contribution was to inculcate in us a lasting respect for other families' cultures and diverse ways, and for the humanity that we shared in common.

Not trusting the adequacy of primary school facilities, Mom and Dad were keen for us to learn to swim, and took us all at a very young age to the swimming baths, persisting until we could all cover a distance of at least 20 metres. Dad wouldn't leave until he himself had completed his mandatory 100 lengths of the 20 metre pool. Dad is fond of recounting that Toussaint took her first strokes holding on to his beard, and how I was fearless in the water, jumping into the pool before I knew how to swim or float. Later, at Smestow School, which had its own swimming bath, I developed a stylish back crawl and, on a number of occasions, swam for the school. A classmate was mystified by my performance, informing me that what I was doing was technically impossible because black people had heavier bones than white and were incapable of swimming so fast!

Having been physically threatened themselves by racists and Nazi thugs, Mom and Dad wanted us to learn self-defence and to acquire the confidence to stand up for ourselves. While still at primary school, all three of us were enrolled to learn martial arts with the Elite Karate Association based in Wolverhampton. One of its dojos was held three times a week in St Chad's church hall on Owen Road. We were required to attend on a regular basis to practise our katas under the direction of our sensei, an athletic young black man named Robert Heath.

On one occasion when walking to the karate class with an Indian boy I knew from school, I witnessed a fight. Two white boys were beating up a young Asian lad and calling him 'a fucking Paki'. I turned to my Indian companion and said "Aren't you going to do anything?"

"I'm from India, not Pakistan," he responded proudly. "It's nothing to do with me."

Unfortunately, I still didn't have enough confidence in my karate to intervene myself.

At karate, we were expected to demonstrate discipline and control at all times from the formal bow to the sensei on entering the dojo, to the dismissal at the conclusion of the class. Students were matched according to their size and skill.

The most unruly young recruits quickly fell into line in awe of the measured movements and routines of the more advanced brown and black belts.

The katas, press-ups, and other physical exercises made us all extremely fit. In addition to the strictly-regulated nature of activities, the other impressive feature of the dojo was its age, gender and ethnic mix. Lined up together were 7 to 70 years olds, matching numbers of girls and boys, and roughly equal proportions of Asian, black and white people, all united and respectful in pursuit of their common goal of systematically improving their karate skills.

The Elite Karate Association was made up of six dojos located in different parts of the borough. In the summer, about three hundred of us students from different dojos would join together, uniformly dressed in our white cotton pyjamas, to participate in a mass demonstration of movement sequences and to receive the results of our grading in the form of coloured belts, each marking a stage in our development of the martial art of karate. I still possess a vivid mental image of numerous figures, clad in white, standing in line on a green playing field in bright sunshine. Later, Dad painted a picture of me, at the age of eleven, in my white pyjamas, displaying my clenched fists and emerald green karate belt against a background of daisies.

.rate Association had been started in 1986 by Shihan sh Johnson, a 7th Dan in the Wado Ryu style. Like ı was a Jamaican, who came to Wolverhampton in 1966, and, through a ruthless commitment in his spare time to and exercise, achieved national and international .tion for his prowess at karate, becoming the English Karate nal Coach.

Mel and Frank were on good terms with Josh and would stop to talk and exchange news when they met in town. Instinctively, we stood back at a distance out of respect for the formidably-built black shihan who presented us with our colour-graded belts.

I know that my parents share a profound appreciation for Josh Johnson and the impact he has had on the discipline, self-awareness and fitness of many generations of Wolverhampton's young people. In hindsight, I think attendance at karate classes has contributed immensely to my own assertiveness and continued interest in physical exercise.

Toussaint had already paved the way for me when I transferred to Smestow School in 1992. Robeson was to follow in 1995. Teachers knew we were a family, and sometimes compared our behaviour and performance, but never in a destructive way. In truth, I relished the strength and support that arose from the three of us attending the same school.

Smestow, in Castlecroft, was one of a circle of 11-to-18 non-selective secondary schools situated on the outskirts of Wolverhampton. It served a western segment of the borough, taking children from the inner wards all the way to the boundary of the town, along the 543 bus route. The building had been erected in 1964 by Staffordshire County Council before the boundary changes that made Tettenhall part of Wolverhampton. The school was situated on open land behind a former council estate and had a large hall, gym, and its own swimming bath.

"Why did you choose to send us to Smestow?" I asked Dad.

"The comprehensive schools to the west of Wolverhampton all seemed very similar to me," Dad replied. "We visited three or four of them and finally selected Smestow because it was conveniently placed on a direct bus route from Merridale. I suppose the other reason was that our neighbour, Paul Willis, was a friend of Mr Hawthorne, the headteacher. Paul considered him to be enlightened and progressive in his approach to education - a person you could reason with."

With just under one thousand students drawn from a wider geographical area, Smestow was four times the size of Merridale. As with other secondary schools, it divided the day into 'periods', each filled with a 'subject', taught singly and separately. The curriculum - mostly determined at national level - consisted of a succession of discrete subjects: English, Mathematics, Science, Geography, History, a modern language (French and/or German), Art, Design and Technology, Information Technology, Physical Education, and Religious Studies.

Smestow, along with other state schools, was expected to provide Christian religious worship and religious studies. As non-believers, our parents could have withdrawn us from these sessions, but were not inclined to do so, explaining that it was important that we understood as much as possible about Christianity, as it was part and parcel of Jamaican and European culture. This did not mean, however, that we were expected to believe literally in its myths about the origin of the universe and of life on earth.

As for ideas, such as eternal life after death, and of people coming back to life who were truly dead, Mom and Dad suggested that we rely instead on what we learned in our biology lessons about the life cycle. Neither did they regard Christianity as an adequate or acceptable moral code for us to live by, making it clear they were horrified by the many aspects of Christian - especially Catholic - teaching, which appeared to impact negatively on the equality of women and gays. They explained that only socialist morality promulgated a public duty to support collective measures to secure the wellbeing of all our fellow citizens, as exemplified by the National Health Service and various other statutory welfare provision. Christianity hadn't managed to achieve this in its two-thousand-year history.

At Smestow, we missed the deliberately integrated themes and projects of our primary school. We also had to wear a uniform with the curious Tettenhall circle badge, said to represent watersheds, windmills and weapons, although one needed a good eye to decipher these themes from the intricacy of the design.

Another noticeable difference from Merridale was Smestow's ethnic composition. It was a mainly-white school, with less than one in five of the students coming from Asian, black, or mixed backgrounds, and with few, if any, ethnic minority teachers.

As most of our time was spent in sets based on our ability, I was often the only person in the room who wasn't white. Even in my form class, which wasn't based on ability, there was only one other pupil, called Curtis, who was of Jamaican descent. Apart from me, him, and one Asian boy, everyone else was white. The consequence was that nearly all the friends that Toussaint, Robeson and I made at Smestow were white.

I still remain in regular contact with many of the friends I had there. On my first day at school in Year 7, I was sitting at a desk with an empty chair, when I heard a shy voice asking if the place was free. A girl sat down beside me. It was Kate Rimmer. Our friendship has lasted to this day. Recently, she travelled all the way to Kenya to visit me.

In Year 9, Johanna, a petite blond Swedish girl, who had lived in the United States, joined my form set. My form teacher, Mrs Timbrell, sat her next to me and asked me to look after her and show her around. Johanna asked lots of questions and spoke very quickly. She introduced me to her parents, Magnus and Suzanne, who invited me to their home and spent time talking to me. Much of their food was of fish and far more plain-tasting than I was used to, but the experience contributed to my growing interest in life in other countries. Johanna, now returned to Sweden, remains a very dear friend.

In the sixth form, I made friends with Ivan who came from Serbia, where his mother and sister still lived. He was most distressed by the events occurring there: the election of Slobodan Milosevic as Yugoslavia president, the war in Kosovo, and the NATO bombing of Belgrade. He spoke of the Muslims in his family and of how he didn't understand what was happening to his country. I was developing an interest in international politics and, out of concern for Ivan, began to follow avidly the news from the Balkans. A fascination in people from other countries and cultures, but also a loathing for the horrors of genocide, have remained with me ever since.

Smestow was designated and equipped to accommodate visually impaired and blind students who were integrated and educated as much as their disability allowed into mainstream classes. There was a blind boy at the school called Craig who was really friendly and intelligent and played the piano very well. While talking to him in a music class, I mentioned casually that my mother was Jamaican. He remarked, "Yes, I know," which, at the time, I found very surprising.

Toussaint and I went on the French exchanges organised by the French teacher, Mr Patch. He inquired about our hobbies and personal interests in an attempt to match us with a suitable French child. When he leaned over my desk with the card listing my details, I noticed the word 'noire' written in capitals. I didn't question him at the time but remember feeling indignant that my skin colour mattered.

When I was in Year 10, a letter appeared in the local newspaper, the *Express and Star*, attacking multi-cultural education and claiming that immigrant children were damaging standards in schools. Dad showed me the letter and asked me what I thought of it.

"Rubbish!" I declared.

"What are you going to do about it?" he asked.

"We could all write to the newspaper to say we were in favour of multi-cultural education," I suggested.

The upshot was that we prepared a letter which I signed and took to school, where I gathered further signatures from sympathetic class mates. My friend, Martha, made the mistake of signing her name above mine. When later, our letter was published, the editor abbreviated the long list of supporting names, to 'Martha Cheesewright and friends'. It wasn't difficult to locate the only Cheesewright family in the Wolverhampton phone book. Martha was sent an anonymous letter full of racist abuse. I believe her parents called the police to report it. By way of contrast, our household was so used to receiving abusive correspondence that a letter of this kind would have been routinely filed to provide further social scientific evidence of the persistence of bigotry and prejudice.

Drawing pupils from across a large area of the town, the school inevitably took in children from a wide range of backgrounds: refined and rowdy, kind and cruel, polite and bad-mannered, well-to-do and poor. There were fights in the play ground, sexual horse-play, drugs, gang fights and bullying, but never on a scale sufficient to make our lives at the school unbearable.

Our mixed-race appearance gave us street credibility. Along with the black kids, it was assumed that we were tough and could look after ourselves. Indeed, being black, or mixed-race, was seen as 'cool', and acting 'black' was something 'cool kids' aspired to, resulting in some very odd Jamaican 'patois'!

Black playground solidarity manifested itself in other unexpected ways. It didn't do to make remarks, either in class or elsewhere, which might be construed as disparaging to black people. Robeson, as Deputy Head Boy, was once obliged to intervene to stop a hapless white youth from being beaten up for expressing allegedly racist opinions. He points out, by way of balance, that he also had to stop black pupils, especially the girls, racially abusing their white classmates.

Although studious, all three of us were tall, strong and good at sport, which helped enormously in the popularity stakes. My sister and I also acquired a well-earned reputation for being gobby and assertive. We would never back down when faced with aggression. Bullies usually gave us a wide berth. We also took it upon ourselves to correct anyone, teachers or students, whom we considered to be showing us disrespect, or who referred to us as 'half-caste' - an expression we hated.

As I progressed through school, it became obvious that the majority of black and mixed-race children had, for whatever reason, been allocated to lower ability sets.

Toussaint, Robeson and I stood out for bucking this trend. Toussaint, as trailblazer was particularly sensitive to teacher attitude. She believes that she had constantly to demonstrate her intellectual worth in the face of the teachers' poor opinion of black and mixed-race children's abilities. Our subconscious recognition of this state of affairs may have motivated all three of us to outshine our classmates in an effort to overturn our teachers' negative stereotypes.

Our parents were also prone to impose their assumptions in the way they behaved to us. They were keen for us to concentrate on academic achievement and largely ignored our sporting prowess. They didn't want us to be channelled towards subjects, usually involving physical exercise, or popular music, that black people are stereotyped as being good at. Toussaint and I were keen netball players, and Robeson excelled at football. We all played regularly for the school. Yet our parents never once came to watch. While they may argue that it was because of their busy work schedules, I suspect it was for another reason.

By the time Toussaint reached the fifth form, she had established for herself a reputation as an intelligent and hardworking student but, judging by her teachers' apparent surprise, they were still unprepared for her GCSE results. According to Mr Hawthorn, the headteacher, these were the most outstanding that he could remember in his time at the school. She took and passed 11 GCSEs in all, 5 at grade A* and 6 at grade A. Even so, my sister was aware that her performance would not alter what she believed to be the persistent negative stereotyping of mixed-race or black students. Troubled when one teacher referred to her as an 'enigma', she concluded that she'd only ever been seen as an unusual exception to the general rule.

Robeson and I somehow managed to live up to the high standards set by Touss, all three of us passing eleven GCSEs apiece, mostly with A*s or As, and certainly with no grade below a B! We also retained the momentum of our success in the sixth form, with each of us passing four GCE A levels, and progressing effortlessly to university. Toussaint went off to the University of Warwick in 1998 to study for a degree in biological sciences, while I took up a place at Lancaster to read law.

What role did the school play in our success? Dad was highly critical of the school's apparent inability to customise the curriculum to students' individual requirements. In particular, he was annoyed at the school's refusal to recognise and develop Robeson's mathematical prowess and provoked to fury at one teacher's suggestion that his son had already reached his 'mathematical plateau'. In Dad's view, Robeson could have passed his GCSE in maths in Year 10. He was clearly bored and losing interest at school in his best subject.

The head of maths, Mr White, proposed 'extension activities', but these never materialised. Dad wrote to Mr Hawthorne, the headteacher, pointing out that neither the learning process for individuals nor the classification of mathematical subject matter, could ever be made to correspond exactly to a school organisational structure based currently on chronological age banding and the requirements of the National Curriculum. All to no avail!

In despair, Dad arranged for Robeson to visit Roger Sanders, a retired colleague and former engineering lecturer, to receive tuition in mathematics. Roger was no ordinary teacher and approached the task by engaging Robeson in the creative application of mathematical principles to practical problem solving, an approach that Robeson uses in his work today. My brother still expresses his profound gratitude to Roger for his inspired and lasting contribution to his mathematical education, which led directly to his reading statistics and operational research at University College London.

The foregoing reflections on our early years and education in Wolverhampton propelled us, inevitably, to investigate our mother's childhood in Jamaica, which we imagined would be very different from our own. Afterwards, we turned to our father's upbringing in Birmingham and his good fortune in passing the eleven-plus examination to grammar school. The stories they told in response to our questions allowed us to compare our lives with theirs, and to tease out the differences and what we shared in common. Our admiration, particularly for our mother's achievements, rose in leaps and bounds.

PART II BEFORE THEY MET

Chapter 11

Growing up barefoot

In 1993, we visited an overgrown plot of family land at a location known as 'Content', high in the hills of Jamaica, where we discovered the graves of our maternal great-grandparents. The tombs of 'Poppy' and 'Aunt' Worrell were capped in concrete inscribed in a spidery hand with their names and burial dates. It is customary for Jamaican peasant farmers to bury their relatives on family land close to where they lived, marking the spot by planting colourful crotons and Joseph coats (colei). By the time of our visit, no commemorative plants had survived. The site was surrounded by shoulder-high marijuana bushes flourishing beneath a light canopy of tall trees. Mom was annoyed at what she perceived as a desecration, but Dad seemed wryly amused. It turned out that, on a previous visit, Dad had been given a guided tour of the family ganja fields by a fierce Rastafarian brandishing a cutlass, who turned out – luckily – to be a relative. Worrell family land was still being cultivated but, in this instance, for commercial, rather than subsistence, purposes.

Mom was born in this tiny settlement called 'Content', to the west of Bog Walk in the Jamaican Parish of St Catherine. There are at least six locations marked on the tourist maps of Jamaica called 'Content', but the 'Content' where Mom came into the world is too small to be one of them.

Her birth certificate, or 'age paper', as it is commonly called in Jamaica, records her place of birth as Bog Walk itself, a five-mile walk from her 'Content', along winding tracks and lanes. Bog Walk was the nearest market town, situated upstream from where the Rio Cobre River enters its spectacular gorge. Mom's date of birth is entered as 11 March 1944. Her name is registered as 'Melhado Chevannes', a curious combination of a Scottish surname serving as a first name, and the French-sounding family name of her father. The certificate gives her mother's name as 'Hephzibah Worrell', the registrar rationally, but wrongly, assuming 'Epsi' to be an abbreviated form of the Hebrew Old Testament name.

ɹamaica was still a Crown Colony and Britain 'the y'. But the year of Mom's birth saw the adoption of a ution which started the island on its eighteen-year , full independence. Every Jamaican over the age of ne, which included Mel's mother, gained the right for the ne to vote in elections for the new House of Representatives. year, the Jamaica Labour Party under Alexander Bustamante s ept the polls, winning 25 of the 32 seats. Grandma still votes for the Labour Party - but a different one – in Birmingham, England.

"Gran," Toussaint asked, "was Mom born at home?"

"Mek mi tell you something," she cackled. "In dem days all di pickney dem baan a yaad."

"Where was that?" Toussaint probed.

"Unu momma baan a Pond."

Mel expressed surprise. "I always thought I was born at Baines," she said.

"A Pond fi sure!" Aunt Epsi retorted.

She had given birth to Mel at a place called 'Pond', in a small timber-framed house complete with wattle-and-daub walls and coconut-leaf thatched roof. It was situated on land belonging to the Chevannes family. 'Baines', built on Worrell family land, was a similar-size property half a mile away, set among fruit trees, with a barbecue, that is, an open floor for drying beans.

Aunt Epsi claimed to remember being attended at Mel's birth by her next-door neighbour. The impromptu midwife gave advice and encouragement, intervening when necessary, and tidying up the mother and baby afterwards. There were no scales to weigh the baby, but Mel was described as 'likl'. Aunt Epsi recalled that the afterbirth was buried and a fruit tree planted at the spot, a widespread custom rationalised in terms of providing food in later life for the new offspring. She was of the view that Mel's 'navel-string tree' had been a banana palm.

We identified Pond nearly fifty years later from its muddy green pool, paddled by ducks and trampled by cattle. Nearby was a garden of sugar-loaf pineapples and ripe coffee beans. But the unromantic impression that has stayed with me is of a place of humidity, heat, and insect bites.

When Aunt Epsi was away in Spanish Town, or Kingston, working as a market trader, or 'higgler', selling the produce grown by family members, Mel and her brother, Lloyd, stayed with their grandparents, 'Poppy' and 'Aunt' Worrell, who lived in Content in another little wooden house with a 'zinc', or corrugated-iron, roof. Mel remembers her grandmother as a strict no-nonsense character, disinclined to display affection towards her grandchildren and merciless in punishing perceived wrongdoing. 'Poppy', in contrast, was kind, sitting his children – or 'pickney' - down and telling them stories.

Mel's mom has always been part of her life. She assumes her mother and father must have separated when she was very young. She has retained contact with Chevannes family members in Jamaica – most notably, her father's sister, Aunt Dine but, when she lived in Content, she saw almost nothing of her father, Fitzroy. Hers was a typical Jamaican maternally-focused experience. She was brought up in Content by her mother, her grandmother and various aunts and older cousins until the age of eight, when she and her brother, Lloyd, were taken by their mother, Epsi, to live in Spanish Town.

Mel's lasting memory of her childhood was of communal living, where everyone in the locality seemed to be related, however distantly, to the Worrell family. 'Poppy', her grandfather, had fathered twelve children by 'Aunt', as well as having two 'outside children'. These uncles and aunts had themselves parented children. Many lived in the immediate vicinity of Content, or had left their offspring there, as they went in search of their livelihoods in the wider world. The family had become so concentrated that an area in Content had acquired the sobriquet, 'Worrell Town'.

While visiting Content, we had called at the houses of Aunt Epsi's brothers: Uncle Andrew and Uncle Willie, and had been amazed, even then, at the number of Mel's cousins and their children present, or in residence. Our branch of the family in England had long lost touch with them. We managed at least to recognise Uncle Willie from the portrait Dad had painted on an earlier visit, showing him sitting proudly astride his donkey.

"So, how has this place changed since you grew up here?" Toussaint asked Mom.

"In lots of ways", she replied. "For a start, it was far more isolated from the outside world. Your father couldn't have driven the car up here as he did today."

The Content in which Mom grew up in the 1940s and 50s was far more difficult to access. It was situated along a narrow pot-holed cart track a mile from the nearest metalled road at Spring Vale. The track to Content rose between precipitous limestone crags along a narrow valley overgrown with tangled vegetation. Wherever the depth of soil and gradient on either side allowed, the local people had planted crops of yam, banana and other staples. After the regular afternoon downpour, the route became slippery and almost impassable until the sun blazed down again.

Away from the track, houses and farmland could be reached only on foot, the main means of transport for most people. Donkeys could be ridden, but were kept mostly as pack animals. A few of the men had bicycles. Carts and market trucks struggled sporadically up the hill. The children became very excited on one occasion when Mel's Uncle Eddy, who lived in St Thomas, turned up riding a motor cycle.

Despite the limited means of transport, the locals were used to making their way down the hill to Spring Vale and following the winding lanes to market in Bog Walk or Linstead, or catching the country buses to Spanish Town or Kingston. They certainly didn't think of themselves as being cut off from the outside world. This was merely Mom's perception from her vantage point in England, fifty years into the future.

Content, in those days, consisted of a row of little houses spread out for half a mile on either side of a pot-holed track. The worst potholes were mended every now and again with limestone chippings. Houses were made of wood: the poorest with one room, the more prosperous with two, comprising a sitting room and a bedroom. Frequently, extra rooms would be built around a central yard to provide more living space for older children. It was customary to erect a completely separate shelter alongside the main dwelling to serve as a kitchen. Another enclosed shelter, covering a pit latrine, was situated at a discrete distance from the main dwelling.

The preoccupation of the residents of Content was the extent and quality of family land and their entitlement to it. Men and women survived by farming, a back-breaking activity that occupied them everyday of the week except Sunday. The men saw themselves as primarily responsible for working the land, while the women took on the extra role of selling any surplus crops at market. Realising that they would remain poor subsistence farmers, squabbling over family land, for the rest of their lives, some of the men signed contracts to work in the United States as agricultural labourers. Among those who went to America were Mel's father, Fitzroy, and her mother's youngest brother, Abraham, known to the family as 'Dadda'.

Mel remembers a shop selling basic provisions such as flour and salt fish, a rum bar, and the Hill Top Pentecostal, a small church built of wood on a base of concrete blocks. It was at the shop that Mel first heard the sound of a radio set, powered by a car battery, for Content was not connected to an electricity supply, nor was there water on tap. There wasn't a telephone service or postal delivery. Letters had to be sent to a post office box number.

Early in the morning, before walking to Spring Vale, Mel, along with other children of her age, went to fetch water from a river half a mile away. She was expected to wash regularly in an enamel bowl with flannel and soap, or to bathe in the river. She had no opportunity to shower until she went to live in Spanish Town. Water for cooking and drinking was stored in the shade of the house in a large, slightly porous earthenware jar – a 'Spanish jar' – the surface evaporation keeping the water deliciously cool.

Both her mother and grandmother worried about Mel, because she was so thin and slight, or 'maaga', as they put it. As a consequence, she was never smacked or beaten. They saw to it that she was regularly fed, and allowed her to carry water only in a small metal bucket, rather than a full-size kerosene pan. Nevertheless, on one occasion, she slipped over and the full bucket of water that she was balancing on her head fell off and cut her badly on her heel, leaving a scar that shows to this day. In common with other children, she went around bare-footed. She wore shoes only on public occasions to attend school and church.

On washing day, the womenfolk, carrying bundles of laundry on their heads, would make their way in line to the river and select a suitable spot with rocks, on which the clothes could be smacked, wrung, and laid out to dry. When the children weren't at school, they would go to the river to play. Fruit and firewood were gathered along the river bank, and crayfish caught in the rock pools. While the washing dried, the women would cook and eat. Mel was fascinated by the way the crayfish turned pink on the fire.

She remembers her meals with relish. She was fed with home-grown yam, sweet potato, coco, dasheen, cassava, breadfruit and banana, as they came into season. Although inexpensive, the fare was varied and tasty. She ate stew peas cooked in coconut milk, goat and pigs' tripe, pigs' tail, salted mackerel or herring, and salt fish (dried cod) served with ackee or calaloo (a type of spinach).

It's obvious to me that our Jamaican family heritage has been retained in the meals we eat now. In England, we regularly consume a thick Jamaican 'soup' or broth, flavoured with chilli and other spices, and containing mutton chunks, yam, coco, dasheen, chocho, and dumplings. It tastes much the same, we believe, as it did in Content. At Christmas, a breakfast of green bananas, ackee and bacon is served, while at other times we eat cornmeal porridge, or hominy. On other family occasions, plates of Jamaican confectionary, such as gizadas (tarts filled with grated coconut) and cut cakes (made of chopped and sugar-coated coconut) are passed round. Dad has come to prefer Jamaican cooking, which he calls 'yard food', and complains when he doesn't get it.

In the Content of those days, family meals were prepared mostly by the women over a wood fire or, less commonly, a coal stove, in the household kitchen, the 'coal', of course, being 'charcoal'. The fire heated the pots, including the round-bottomed dutch pot, or dutchy. Breadfruit would more usually be turned and roasted over the embers. Mel recalls how the men would sometimes gather late in the night to cook their own special feasts, washed down with beer and rum. Lying awake listening, the children would make their presence known, and be rewarded with the left-overs.

In the tropics, night fell rapidly and the twilight lasted barely twenty minutes. Before the moon rose, or at the new moon, it could be very dark indeed. In those days, when the sun set in Content, the only natural light came from the moon, the stars, the peeny wallies (the luminous spots of a click beetle) and the blinkers (fire flies). The blinkers hovered above the bushes, giving off short pulses of light, like sparks from a bush fire. Artificial light came from burning wood, candles, common kerosene lamps and the rarer, and recently-introduced, pump-up primus lamps.

Intense nocturnal darkness, punctuated only by feeble lamp light, provided the ideal setting for lurid tales of the supernatural. At night, the children were frightened to sleep by stories of 'duppies', the restless ghosts of the dead. Some duppies were protective when they happened to be family ancestors, but the majority was malignant, if not treated with the utmost caution and respect.

One demonic form of duppy, rumoured to roam the hills of Content, was the dreaded 'rolling calf', a roaring calf-like monster with fiery eyes, which dragged along a clanking chain. The older men sometimes confided how they had terrified gullible passers-by by groaning and rattling chains in the bush at night.

Unlike some other family members, Mel's mom was not superstitious and had no truck with obeah men – the traditional Jamaican witchdoctors, who wielded considerable influence in country areas. Instead, Mel's mom was, and still is, a devout Christian, currently attending the King's Christian Centre, a Pentecostal church in Sparkbrook, Birmingham. Aunt Epsi learned to read and write, and studied her bible and the church magazines.

Mel was sent at a very young age to the church school in Content and, later, attended the primary school at Spring Vale. She practised her alphabet on a slate at the church school, but was given her first paper exercise book at Spring Vale. Because of the heat, many of the classes were taken out of doors in the shade of a tree. She remembers learning her multiplication tables by rote at Spring Vale and being selected by a kindly teacher called Miss Henry for extra tuition after school hours. Mel was considered a quick learner. All the teachers and pupils she encountered before she left for Spanish Town were black Jamaicans.

"Mom, when did you first meet a white person?" Toussaint asked.

"For as long as I can remember", she replied unexpectedly. "Uncle George was a white man."

"Who on earth was Uncle George?" Toussaint inquired.

Uncle George, she was told, was white, or very light-skinned, but not an albino. He lived in Content and made his living as a farmer, the same as everyone else. He was related in some mysterious way to the Chevannes family, hence the 'uncle'. But Mel was conspicuously vague on the details.

"Why was he living in Content?" Toussaint persisted.

"He was said to be an English sailor who jumped ship in Kingston and ran away to hide in bush."

"Did he have an English accent?"

"No", Mom replied, "he spoke Jamaican patois like everyone else."

"Was he married to a black woman?"

"I think he lived on his own," she said.

In her eighty-ninth year, Aunt Epsi, our grandma, recalled experiences from her childhood more vividly and with greater accuracy than events in later life. One day, without warning, she told us that when she was about six years old, her mother had given birth at home in Content to a baby called Isabella. Epsi's new sister came into the world with a sixth digit on each hand and foot.

I googled 'six fingers' to discover that in medical circles this congenital condition is referred to as 'polydactylism' and is found in 1 in every 500 live births – though 10 times more frequently among black children than white.

Epsi's mom, Miriam, believed the anomaly to be a result of obeah (sorcery), and sought to rid her child of the extra appendages by binding them tightly with thread in the hope that they would wither and drop off. Starved of their blood supply, baby Isabella's extra fingers and toes putrefied and poisoned her blood stream, causing her to die soon afterwards of septicaemia. Thus, my great-grandmother Worrell brought about the death of her twelfth and last child through ignorance, superstition, and the absence at that time of modern medical care for poor rural Jamaicans.

Chapter 12

Growing up on chocolate

Bournville had been conceived in 1893 by the Quaker, George Cadbury, and built on land he acquired next to his new chocolate factory. The name 'Bournville' was coined originally for the factory, from 'Bourn', the brook that ran through the area, and 'ville', chosen for its French connotation at a time when the French were thought to make the best chocolate.

The model village was intended to improve living conditions for the working-class people of Birmingham, not merely the employees at Cadbury's. Families were expected to benefit from the advantages of an Arcadian outdoor village life: sun, light and air, with unlimited opportunities for gardening and other self-improving activities. The countryside was brought to town by planting trees and preserving patches of woodland and open green spaces. The place certainly had a rural feel to it. Dad recalled how in the 1950s a gaggle of geese was driven on a daily basis down Sycamore Road to graze behind the church.

The ample cottage gardens, each averaging 500 square meters, were meant to encourage residents to grow their own food and to achieve a measure of self-sufficiency. The Cadbury strap line 'factory in a garden' carried the ring of truth. Granddad and Grandma Reeves were not enthusiastic gardeners, but they still managed to grow cabbages, keep bees and chickens, crop the fruit from the orchard, mow the lawns, and cut the hedges.

The implicit assumption was that, when not at work, a man's place was in the garden, and a woman's in the home. It was certainly not in the pub. The deeds of the Bournville Village Trust, set up in 1900, prohibited the erection of any building for the manufacture, sale or distribution of beer, wine and spirits. This was of no concern to Granddad and Grandma Reeves who drank very little. On occasion, they accepted a bottle of elderberry wine from a neighbour in exchange for a jar of honey produced from the hives in their garden.

Our father, Frank, was born in the maternity ward at Selly Oak Hospital in Birmingham, England, on the 7th February 1945. According to our Grandma Phyllis, he weighed in at 9lbs 10oz, whatever that might be in grams. The doctor and nurses were particularly alert because, some two years earlier, an older brother, Thomas, had died in his cot a week after birth. This time, Phyllis, his mother, returned in triumph with her baby to her home at 13 Sycamore Road, Bournville, to be greeted by a birthday cake, candles, a thanksgiving prayer, and a warm room – the last a considerable achievement, given the rationing of coal.

When Dad was born, the Second World War was raging, Berlin was being bombed to the ground, and 'the big three' – Roosevelt, Stalin and Churchill – were meeting in Yalta to decide on what to do when the fighting finished. Victory in Europe was still three months away. While the new baby would not have been aware of this, one consequence of the war was that food and other goods were severely rationed. Dad's birth certificate brought with it a ration book, a National Registration Identity Card, and other paraphernalia, such as a baby's gas mask (discovered many years later in the cellar).

The child was registered as Francis William Hugh Reeves – quite a mouthful – but revealing of our English grandparents' determination to make sure the baby was protected by a triumvirate of saints: all of them Catholic. (Despite his parents' preference for 'Francis', his mother's irreverent family managed immediately to subvert the baby's name to 'Franky'.) The baby's mother was recorded as Phyllis Marie Reeves, and the father as Norman Charles Reeves (occupation: works chemist), both of them resident at Sycamore Road, in the sub-district of Selly Oak, in the County Borough of Birmingham.

Thereafter, the Reeves family grew quickly. Frank acquired three sisters. Margaret (our Aunt Maggie) was born in 1948, Angela (Aunt Annie) in 1949, and Philippa (Aunt Pip) in 1951.

The house at 13 Sycamore Road was situated near the centre of the Bournville Village Estate, on the same road as the timber-framed row of shops, the re-erected Elizabethan Selly Manor, the Day Continuation College, and the Anglican Church. Within view were the picturesque Village Green, with its distinctive octagonal Rest House, featured on chocolate boxes, the Quaker Meeting House, and the Village Schools, topped by the landmark tower and patinated carillon.

Frank, our Dad, describes growing up on Bournville as like living on the film set of William Morris's utopia, *News from Nowhere.* But, from a practical point of view, the village had its deficiencies. The nearest department store, public library and reading room were in Stirchley, the swimming baths were reserved for Cadbury workers and, of course, there was no pub (although Davenports - 'Beer at Home' - did a roaring trade).

The semi-detached house to which Frank was brought home was designed, in Arts and Crafts style, as a 'large cottage' by the Trust's architect, Alexander Harvey, and erected around 1904. It had three floors: a front room, dining room, kitchen and scullery on the ground floor, and four bedrooms, a bathroom, and water closet on the two upper floors. A coal chute sloped down into a large double cellar. Years later, Dad was surprised to see a picture of the same house featured in the Shell Guide to Warwickshire.

The windows at the back of the house looked out over a long garden, stretching down to the railway sidings in a deep cutting, with the massive Cadbury factory buildings in the distance. The windows at the front provided a view of the front garden, Sycamore Road, and the timber-framed Elizabethan Selly Manor. Our great-grandfather, Edward Fortey, and afterwards our grandma, Phyllis, kept the keys to both Selly Manor and Minworth Greaves (the fourteenth century cruck-framed hall behind). They were expected to open the windows to air these historic buildings, as well as to show round the occasional visitor.

Water and gas were piped into the house from a mains supply and there were electric plugs and light sockets in every room. Like most other houses at the time, Number 13 was not centrally-heated or double-glazed. Each room was provided with a fireplace and chimney. During the winter months, however, because of the cost and the limited supply of coal, on weekdays only the kitchen could be kept warm. When the need arose, an electric fire could be switched on in the dining room and a portable paraffin stove used to heat the bathroom or study.

Granddad used to get up every morning at 6.30am to light the fire under the kitchen range before leaving for work. Grandma, apparently, regarded this as the proof of his love and devotion! A back boiler in the kitchen produced hot water but, because of the cost, hot tap water and a hot bath were available only on Saturdays.

At other times, Frank washed – or more probably said that he washed – at the bathroom sink, with water in winter poured from a hot kettle heated on a gas ring. The cooking stove and the wash boiler, both situated in the scullery, were heated by gas. It was not until the mid 1950s that the boiler, wringing board and mangle were replaced by a washing machine, the result of one of Grandma's more successful campaigns for women's rights.

Dad has vivid memories of climbing the stairs reluctantly on winter nights to a bed made up with layer upon layer of blanket. Before the light was switched off, he would watch his breadth condensing in the cold air of the room. By morning, a deposit of ice would have formed on the inside of the window panes. He remembers the chilblains on his hands and feet, and the daily dose of cod liver oil to keep them at bay.

Milk and bread deliveries were made in those days by horse-drawn carts, replaced in the mid 1950s by electric milk floats and motor vans. Every three weeks, the coalmen arrived in their truck, lifted the coal sacks onto their backs, and emptied them down the chute. Other tradesmen who called at the house were the window cleaner and chimney sweep.

As in other suburbs in England, the families living in Bournville valued their privacy. Tall privet hedges had grown up to separate gardens, both front and back. While always polite and helpful to their neighbours, people kept themselves to themselves.

Frank, however, was part of the large extended Fortey family which formed a community in itself. His grandparents, Edward and Florence, had reared nine children, six of them taking up residence in, or close to, Bournville, which was especially convenient for the three family members who worked at the chocolate factory. Sycamore Road, in particular, became a Fortey hotspot.

There were advantages of having family members working at Cadbury's, particularly in the immediate post-war period. Employees were entitled to cards allowing them to buy chocolate waste and other items at the factory shop. The whole family took advantage of this perk, to the extent that the children were used to gorging chocolate biscuits when they came home from school each day. The sight of a chocolate biscuit makes Dad feel sick!

The local, tightly-knit Fortey collective of five sisters and their mother – an older generation all now deceased – has left a lasting impression on younger family members. Frank, his sisters, and their maternal cousins, still remain in touch. They gathered recently in 2009 to plant a commemorative Fortey family tree on the Green itself. Cousins Janet and Tony still live on the estate, representing an unbroken 88 years' association with Bournville.

Dad says the place looks much the same as it did when he was growing up, except that it is now more 'open plan'. The railings around the Triangle have been dismantled, hedges uprooted, and front gardens paved over for car parking. The once wide and empty Sycamore Road is now cluttered and congested with motor vehicles.

The strength and durability of relations on our Grandma Phyllis's side of the family can be compared with Granddad Norman's. Norman had been brought up in Sparkbrook, Birmingham. He had two brothers and three sisters, but only one of them, Granddad's brother, Horace, lived close by. He was married but had no children of his own. Frank was a favourite of his Uncle Horace, who fought at the Somme, had medals, and was styled 'Major Reeves'. In civvy street, he worked as a clerk on the railways, but remained a marksman, teaching Dad how to shoot his air rifle to hit tin cans every time.

Little day-to-day contact was possible with Granddad's other relatives, who lived much further afield, in Lincoln, London and Bexhill-on-Sea. Their impact on the family at number 13 was imperceptible compared with that of the Forteys settled nearby. In the 1940s and 50s, family members separated by distance could retain contact only by writing postcards and letters, or by making regular visits. Few people had their own car, and travel was mainly by bicycle, bus, and train.

Dad's family did not have a telephone line until 1958, a television until 1960, and a car until November 1962. The Reeveses were avid radio listeners instead, tuning in to programmes such as Mrs Dale's Diary, The Archers, and Children's Hour - a great favourite of Frank's. Grandma Phyllis was of the view that radio stimulated the imagination, whereas television rendered it superfluous. Children were better off without TV.

Dad's childhood in Bournville led directly to the development of his interests in, for example, nature and the countryside, beekeeping, architecture and town planning, topography and meteorology, the peace movement, and comparative religion.

He has a vivid image of being taken by his father to the park to catch newts and coming back plastered in mud, but proud of his jam jar full of them. With his cousin Janet, he went for walks in the fields to the west of the estate, where they would pick wild flowers and hunt for sticklebacks and caddis lava.

Every year, the family participated in the Bournville Village Festival held on the sports ground in front of the factory. It was a grand affair, with maypole dancing, a fancy-dress parade, free cakes and pop, a film show, a fair, and a fire work display: the grand finale. A family photograph exists of a very young boy dressed up as a pirate. My aunts, as young girls, took part in the maypole dancing.

Enrolled for many years as a London University external student, Norman studied at home in a systematic and disciplined way but never had the opportunity to experience the intellectual cut and thrust of campus life. Around the time Frank was born, he completed a bachelor's degree in German and decided to explore the possibility of becoming a language teacher, acquiring a job soon afterwards as a master at Holly Lodge Grammar School in Smethwick. The boys behaved so badly towards him that, for the sake of his health, he soon transferred to an all-age school, where he got on much better with the children and staff. In 1952, he joined the Chance Technical College as lecturer in English and Modern Languages. We remember Granddad as a kindly man, always interested in explaining to us the meaning of words or the history of the buildings around us.

Our grandmother, Phyllis, had worked for a short while during the war as an assistant teacher of young children at Miss Payne's Woodlands Park School, but had been obliged to leave when her first child was born. As was expected in those days, she remained at home caring for the family as a full-time housewife until her children were grown up. She eventually took a part-time job at Cadbury's in the mid 1960s.

Dad was brought up in a home full of bookcases and books, where great store was placed on the value of education and ideas, not for occupational advancement, but for its own sake.

The Reeves household stood out from those of relatives and neighbours, not so much because of its interest in education, but because of Norman's ardent commitment to Roman Catholicism and his determination to bring his children up as devout members of that faith. He had converted to Catholicism in 1923, aged only 17, and took his new religion very seriously. For him, it was a matter of eternal life or death.

When Phyllis first informed her father, Edward, of her intention to convert to Catholicism in order to marry Norman, he showed a distinct lack of enthusiasm.

"I suppose a Catholic is a Christian," he remarked. Our great-grandfather had an alternative vision of Christianity which he chose to express in his ceaseless efforts to build the Birmingham Labour Party. Along with Alderman Alfred Bradbeer, he was a founding member.

Regarding religious belief as a private and personal matter, the Fortey family found Norman's in-your-face avowal of Catholicism difficult to comprehend. For Frank and his sisters, it meant praying every night before going to bed, attending morning mass and evening benediction on Sundays and holy days, eating fish on Fridays, and being sent to Catholic schools, thus distinguishing and separating them from the children who went to school on the Green.

Norman's initial ambition was for Frank to become a priest. From a young age, Frank managed to disappoint with his reluctance to serve as an altar boy and his protestations of boredom with the repetitive nature of the mass. With the benefit of hindsight, it seems obvious that Norman's prayer-inspired transcendental spirituality could never sit comfortably with his son's propensity for rational analysis and argument. In matters other than religion, however, Frank admits he gained a great deal from his father, including some of his basic political values.

As a young man, Norman marched for 'no more war', and went from house to house persuading people to sign the 'Peace Pledge'. He was active in the League of Nations Union, becoming a committed internationalist. On holiday in Germany, he once challenged, at great personal risk, the ranting of a brown-shirted thug. He used his language skills to assist Jewish refugees to settle in Birmingham after their expulsion from German and Austrian universities. He detested Hitler's anti-Semitism and nationalism, but was convinced that they would never have prevailed had the Germans been treated reasonably at the Treaty of Versailles. (His ambivalence towards the Spanish Civil War arose directly from his Catholicism: although a Republican by temperament, he had no time for the Republic's anticlericalism.)

My father and paternal grandfather disagreed bitterly over the value of religious belief. Norman saw religion as indispensable for leading a life of integrity, while Frank regarded it as damaging the human capacity for accepting moral responsibility. In this essential respect, they grew further apart and were never reconciled.

In the course of Dad's account of his early life on Bournville and his digression to explain the differences he had with his father, Robeson interrupted to inquire:

"When did you first meet a black person?"

"Do you mean 'see', or 'get to know'? Dad replied. "They're very different."

This hair-splitting was vintage Dad. After a moment's thought, he elaborated:

"I don't recall a single black family living in our immediate neighbourhood until I left in 1967. We first saw black people in the mid 1950s on the buses: on the outer circle route and along the Bristol Road. Coming home from school, I was approached on a few occasions by black men asking directions. I took them, I recall, to houses on Katie Road, or thereabouts, in Selly Oak. I also remember black nurses from the Woodlands Nursing Home attending St Edwards, our Catholic church on the Raddlebarn Road. Sometimes, we saw black students from the Selly Oak Colleges strolling by the Yachting Pool."

Robeson didn't anticipate what Dad told him next. Frank's father, Norman, had been friends with an African priest. The friendship had developed after Norman was encouraged by a missionary friend to correspond in German and English with a young man training to be a priest in a seminary in Tanganyika.

Father Christian Kapinga, and his cousin, Werner, from Songea in Tanganyika, had stayed with the Reeves family in Bournville on a number of occasions and were popular guests. It was in 1958, when Christian's cousin, Werner, who had gained a place at the Co-operative College in England, came to stay for Christmas.

"I was only thirteen years old," Dad said, "but Werner and I became friends. I think he found it easier to relate to me than to my father, for whom he had an excessive respect. Werner visited again in 1963 on his way back from the Soviet Union. He told me about the disagreements he'd had with the communists there over the value of the co-operative movement in Africa. He was the first person to tell me about socialism and to explain why he was a socialist. When he visited next, he'd become General Manager of the Tanzanian Cooperative Union."

Robeson inquired about Fr Christian Kapinga, the other visitor.

"I was sent to fetch him from the station. He was on his way to Dublin in 1962 to attend a course in theology. He was an extremely bright and interesting chap, and we talked politics and religion incessantly. Fr Christian was far more open-minded about religion than my father. As a visiting priest, he was expected to say mass at local Catholic churches, although I think he would have preferred to have done more sightseeing.

When he visited again the following year, I went sightseeing with him to Oxford and Stratford. We also visited the Bournville Village Festival where, to my father's unease, Fr Christian pointed out that the maypole dancing was a pagan fertility rite. He asked my father about his attitude towards it. Apparently, Fr Christian, as a Catholic priest in Africa, was expected to suppress rituals of this kind. Until that moment, I don't think my father had been even vaguely aware of the maypole's sexual symbolism. If he had, he might have agonised over whether to allow my sisters to participate in the dancing."

After studying in Ireland and Canada, Christian returned to Tanzania to become a Catholic bishop. Some years later, he converted to Islam, a decision he took, according to Norman, in order to take a wife. At least, that's how Granddad chose to rubbish his decision to become a Muslim. Granddad subsequently wrote him a reproving letter and broke off all contact.

We retain, nevertheless, a memento of the Kapingas' friendship. Early in 1960, Fr Christian wrote to Granddad telling him of a visit he had made to Ndanda, near Lindi, in what is now Tanzania. He had seen a sculptor from the Makonde tribe carving a head of a young woman in ebony.

"The thought of sending you the carving came at once to my head, so I began trading with him… The carving might make a good remembrance of Africa and me."

Some months later, the exquisitely carved bust of a finely-featured African girl arrived in the post. Granddad knew that Frank had always coveted the object and made him a present of it shortly before he died. It is displayed now in the study at Blue Roof. I suspect it's my father's most valued possession. I know it's a far-fetched supposition, but I've always wondered whether Dad's fondness for this carving had any bearing on his appreciation of my mother.

Chapter 13

From Spanish Town to KT

At midnight on 5 August 1962, Jamaica became a free independent nation within the British Commonwealth. Mel was just about to enter her fourth and last year at High School. She remembers the great excitement at the school and on the streets as the time approached. A grand ceremony attended by 35,000 people was held in the newly constructed National Stadium in Kingston in the presence of Princess Margaret (on behalf of the Queen), Sir Alexander Bustamante (Jamaica's first Prime Minister) and Mr Norman Manley (leader of the Opposition).

On the stroke of midnight, the Union Jack was lowered, and the green, yellow and black Jamaican flag was hoisted. This was followed by a magnificent firework display at the Stadium, with lesser displays at other places on the island, including Spanish Town. Everywhere was decorated with flags and bunting, and Kingston was lit up at night, with dancing in the streets and two days of public holiday.

Mel has always been intensely proud of her Jamaican nationality. While we were growing up, the green, yellow and black flag was displayed as a sticker on the rear window of our car.

In 1952, Aunt Epsi sent for Mel, now aged eight, and her brother, Lloyd, living with their grandmother in rural Content to join her in Spanish Town, the old capital of Jamaica. Aunt Epsi had managed her business as a 'higgler' sufficiently well to enable her to rent a little shop built from wood, with a painted front. The living accommodation at the rear had two bedrooms, an outdoor kitchen, wash area, and latrine. Their new home was situated on March Penn Road to the south of the Spanish Town train and bus station, on the far side of the railway line and the Rio Cobre irrigation canal.

As a single mother on her own, Aunt Epsi had to work extremely hard to make a living for herself, and a home for Mel and Lloyd. She sold food and provisions to passers-by making their way on foot, or on bicycle or cart, towards the town centre. She would cook food and, later in the day, push a hand cart, loaded with fried dumplings, fritters, salt fish, plantain, and cornmeal pudding, to the surrounding sugar-cane fields to sell lunch and syrup drinks to the cane cutters. The overseers were still mainly white, while the cane cutters were black, but they all appreciated and partook of Aunt Epsi's cooking. In the school holidays, Mel was expected to accompany her mother to the fields and help serve the drinks, making her feel happy and important, as she poured the syruped water and added the chipped ice for the customers.

Aunt Epsi supplemented her income by making dresses for women and children, and shirts for men on her trusted Singer sewing machine. She was a skilful seamstress, measuring people carefully, and accurately recording their sizes. She sometimes sketched the style that her clients specified but, more often than not, committed it to memory. She was an accomplished artist in cloth and could cut and tailor it without the help of a pattern. This was even more remarkable given that crinoline dresses were in fashion.

As Mel grew older, she acquired a bicycle with a basket and was entrusted with the job of cycling to Spanish Town market to purchase goods which Aunt Epsi didn't, or couldn't, keep in stock, such as fresh meat, pumpkin, Irish potatoes, and yellow yam. With the bicycle loaded down, she often had to balance the produce on the handlebars with one hand and use the other to steer.

Not very far away from where Mel lived, spanning the Rio Cobre, on the outskirts of Spanish Town, was the Iron Bridge, uncannily resembling the bridge with the same name at Ironbridge in Telford, near to Wolverhampton. It had been built in 1801 from cast-iron pieces shipped from England. It is said to be the first and only surviving one of its kind in the Americas. Whenever Mel and Frank take visitors to Ironbridge in England to marvel at Abraham Darby's achievement, Mel is reminded of her beloved Spanish Town and becomes nostalgic.

When they first arrived in Spanish Town, Mel and Lloyd were expected, as they had been in Content, to go to school, although school attendance in Jamaica at the time was neither compulsory nor enforced. The children realised from an early age, however, that their future job prospects and economic wellbeing depended on their education.

There were two free all-age schools in Spanish Town which they could attend: one government-funded and the other Roman Catholic, the latter carrying the expectation that pupils would belong to the Catholic faith. For some reason that we haven't been able to discover, Mel and Lloyd, neither of them Catholics at the time, determined to go to the Catholic school and to covert to Catholicism as a condition of their admission.

St Catherine's School took children between the ages of five and fifteen, and was similar in kind to the all-age schools found in the United Kingdom prior to the passing of the 1944 Education Act.

Run by nuns and priests from the United States, the school was situated next door to the town's Catholic Church, between Red Church Street and White Church Street, the Red Church being the old red-brick Anglican cathedral founded in the 1660s and sited prominently in front of the school gates on the other side of the square.

Mel used to walk to school along the dusty streets, past the Old Barracks and the Cenotaph. Centrally located, the school was not far from the Spanish Town Square and its grand old buildings: the King's House, Court House, former House of Assembly, and the Memorial to Admiral Lord Rodney. The historic townscape was in stark contrast to the forested limestone gullies of Content, but Mel soon grew used to the new urban environment and her regular eight-mile walk in the baking heat to school and back.

At St Catherine's, Mel was taught the normal three Rs curriculum of reading, writing, and arithmetic, and other general topics, which became separate subjects as she grew older. She also received religious instruction and learned about becoming a Catholic, studying the catechism, the roll call of saints, how to confess, and to receive the holy eucharist. She liked the Catholic atmosphere of the cool dim church, with its crucifixes, candles and incense, and the repetitive chanting of the mass. She began to attend evening mass on Sundays, walking to church and back with her friend Vivienne, a fellow pupil, who also lived on March Penn Road. Attending mass was fun. They met other school friends there and, afterwards, visited the cinema, where they treated themselves to ice cream and freshly-roasted peanuts.

Most of the pupils at the school were black like Mel but, reflecting Jamaica's long history of racial mixing as encapsulated in the country's motto, 'out of many, one people', there were also children of Chinese, Indian and Syrian descent. All the teachers were black, except for one white nun who taught religious knowledge.

Mel remembers feeling happy, contented, and safe at the school, and recalls with gratitude the help she received from the head teacher, Mr Neal, who encouraged her to continue with her studies. It was he who entered her for an entrance examination to a Roman Catholic High School in Spanish Town. She was not successful but, shortly afterwards, in July 1959, she gained a free place at a government school in Kingston: Kingston Technical High School, referred to by its alumni as 'KT'. Her achievement was not simply to pass a highly competitive entrance test, but to qualify for a government grant to meet the tuition fees for the whole of her four-year course.

Mel's ambition at St Catherine's was to become a teacher. When she finished at the school at the age of fifteen, she had achieved the educational entry standard for teacher training - the Ministry of Education Third Jamaica Local - but couldn't be accepted at a training college until her eighteenth birthday.

In 1959, when Mel was fourteen and still at St Catherine's, revolutionaries, led by Fidel Castro, seized power in the neighbouring island of Cuba, and began to nationalise industries, including those owned by Americans. Cubans hostile to the new socialist regime began to leave the country, most of them heading for the United States. Some found their way to Jamaica.

Mel remembers the hysteria generated in Jamaica at the prospect of having a communist state on the doorstep and encountering Spanish-speaking Cuban refugees on the streets of Kingston. During the Autumn of 1962, when it was learned that Soviet missile bases had been sited in Cuba, fear grew of an all-out war centred on the Caribbean. President Kennedy announced that he intended to impose an American blockade on the island. Exercising significant influence over public opinion, the Jamaican churches denounced communism as a godless philosophy that epitomised everything that was evil in society. This was the impression that Mel took with her to England.

In 1983, nearly twenty-five years after the Cuban revolution, Mel and Frank were in Spanish Town visiting Mel's aunt, Velma. Bored with the family gossip about relatives he did not know, Frank went sightseeing by himself to photograph yet again the ancient buildings in the main square. He was dressed in khaki, his hair was fashionably long, and he had a pronounced and unkempt beard.

As he returned from the walk, he noticed he was being followed by a growing band of youths who began to chant: "Cuban! Cuban!" As he quickened his step, they quickened theirs, their voices growing louder and louder. He was much relieved when he reached the safety of Aunt Velma's yard and the shouting faded away.

"Which is it better to be around here?" Frank inquired of Mel's Uncle Dada. "Cuban or English?"

"Me tink it better you is a Hinglishman," Uncle Dada replied unhesitatingly.

Under Michael Manley's democratic socialist government of the 1970s, Fidel Castro, the Cuban leader, had sent doctors to Jamaica to augment primary and secondary health care in compensation for the brain drain of Jamaican doctors to the United States. This humanitarian aid project had been denounced at the time by the leader of the opposition, Edward Seaga, amid claims that the Cuban doctors had been responsible for a series of wrong diagnoses and deaths. Succeeding Manley as Prime Minister in 1980, Seaga soon terminated these fraternal ties with Cuba and took measures to improve relations with the USA.

In September 1959, Mel started her new school: Kingston Technical High. She was dressed in the school uniform of pleated navy blue pinafore with white blouse and gold and black belt. Every week day, she had to make the thirteen-mile train or bus journey from Spanish Town to central Kingston. This was preceded by a two-mile walk from March Penn Road to the Spanish Town station and a three-mile walk from Kingston station to the school in Hanover Street, and then, of course, there was the return journey.

Kingston Technical High School took in students whose parents could afford to pay the school fees, other children who had gained free scholarship places, and those, like Mel, whose fees were paid by a government grant awarded on the basis of a competitive examination. Students followed a four-year full-time day course, with a chosen technical specialism which, in Mel's case, was Home Economics.

The school was co-educational, although the intake of girls outnumbered boys in a ratio of more than 2 to 1. Girls and boys were taught general subjects together, but were separated for their technical and, therefore, gender-determined and occupationally-related specialisms. Girls took cookery and dressmaking, while boys did woodwork and construction.

"What subjects did they teach at the technical school?" Toussaint asked. "Were they mainly technical?"

"No," Mom replied. "Apart from the technical subjects, we followed the same curriculum as students in England."

"What subjects?" Toussaint persisted.

"We studied English language, English literature, maths, science, geography, history, Spanish, and Latin."

"Latin!" Toussaint exclaimed. "Even we didn't learn that!"

"But your father did," Mom retorted. "The subjects like Latin that I studied were heavily outweighed by practical subjects like cookery, dressmaking and typewriting."

"What was your best subject at school?" Toussaint queried.

"My best subject and the one that interested me most was geography," Mom replied.

As at St Catherine's, the students were racially very mixed but predominantly black Caribbean. The majority of the staff was also black, but there were a few white teachers from England.

KT encouraged extra-curricular activities of a cultural, artistic and sporting nature. For one week in August every year, the school held a cultural festival which was called the Eisteddfod, after Welsh festivals, such as the Royal National Eisteddfod, in which participants compete for prizes in music, poetry and drama. The KT celebrations involved square dancing, folk singing, team games, the recital of Jamaican poetry, and arts and crafts. We were, of course, all familiar with eisteddfodau from the holidays we spent in Wales, but were surprised to hear of a festival known as an eisteddfod taking place in Jamaica nearly 5,000 miles away.

The teacher who taught Mel Spanish worked at the National Little Dance Theatre in Kingston and invited Mel and some of the other girls to come to her home on Saturdays to help make the costumes for the dancers at the theatre. They ate lunch at the house and sat out in the garden, where they met some of the dancers, including Rex Nettleford, the Rhodes scholar, dancer, choreographer, and founder of the Jamaican National Dance Theatre Company, later to become Vice Chancellor of the University of the West Indies. Such was Mel's excitement at being involved in the theatre that, with Aunt Epsi's agreement, she made the long journey to Kingston on Saturdays as well.

As in most secondary schools in England and Jamaica, sport formed an essential part of weekly activities, both in, and after, school hours. The girls played volley ball, netball and softball and a host of other games. Mel preferred team games to individual games and was a member of the school softball team. (Softball is a variation of baseball that makes use of a larger, softer ball, pitched underhand.) Mel was the team's 'catcher', while her friend, Viv Lennard, was its 'pitcher'. For the team to stand any chance of success, the pitcher and catcher had to develop a thorough understanding of each other's actions. The members of the KT softball team travelled all over the island, winning most of their matches and becoming all-island champions.

At the end of the course at KT, examinations were taken that had been set by English examining boards, such as the Associated Examining Board – which awarded Mel her GCE O levels – and the Royal Society of Arts. She also received a school certificate detailing the course she had followed, and her grades in the various subjects taken.

In Mel's last year at the school, 1962, Aunt Epsi emigrated with her two-year old daughter, Carmelita, to England to join Mr Son, her husband. To help pay for their fare, Aunt Epsi had to sell her little business. Mel and Lloyd were obliged to take lodgings with neighbours, where they stayed until they were sent for in 1964. On completing her studies at KT, Mel found a job as a telephone operator at the prestigious Jamaican Telephone Company, where she worked for almost a year before joining Aunt Epsi, Mr Son, and Carmelita in England.

During the late 1950s and early 60s, large numbers of Jamaicans migrated to Britain in search of work and better prospects. In 1960, the figure for those leaving reached 32,000 and, in 1961, exceeded 39,000 – encouraged by the UK government's threat to impose restrictions on the entry of Commonwealth citizens.

The scale of Jamaican emigration to Britain, Canada, or the United States, was prone to disrupt old school friendships and cause people to lose contact, in many cases, forever. Mel has managed, nevertheless, to stay in touch with one old school pal and colleague at the Jamaica Telephone Company. Sonia Phillips chose not to emigrate and still lives in Kingston, Jamaica. Mel and Frank go to stay with her whenever they visit Jamaica.

On one occasion, they persuaded Sonia and her young daughter, Tamika, to come to Wolverhampton for a summer holiday. Seeing England through Sonia's eyes was a disturbing experience. She was terrified by the speed of the electric train from Euston to the West Midlands. She couldn't understand the English love for brick houses, much preferring modern concrete structures. She showed more interest in the escalators of department stores than in historical buildings. She complained most of all about the weather, which she repeatedly damned as 'bleaky'. When taken to visit St Peter's Parish Church, the stately 13th century red sandstone edifice at the centre of Wolverhampton, she remarked, to everyone's shock and amazement, that it looked filthy and could do with a good coat of whitewash.

In the summer of 1999, Mel's face appeared on the cover of the Nursing Standard, which was running an article on the careers of nurses from ethnic minorities. Shortly afterwards, Mel received a telephone call:

"Are you the Mel Chevannes who was the catcher in the KT softball team?" a voice inquired.

It was Mel's old school friend, pitcher and team mate, Viv Lennard. Reunited after 35 years, Mel and Viv exchanged notes, realising that separately they had each ended up in England and gone on to become health visitors. While Mel had subsequently pursued an academic and teaching career, Viv continued working as a health visitor in the East End of London. They remain close friends to this day, still happily recalling the time they spent together as pitcher and catcher.

Chapter 14

Pietas in the coal hole

On the first day of the new school year, boys at the Grammar School filed into the Church of the Oratory to attend mass celebrated in full regalia at the high altar. One of the School's attractions lay in its proximity to this glittering baroque marble-clad basilica, where the famous Roman Catholic convert, Cardinal John Henry Newman, celebrated mass until his death in 1890. After the ceremony, the student congregation discharged into the crowded school yard, sandwiched between the Church and the School buildings. On his first day at secondary school, Frank was about to learn that new boys were called 'fags', who had to show respect for those in upper forms by accepting the verbal insults, punches, shoving, slapping and wrestling directed at them.

Frank, along with his classmates, was seized and hurled down a flight of steps into a coal hole next to the school boiler room, where the older boys, leaning down from above, spat on them and showered them with burning matches, to the chant of "Light up a fag! Light up a fag!" Other unfortunate 'fags' were marched off 'to receive the baptism of desire', an expression referring to the practice of thrusting a boy's head down into the bowl of a water closet and flushing it.

The worst aspect of these unpleasant initiation ceremonies was that you were deemed to have undertaken them successfully only if you accepted the humiliation stoically, and refrained from grassing to authority afterwards. This made you 'a sport' and allowed you to become a bona fide (but still inferior) member of the school fraternity.

Norman and Phyllis, Dad's parents, valued education for its own sake, but they were also aware that it provided access to a middle-class profession, salary, and lifestyle. Both of them had made considerable personal effort to better themselves through study. Having left school at fourteen, Norman studied at evening class, going on to graduate in modern languages in the year Frank was born. Phyllis attended Kings Norton Grammar School, showing such promise that she was persuaded to continue into the sixth form. Her brothers and sisters, already working for their living, were reluctant to contribute to her upkeep and she was pressured to leave and take a job. Norman and Phyllis wanted their four children to achieve more through education than they themselves had managed.

The obstacles were threefold. As a Catholic, Norman wished to comply with the Church's instruction to send his children to a Catholic school. As a teacher and the family's sole wage earner, he couldn't afford to educate them privately. And his choice of school was restricted by the nationwide tripartite system of state education formalised by the 1944 Education Act.

To stand any chance of progressing to higher education, children had to pass a competitive examination at the age of eleven to win a place at a grammar school, take GCEs at sixteen, and then stay on in the sixth form for another two years. Those who didn't pass the eleven plus – roughly four fifths of the school population - went to the secondary 'modern' school. Most secondary moderns did not teach the ancient or modern languages necessary for university entrance, nor provide fifth or sixth forms. The statutory school leaving age at the time was a child's fifteenth birthday (raised from 14 in 1944, becoming operative in 1947).

When he was five years old, Frank was admitted to St Mary's Roman Catholic School in Vivian Road, Harborne, three miles distant from Bournville where he lived, on the Outer Circle bus route. The school was accommodated in two high pitched-roofed brick buildings to the side of the church and house run by the Passionist Fathers, an Order dedicated to promoting the suffering of the crucified Christ. The children were taught in barn-like Victorian classrooms, furnished with rows of wooden desks. The toilets were situated in a separate block in the tarmacked yard outside.

St Mary's had just completed the process of converting itself from a 5-to-14 all-age school into a primary school for 5 to 11-year-olds. Despite having shed its older age bands, it was struggling to meet the demand for places arising from the post-war surge in births. It was a time of austerity, with basic school materials, such as exercise books, pencils and pens, in short supply. Sweets remained rationed, although Dad said that as he'd never had them, he never missed them.

After the first few days of being taken to the school gates, Frank was expected to make the journey to Harborne and back on the bus by himself. He was allocated to a reception class of nearly fifty pupils, seated at rows of desks and taught formally from the front by a teacher making extensive use of a blackboard and chalk.

At the morning break, the children were sent out into the yard to drink their third-of-a-pint bottle of free school milk, a provision introduced under the School Milk Act 1946 by the first woman Minister of Education, Labour's Ellen Wilkinson. Frank recalls that his entitlement was usually drunk by older boys who also consumed his packed lunch which he was forced to hand over in return for their 'protection'. Boys who didn't comply were taken to the toilet block to suffer further intimidation.

Even by the standards of the day, the School was considered 'rough'. Phyllis was forced to complain to the headmaster when her son came home with cuts and bruises. If the culprits could be identified, they were given the cane, with the result that Frank was bullied afresh for being a 'tell-tale rat'. A lesson soon learned was that it was best never to tell parents about anything that happened at school.

Frank was prepared by the Passionists for his first communion and confirmation into the Church. The success of the religious curriculum was insufficient to reduce his parents' concern over his lack of academic progress. Phyllis had taught him to read before he started school, and they believed him to be a bright little boy. But they could not discern much improvement in his performance during the three years he had spent there, apart from the addition to his vocabulary of a few naïve swear words.

Phyllis's sister, Meg, annoyed them when she candidly observed: "You'd have been better off sending him to the school on the Green than to that Catholic dump".

Accused of religious bigotry, she remarked: "You won't say that when he fails to get in to a grammar school".

Her comments were reinforced when Maggie, Frank's sister, came home crying every day for the first two weeks of her brief attendance at St Mary's. This stung his parents into action. Without more ado, Frank and his sister were removed from St Mary's and enrolled at Eccleston, a small fee-paying establishment with a

Catholic ethos, situated in a large house in Harborne. They were followed by Angela and Philippa, when they reached school age.

(Incidentally, Frank was delighted to read that St Mary's Primary School recently received an 'outstanding' OFSTED inspection report nearly sixty years after he'd been a pupil there.)

Eccleston had no more than 180 pupils on roll, the classes were much smaller, and the teaching methods progressive. The School's main clients were professional people, aiming to ensure that their children passed the eleven-plus examination and gained a place at grammar school. Though granted a 'sibling discount', Norman, with two children enrolled and two others queued up, had difficulty meeting the school fees, and was obliged to take on extra evening classes and book translation to supplement his income. It was at Eccleston that Frank showed aptitude for writing stories and painting pictures.

In Autumn 1955, at the age of ten, the time came for Frank to go along to St Philip's Roman Catholic Grammar School, his parents' preferred choice of secondary education, to sit the eleven-plus examination, a series of reasoning, language, and arithmetic ability tests. Frank had been conscious for as long as he could remember that his future prospects depended entirely on his success in passing this exam and gaining a place at grammar school. To everyone's relief, he passed.

This encouraged Norman to embark on an innovative scheme that he'd heard about, to ensure Frank became fluent in a modern language. He wanted his son to learn French through 'immersion'. In the six months prior to the September start at secondary school, Frank was sent to stay with his father's friends, the Cabuts, who lived at Villars les Dombes in Ain, France.

Oncle Jean and Tante Simone were given the unenviable task of ensuring a ten-year-old boy, without a word of French, returned home six months later with some proficiency in the language. They began, as agreed, by sending Frank to the local school, an arrangement abandoned after the first day, when the other pupils, realising he couldn't understand what they were saying to him began shouting:

"Nous detestons le sale petit Anglais!...Espece d'idiot!...Albion perfide!...Petit merdeux!," and proceeded to beat him up.

For the rest of his stay, he lived on the Cabut farm, 'Domaine-du-Clou'. The house had an odd boat-shaped roof and was surrounded by a farmyard full of animals. Frank learned about farming: how to milk a cow, find free-range eggs in haystacks, and to catch edible frogs in a flooded silo, but he did not learn much French, nor get to practise his English, either. Feeling lonely and homesick, he became very attached to the farm-yard dog, Bichette.

On one tragic occasion, he took Bichette for a walk on the main road, a mile away from the farm, where the excited animal began to chase the passing motor vehicles until it was fatally struck by a car. Unpopular and remorseful for causing the death of the family pet, Frank coped with the situation by running off every day to play by himself in the fields and the woods.

Dad regards Norman's educational experiment a disaster, but admits that he did manage to learn enough French to give him a head start in the language classes at secondary school. In hindsight, he considers that the six months spent in France had a profound and lasting effect on his life. He found himself isolated and entirely enveloped in an alternative, alien, nationalistic culture. And he became more emotionally self-reliant, similar to the effect of being sent to boarding school.

Founded in 1887, St Philips, the Grammar School that Frank was to attend for the next seven years (1956 -1963), was situated next to the Oratory Church and House, in Hagley Road, Edgbaston. It had occupied the site since 1923, when the former occupant, the Oratory Public School, had relocated to Caversham. Since then, under its headmaster, T J Larkin, the Grammar School had expanded in numbers to meet the growing demand for secondary education.

By the time Frank became a pupil, there were around 800 boys on roll and a staff of 45. To accommodate the extra numbers, prefabricated wooden huts had been erected on the yard and a new teaching block was under construction. The new wing was completed in 1957, well in time for Frank to make use of its facilities.

The School had a three-form entry of 120 eleven-year-old boys, 40 per form, all of them having passed the entrance examination at the requisite level. The form sets in which most standard subjects were taught were coded 1x, 1y, 1z. Each school day was divided into 40 minute periods allocated to the subjects taught at the school. For at least the first three years, all pupils had to study nine academic subjects: English, mathematics, Latin, French, history, geography, physics, chemistry, and art, plus essential religious instruction and physical education.

Frank started at the Grammar School with 119 other boys in September 1956. He was dressed in a school uniform consisting of black blazer and cap (both emblazoned with the St Philip's coat of arms), standard grey shirt, and grey short trousers. I notice that on most days my father still wears a dark blazer, striped tie, and grey flannel trousers, but no longer at knee length!

On their first day, the new boys were shown to their classrooms, where they met their form master and classmates. Frank was assigned to Form 1Y and its form-master, Mr James Mulholland, who was to be in charge of him for the next four years. A surly Geordie, with a grim sense of humour, he was nicknamed 'the Masher'. He taught Frank English for the duration of his time at the School. After the administrative tasks were completed, the boys were allocated individually to one of the four School 'houses' (named after Catholic saints).

Next came an exhortatory talk on the ethos of the School, always pitched around the meaning of the School motto, 'pietas', which was translated elastically to mean 'piety', 'holiness', 'spirituality', 'duty', 'loyalty', 'mercy' and 'concern for others' – indeed, almost anything to which a good Catholic might aspire. When asked by family and friends to explain the motto, older boys would always hesitate, knowing that, if they obliged, they were likely to be greeted with guffaws of derision.

Having passed their eleven plus, all pupils in theory should have found learning easy and enjoyable. In reality, their interest in a subject area depended heavily on the personality, enthusiasm, and consistency of approach of its teacher. Frank believes that the masters' differing ability, and the prevailing methods of teaching a given discipline, affected his subject preferences, intellectual development, and future course of study.

The subjects he excelled in – English, Geography and Art – were taught through participative methods, with principles explained, opinions sought, and controversy entertained. Often a project was set which the boys could take charge of. The languages, on the other hand, – French and Latin – were taught largely by rote, with the class expected to memorise seemingly endless lists of vocabulary, irregular verbs, conjugations, and declensions. Mathematics and Science could be taught excitingly but, more often than not, were reduced to page after page of repetitive formulae and calculations.

In English lessons, the boys were set essays on topics, such as 'Will atomic weapons prevent or provoke a third world war?', 'Should mothers go out to work?', 'Should the death penalty be abolished?' and 'Is it better to be English or American?'. We discovered Frank's answer to the last question in an old exercise book that his mother had kept. He'd written:

"Although most people think Americans are rich, they are not all millionaires. Many people there live in appalling conditions, especially coloured people. In our slums there is not such a colour-bar attitude. Most people do not try to outdo their neighbours. Not so in America. There is a strong colour bar and people can fall into debt for trying to rival their neighbours' cars or television sets."

A foretaste, perhaps, of Dad's future interests and concerns!

The attention to current affairs was limited. Teachers were attentive, in the main, to spelling and syntax, ignoring the substance of the opinion itself.

To justify its Catholic status, the School devoted appreciable time and resources to religious instruction (RI), devotions, and week-long spiritual retreats. After four years of RI, Frank, along with the rest of the class, took an exam and was awarded the Religious School Certificate by the Conference of Catholic Colleges. The School's religious curriculum was loosely based on learning the essentials of the Catholic catechism and was properly described as instruction rather than education. Christianity was presented as an elaborate but rational world picture, featuring a taken-for-granted god and his self-evident purpose for mankind. Reason, rather than emotion, was central to the formula. The effect was that the School excelled in the rhetoric of religiosity, but retained an indifferent secular ethos, much like that of other grammar schools.

St Philip's prided itself on its sporting prowess, believing it excelled in the fields of football (soccer), swimming, and chess (if that counted as a sport). One afternoon a week was spent on the school playing fields, even in midwinter, when snow was on the ground.

On one occasion, Dad was caught dawdling at a goal post on a cold gloomy day, waiting for four o'clock when he could go home. When asked why he wasn't chasing the ball like the other boys, he said he couldn't see the point.

"Go to the pavilion," the PE teacher told him, "and wait for me there."

He was given six of the best with a cricket stump, and forced to say after each stroke: "Boys at this school play up and play the game."

"Did it hurt?" Robeson interjected.

"The stump hurt a lot more than the plimsoll," Dad admitted, "but to tell the truth, although you'd always choose to avoid a whacking, you soon came to accept it as an inevitable part of school life. Besides, you had to pretend to the rest of the class that you were tough, and that your free spirit would never be broken by a teacher tyrant with a plimsoll. Any boy who could take a sound beating without a murmur was admired for his courage."

Most masters administered physical punishment, often with a plimsoll or pump but, by the standards of the time, this sanction, while frequently dispensed, wasn't applied arbitrarily or excessively. James Mulholland, Frank's form master, would routinely plimsoll any pupil who failed to submit his homework on time, or to the standard demanded. The number of boys who failed to comply with his exacting criteria soon fell, causing him to raise his requirements, and to beat all those that he felt guilty of 'sitting on their laurels'. His punishment regime, at least, was rationally conceived and related to educational outcome. The same couldn't be said of one or two of the other masters at the school, who, in hindsight, Frank felt, exhibited distinctly sadistic tendencies, and succeeded in traumatising many of the younger boys. The head teacher, known to be strict but fair-minded, made use of a cane as a last resort before the ultimate disgrace of expulsion. Corporal punishment wasn't made illegal in state schools until 1987.

Younger boys went every week to swimming lessons at the Monument Road Baths. Everyone was expected to learn to swim. Swimming was regarded as an essential survival skill, rather than as a means of keeping fit. Frank had been taught by a family friend to swim by the age of seven.

Sixth-form boys could learn life-saving as an alternative to games or athletics. Classes were held at Woodcock Street Baths, where Frank trained for his Royal Life Saving Society Bronze Medal, Bronze Cross, Award of Merit, and Instructor's Certificate, thus satisfying his desire 'to do something useful in sport'.

After five years of extremely variable subject teaching, Frank chose his sixth-form subjects solely on the basis of the stimulation and enjoyment they afforded him, without any thought to his future career prospects. The subjects were, predictably, English, Geography and Art, which also happened to coincide with his extra-curricular interests. In his spare time, he wrote journals, stories, stage plays, and poetry, collected rocks, minerals and fossils, and tried his hand at drawing, painting, modelling and lino cuts.

Towards the end of his sixth-form studies, Frank took his portfolio of art work to the Birmingham School of Art and was offered a place there. His father and Mr Larkin, the headmaster, had other ideas. Frank was summoned to a meeting in the headmaster's study where the two men told Frank that artists were 'ten a penny', and that he must make proper use of his intelligence by going to university. He could always pursue art as a hobby.

Dad passed four GCE A levels and secured a place at Lancaster University to start in September 1964. This left a gap of eight months for him to find a job and earn money.

Dad used to believe that his Catholic secondary education and upbringing had shaped his intellectual identity. Throughout his life, he has wanted to explore abstract, existential questions about the natural world and the human condition. He is always drawn to questions about causality, determinism, design, chance, probability, and free will, and the relationship of parts to the whole. For many years, he attributed this trait to his exposure from an early age to a

Catholic interpretation of the universe, or 'Creation'. More recently, the discovery of the curriculum choice of someone very closely related has led him to conclude his intellectual disposition may well have an alternative genetic origin.

"Dad, were there any black or Asian pupils at your Grammar School?" Robeson asked.

"I don't recall any," he said, "But you can check for yourself." He disappeared into the garage, emerging half an hour later with what looked like a scroll. It was the St Philip's Grammar School official photograph, a picture strip 190cm long, taken in July 1962.

Robeson decided to count the faces staring out at him, arriving at a grand total of 764 pupils and 45 staff. Compared with the photographs taken of pupils at our school, Smestow, the most remarkable aspect was the complete absence of girls and women teachers. Neither were there any pupils in wheelchairs!

Only two of the boys appeared to be black or Asian. This was indicative, no doubt, of the ethnic composition and age profile of the Birmingham population at the time and of the highly selective nature of the school intake. The photograph predated the demographic shift which was to lead some thirty years later to the growing Asian presence at St Philip's Sixth Form College and the threat this was assumed to pose to its Catholic ethos.

Nevertheless, even in those days, St Philip's, as a Catholic school, provided for sizeable numbers of minority ethnic children from traditionally-Catholic Irish and Polish communities. Dad is still in touch with two of his old school friends, Pat Finucane and Mick Moran, both, it happens, of Irish descent. As far as Dad can recall, however, there weren't any pupils with either physical disabilities or special learning needs, the latter automatically debarred by the School's deliberately selective intake.

Chapter 15

On telephones and tapping

When he was fifteen, Dad wrote to Cadbury's chocolate factory near to where he lived in Bournville to ask for a holiday job, explaining in his letter that he was a pupil at school who wanted to become a journalist. With a wry sense of humour, the personnel officer obliged by offering Frank employment in the printing department, where he was put to assist a one-eyed workman complete an order to cut and print four million cardboard boxes.

Disturbed by the tedious and repetitive nature of his job, Frank's elderly workmate had developed the compulsive habit of tapping the glass eye on his blind side with a hammer when parties of visitors to the chocolate factory passed by on a raised walkway overlooking the print shop. The squeamish among them complained repeatedly about his eye-tapping, and after a succession of warnings from management, the one-eyed man was sacked.

"The only person I ever knew," Dad said, "who was dismissed for tapping his eye with a hammer!"

"Even were I to believe your story," Toussaint remarked, "which I don't, he wasn't sacked for tapping his eye, but for disobeying a reasonable instruction!"

Frank, himself, found the job so boring that he left voluntarily after a month with a few million boxes to go. This, his first experience of paid work, convinced him once and for all that he needed to study hard and pass his exams to ensure he didn't end up operating a cardboard box machine!

As teenagers in Wolverhampton in the late 1990s, Toussaint and I went in search of part-time work to supplement our pocket money. Toussaint followed a short evening course at Bilston Community College to train as a silver service waitress and was taken on at the Molineux Football Stadium to serve meals in the restaurant before the Wolves' home games. Waitresses with silver service skills were paid a little more than the minimum wage. Toussaint then showed me how to set and serve and I, too, was taken on. We spent two years on Saturday afternoons serving meals to Wolves supporters in the restaurant next to the terrace, or in the boxes overlooking the pitch.

The customers, who were mostly men, were generally well behaved, but usually surprised to discover we were studying for GCE A levels and had our eyes set on university. In the next few years, Toussaint and I took on a series of part-time and holiday jobs, usually as barmaids and clerical assistants. For example, Toussaint worked in customer services at British Telecom and in a Druckers Cake shop in Leamington, while I worked in the college bar at university and temped at NPower in Sandwell.

We were curious to know about our parents' first experiences of work and how they compared with our own.

"Mom," Toussaint quizzed, "I know you helped Aunt Epsi in the shop in Spanish Town. But did you have a proper paid job before you came to England?"

"My first job was in a small department store in the centre of Spanish Town," she said. "I was employed as a shop assistant on a Saturday morning and later for the full day. I needed to earn some pocket money while I was at KT."

"Was it hard to get work in Jamaica?" Toussaint inquired.

"Very difficult," Mom replied. "Jobs were in very short supply. My school friend already worked at the store and she put in a word for me when another girl was sacked. The business was owned by a Syrian who used to watch us all very closely while we were serving the customers."

When, in 1963, at the age of nineteen, Mel finished at secondary school, she applied for work at the Jamaican Telephone Company and was employed on the strength of her school record and qualifications. She was trained to manage the national switch board, plugging and unplugging the cables and flicking switches to make the connections, while at the same time listening on headphones to callers. Only the more experienced staff were allowed to work on the international switch board.

Toussaint, inevitably, drew comparisons with her time at British Telecom.

Based at a large office in central Kingston, the workforce at the Jamaican Telephone Company was kept under constant surveillance, with supervisors phoning in regularly to make checks on how calls were being answered. Operators were disciplined if they failed to greet callers with the standard response and patter, or if their telephone manner was judged to be curt or impolite.

The switchboard was staffed night and day, seven days a week, requiring employees to work shifts. Along with the other operators, Mel had to serve her turn on nights. Within the Jamaican context, working for the telephone company was seen, nevertheless, as a prestigious and well-paid job for a young woman.

"I enjoyed it there," Mel admitted, "and never wanted to leave. My school friend, Sonia, stayed on at the company for the whole of her working life and she's only just retired."

"It's just as well you came to join Aunt Epsi, Mr Son, and Carmelita in England," Toussaint teased, "or none of us would be around to argue with you now."

We turned to Dad.

"Did you have a Saturday job?" Toussaint asked. "Or were you spoiled with too much pocket money?"

"My father was the sole breadwinner with a wife and four children to maintain," Dad replied defensively. "We were by no means well off. Like everyone else, I had to do my best to support myself. Unfortunately, Saturday jobs weren't easy to come by. Most shops preferred to take on female employees."

"So you didn't work before going to university?"

"On the contrary," he said. "I had a succession of holiday jobs from the fifth form onwards. I was also employed as a teacher from the time I left school until I started at university. We were all expected to pull our weight."

After his first job producing cardboard boxes for Cadbury's, Dad got a job on a building site, where he narrowly avoided the humiliating ritual of initiation into the building trade meted out to the young apprentices. The workmen were worried about the consequences of picking on a young man who attended a grammar school, so nailed him up instead for the day in the dark under the joists of a newly-built house.

The best-paying holiday jobs were to be found stocktaking and deep-cleaning in the factory closure periods. From the age of sixteen, Frank worked at the Austin, or at Fort Dunlop, engaged in some very dirty and greasy, but lucrative, activities. On a couple of occasions, he found himself in the midst of an industrial dispute.

"You mean you went on strike over your holiday job?" Toussaint quizzed.

"Yes," Dad confirmed. "It happened twice: once at the car factory and once at the tyre factory."

We found the prospect of a school boy going on strike during his holiday jobs hard to believe, particularly after his last tall story.

"It was a surprise to me, too," he admitted. "So much so, that I wrote an account of events at the Austin Motor Company, or BMC, for the family newsletter we were compiling at the time. I came across it only the other day."

Sure enough, he found and showed us a hand-written report that he'd set down at the age of seventeen about an incident during the summer 1962 factory closure period. I quote:

"We were told that as we had worked so hard over the five days, the week's work had run out and we were to be laid off. We'd been guaranteed a week's work at £2 a day, meaning we would now receive only £10. We'd worked hard only to discover we were to be penalised for our efforts. We wanted a week's wage for a week's work.

Feelings ran high, and the Austin men offered to call in their union officials. Sheldon's (the subcontractors), our employer, was being paid £8 per person per day for a seven day week by the Austin. Small groups of men gathered round the press shop and began muttering, the noise eventually reaching a crescendo. Sheldon's stood to gain an extra £2 x 2days x 300 men = £1200 by sacking us. The Austin men didn't like that and neither did we.

About fifty of us gathered and, after advice, appointed Michael Shaw, one of the pleasantest boys at our school to speak on our behalf. The boss eventually condescended to see us. He began by abusing our spokesman with: "I've never set eyes on you before, but you look like a nasty piece of work". He then told the lie that the company would only be paid for our five days' work, even though we all knew Sheldon's had a contract for £20,000.

This led the Austin men to 'stop in sympathy' with us. We all roared out our demand for the wages we'd been promised. This time, he didn't dare say no.

Somebody shouted out: "How much are we getting?"

He promised us our £14 on Friday afternoon, and we no longer had to work the extra two days."

Frank concluded, in hindsight, portentously:

"I shall always think very carefully when I read about strikes in the car factories. The capitalist manager has seldom got clean hands."

Frank's holiday jobs appear to have inspired the poetry he wrote at the time which, even while he was at school, frequently adopted a theme - unusual, surely, for a seventeen-year-old – of industrial alienation. Maybe this arose from the lasting trauma brought on at Cadbury's by the order for four million cardboard boxes!

> 'If I should die,
> My hands would rattle
> For at least a shift
> Upon the guard before
> The management would say:
> 'It's number five-o-four;
> Cross him off the list;
> He won't queue up again
> On Friday nights.'
> Another corrugated face
> Would scrape my monster's teeth
> And feed him steel
> With soul for sweet on Sunday.'

(Summer 1962)

Frank worked each Christmas for the Royal Mail, loading and unloading bags of cards, letters, and parcels from the steam trains passing through Birmingham's Snow Hill Station.

On another occasion, he got a job finishing and crating giant industrial mixers en route for destinations in Africa, where they were used to prepare food for workers in the mines. He remembers being warned severely against tampering with the packaging. The students who preceded him in the job had caused the company major political embarrassment by concealing anti-apartheid posters and literature inside the wooden crates.

In the gap between school and university, Dad worked as an Assistant Teacher at Cardinal Newman's, a Catholic Secondary Modern School, in Birmingham. For the first week or so, he found life as a teacher very tough but, with the help of a plimsoll, personal determination, and a love for his subject matter, he gradually began to establish his presence.

The school was rigorously streamed on the basis of ability into five classes: a, b, c, d, and e. The most troublesome children were to be found in classes c and d, with e containing more placid children with special learning difficulties. Being new and inexperienced, Frank found himself timetabled in the main with the cs and ds – a very challenging experience.

Hot from the grammar school, he rapidly came to the conclusion that the main difference between the pupils he was teaching and the ones who had passed their eleven plus was not their intelligence, but their family background, their motivation and self-discipline, and the time and attention given to their earlier education.

Before he left Cardinal Newman School, Dad had become a passionate advocate of comprehensive, non-selective, and open-access schooling, and a fierce critic of the eleven plus. He believed that he himself had only managed to gain a place at grammar school because his parents had paid his fees for Eccleston, where he'd been drilled relentlessly for three years to pass the entrance examination. Nevertheless, he professed himself profoundly grateful to have been one of the lucky ones.

Chapter 16

The laying on of black hands

"Mom, how old were you when you left Jamaica to come to England?" Robeson inquired.

Mom answered without hesitation: "I was twenty years old and Lloyd, my brother, was twenty-one."

"Can you remember the day you first arrived?" Robeson asked.

"Of course I can!" she replied. "The plane touched down at Heathrow airport on Sunday morning, the 29th August 1964."

Robeson, always fond of numbers, was impressed.

"What else can you remember?" he quizzed.

"I can recall my first impressions as we came into land," Mom said. "I could see from the air what I thought were little factories. Later, I realised they were just terraced houses, each with its own chimney."

He looked puzzled. "Weren't there houses in Jamaica?"

"The houses there," she explained, "don't have chimneys like that. There isn't any need in Jamaica for artificial fires to increase the heat from the sun. The problem there is how to keep cool. Until I came here I thought factories were the only buildings that had chimney stacks."

"Did you want to come to England?" he queried.

"To be honest," Mom confessed, "I never wanted to leave Jamaica. I'd heard how cold it was in England, even in summer. But Aunt Epsi and Mr Son had sent us the air fare and we weren't in a position to refuse. We were both looking forward to being reunited with them."

Mr Son was the first member of the family to come to England in 1959. He had a succession of factory jobs before finding work at the Austin factory in Birmingham where he worked long hours and shifts as a plant attendant on the ovens used to heat the car bodies. He was joined three years later in the freezing January weather by Aunt Epsi and their baby daughter, Carmelita. Aunt Epsi had obtained work as a seamstress in the Accident Hospital, adapting clothes and making slings for patients, altering nurses' uniforms, and repairing curtains and bedding.

"Mom, was England very different from what you expected?" Robeson persisted.

"I wasn't sure what to expect," she replied, "but I do recall being surprised by the sight of white men sweeping the roads and cleaning windows. You couldn't have imagined that in Jamaica! Of course, I soon came to take it for granted that white people were capable of manual work."

Lionel – Mel and Lloyd's cousin – met them at the airport and drove them to Cheswick, where their Aunt Miriam cooked them Jamaican food. Delvin, a Barbadian friend of the family, had hired a car to take them on the new M1 motorway to Birmingham.

Aunt Epsi, Mr Son and Carmelita were living in a small rented property next to a jeweller's shop in Stoney Lane, Sparkbrook, an inner-city district of Birmingham. Two rows of red-brick terraced housing and shop fronts faced each other across a road crowded with noisy traffic. The landscape was a labyrinth of brick walls, shutters, passageways, and asphalted surfaces, with hardly a tree or green open space in sight. Mel was expected to share a small bedroom with her little sister, Carmelita.

Researched at roughly the same time as Mel and Lloyd's arrival, Rex and Moore's study of Sparkbrook described the area as 'a twilight zone', occupied by four main ethnic groups: English, Irish, West Indian, and Pakistani. West Indians (8.7 per cent of the population) and Pakistanis (3.6 per cent) were still a small minority. Most of Mel's neighbours, and the people with whom she came into contact at that time, would have been white English or Irish. The West Indians interviewed for Rex and Moore's study had come to England between 1956 and 1964, more than a third since 1961, giving as their main reasons for migrating the need to find work and earn money, a wish to improve their way of life, or the desire to join relatives or friends. In all these respects, Mel and Lloyd were entirely representative of the West Indian population of Sparkbrook in the early 1960s.

"How did you manage to get in to the country in the first place?" Robeson asked. "Was it before the government brought in immigration controls?"

"A good question!" Mel remarked. "The Conservative government put an end to our right as Commonwealth citizens to come to this country in 1962, when it passed the Commonwealth Immigrants Act. It was, in effect, a colour bar. Black and Asian people had to obtain a work voucher before they were allowed in."

"So how did you get round that?"

"Work vouchers were granted so that employers could still recruit workers from the Commonwealth in labour shortage areas, such as health and transport," Mel explained. "Aunt Epsi worked in the sewing room at the Accident Hospital and knew the matron. The hospital was short of nursing auxiliaries, so Lloyd and I were eventually issued with permits to work in the health service."

The arrangement was such that, having arrived in Birmingham on Sunday evening, Mel and Lloyd were required to report for work at the hospital on Monday morning, the next day, allowing no time for them to acclimatise to their new environment. The work was pretty basic stuff: bed pans, bed baths, hygiene routines, and pushing around the food and medicine trolleys.

On her way home from work one evening, soon after she started her job, Mel was followed by two little white boys who shouted 'blacky' after her and made 'nigger lips' gestures. On reaching the safety of the house, she burst into tears, only to be told by her mother that she would have to start standing up for herself. Aunt Epsi had long since become hardened to this commonplace hostility, and had little patience for her daughter's sensitivity.

On another occasion, while washing a woman who had a leg in plaster, Mel was startled when the patient gave her a kick with her one good leg and told her not to touch her with "those dirty black hands".

Mel was once more reduced to tears, but was heartened when the white sister, on hearing what had happened, told the woman that she would have to behave herself if she wanted a wash.

Soon after starting work as an auxiliary, Mel discovered that she wasn't after all being trained to become a fully-qualified State Registered Nurse (SRN) as she had been led to assume. To train, she would have to start on a recognised course.

She applied to the School of Nursing at Selly Oak Hospital, where she was made to take an entrance test before being accepted, even though she had already met the minimum entry requirements for the course with the British GCEs she had taken and passed in Jamaica. Even then, at interview, the Head of the Nursing School tried to persuade her to lower her sights, by suggesting she would be more suited to the two-year State Enrolled Nurse (SEN) training, rather than the more demanding three-year State Registered Nurse (SRN) curriculum. Fortunately, Mel was savvy enough to insist on the three-year training. When she started on the SRN course at Selly Oak January 1965, she found out that some of the students had been accepted without either GCE O levels, or passing the entrance test. She discovered later that she was one of the best qualified students on the course.

She remembers feeling aggrieved at the self-evident unfairness of the selection process as it was being operated at the time. This partiality extended to the hospital work place, where the black nurses were more likely to be allocated menial tasks and denied opportunities associated with the stage they had reached in the training process. If, for example, a black and a white nurse were both working on a ward, the white nurse would be put in charge, given custody of the keys to the medicine cabinet, and allocated the tasks of meeting visitors, talking to the nursing officer, and writing the ward report. Without these opportunities to assume responsibility, it was difficult for a black nurse to demonstrate her abilities and perform well in the examination and upon qualifying.

Black nurses' daily experience was blighted still further by the frequent racist abuse they received from patients and visitors, and the insensitive banter of staff - generally excused as 'harmless fun.'

Towards the end of Mel's period of training at Selly Oak Hospital, Enoch Powell began making his infamous speeches opposing black immigration. His rhetoric served to stimulate, still further, patients' vilification of the black nurses, and even, on occasion, to incite the white nursing staff to join with their patients in racial abuse. When, as happened regularly, patients behaved badly to black nurses, people in authority – doctors and ward sisters alike – frequently pretended that they hadn't seen what had taken place.

Rarely receiving moral backing, and learning never to expect any, the black nurses would seek out and share their experiences with other employees in the same situation, regardless of their country of origin. Without firm intervention by management, however, there was little they could do to stop their ill-treatment, other than to 'grin and bear it'.

It wasn't until Mel met Frank that she learned he'd been born in the maternity ward at Selly Oak – where she'd gone to train a quarter of a century later – and that he'd grown up at Bournville close by.

Mel completed her three-year general training and worked for a short period as a staff nurse before embarking, in the Autumn of 1969, on a midwifery course at Sorrento Maternity Hospital in Wake Green Road, Birmingham. The hospital, fronted by high-gabled, red-brick Victorian buildings, became a maternity home in 1929, and was a well-established NHS maternity facility during her midwifery training there. This increasingly antiquated NHS facility was eventually closed in 1993.

Mom showed me the meticulous records she had kept of all the babies she had delivered in her year at Sorrento. She told me that, although black midwives were employed at Sorrento while she was there, she couldn't recall seeing any of them occupying the position of a midwifery sister. Nevertheless, she enjoyed her midwifery training immensely and wasn't subject to any overt racial prejudice, although she left with the impression that black midwives were given more than their fair share of night duty.

When she won an award as best student of the year, one of the matrons expressed her astonishment. She found it difficult to believe that a black girl like Mel had done so well! Mel was reprimanded by the same woman for using her employer's name as a referee on so many occasions. Why couldn't she aim for something within her reach? Mel was applying for health visitor training but experiencing great difficulty in obtaining a place on a course. Hence, the numerous applications for which the matron was obliged to act as referee.

The health authorities were taking up the references but not proceeding to interview. The spate of straight rejections came from health authorities from whom she requested financial sponsorship, not from the educational establishments where the health visitor courses were based. Nevertheless, acceptance by both parties - employer and training establishment - was required before a student was able to take the course.

Mel's perseverance paid off. She was invited to an interview, at last, only to be told pointedly that health visiting was for 'our girls' and that she should consider working as a domiciliary midwife instead. The panel wished her luck but judged her aspirations to be unrealistic. They were perturbed at the prospect, or feasibility, of a black woman giving advice on child rearing to white families within their own homes.

Mel was eventually offered a place on a course in Nottingham. A sympathetic interviewing panel asked her directly about the number of applications she had made and were visibly shaken by her answer.

Acceptance on the course was only the first hurdle. The next was to find somewhere in Nottingham to live. Mel looked for accommodation advertised for rent in the local paper and then phoned to express her interest. When, half an hour afterwards, she went round to view the property, the landlady would tell her it had just been let. She soon became tired of wasting her time and started to mention her colour on the phone.

"I understand you've got a bed sitter to let," she would say.

"Yes, that's right," would come the response.

"I'm Jamaican. Do you mind?" she would ask.

"You mean you're coloured?"

"I'm black."

"Oh no! I don't think our other tenants would like that."

On another occasion, she remembers:

"I saw in the paper you've got a flat to let."

Picking up on her Jamaican intonation, the voice at the end of the phone asked:

"Are you Welsh?"

"No. I'm Jamaican."

The reply came: "My God, that's even worse!"

When at last she became so desperate she didn't know where she was going to sleep that night, she resorted to stopping a black man in the street and asking if he could help. He took her to his brother who let a room to her in his family home. This arrangement lasted until she told her course tutor about her difficulties. The institution contacted an estate agent on its books, without referring to her colour, and straight away secured her suitable accommodation.

"Why were you so keen to become a health visitor?" Robeson queried.

"As I pursued my nursing career," Mel explained, "I found myself increasingly interested in the business of keeping people healthy in the first place, rather than in treating them for disease. In other words, I wanted to pursue a career in preventive medicine, and health visiting seemed the ideal job. Besides, you have far more freedom and autonomy working with families in a community setting than in the restrictive context of a hospital ward."

"What exactly does a health visitor do?" Robeson wanted to know.

"We work with families in the community," Mel replied. "A lot depends on local arrangements. You could be working with mothers and babies, or with older people, or even providing health education in schools."

"Doing what?" he persisted.

"Most of the time," Mel went on, "we give advice to mothers on how to look after their young babies from when the midwife hands over responsibility to us at 28 days, until the child is old enough to go to school. Mothers want advice on how to feed, wean, clean, wash, and what to expect as their child develops. We deal with the health of the mother and the growth and development of the baby, by visiting families at home and providing facilities such as well-baby clinics. Is that enough?"

Mel began studying for her Health Visiting Certificate in 1970, completing her course in 1971. For her placement, she worked in Hucknall, and did supervised practice in the mining area of Mansfield Woodhouse where, on completion, she was employed by Nottinghamshire County Council in a joint post of Health Visitor and School Nurse. She enjoyed her time visiting families in Mansfield Woodhouse and, in general, found the people friendly and accepting of her, despite traditional working-class suspicion of busybodies sent by the council. On one of the few occasions that her colour came into the conversation, she recalls a miner's wife remarking: "You look no different from my old man when he's been at pit."

Robeson wondered what Mel, having come straight from Jamaica, had made of the English families she'd gone to visit.

"It wasn't always pleasant," she admitted, "and like most people in these situations, I jumped to conclusions on the basis of my first and only impressions. Of course, I'd never done health visiting in Jamaica, so I had nothing with which to compare."

"So what did you think?" he persisted.

"Oh! I arrived at a very dim view of white English people," she said. "I thought they were dirty, immoral, irreligious, unfriendly, ignorant and insincere. I found a large number of them to be colour prejudiced to boot."

Mel explained how once, when she was invited to eat in an English home, she went into the kitchen afterwards, and saw her host washing up. The plates were placed on the draining board with traces of food and soap suds still adhering to them. Jamaicans insisted in washing and rinsing their dishes.

At the hospital, she had noticed how infrequently the English women patients changed their nightdresses, wearing the same nightdress for three or four days at a time. She felt it was a matter of pride and respect that a clean nightdress should be worn each day.

She had visited English homes where the family pet was treated in the same way as a human being. She had seen dogs fed from the husband's dish during and after the meal. Dogs were also allowed to sit on the settee, as well as to sleep on, and in, the beds. In Jamaica, dogs were treated normally: they were kept out of doors and out of beds, and fed from their own containers.

As for English morality! Couples kissed in the streets and lay together in parks and public places. They had affairs even when they were legally married. She'd come across instances of incest in families she'd visited. And the English were so much more relaxed about divorce: unlike Jamaicans, who were prone to ostracise divorcees.

Many English people didn't bother to go to church and never mentioned religion except to disparage it. To Jamaicans, who saw religion as part and parcel of a whole way of life, this was sacrilegious and unchristian.

Mel had worked closely and in a friendly manner at Selly Oak Hospital with an English girl. At the end of the shift, the same girl had stood next to her at the bus stop and turned her head away. The girl had also passed her on the road and pretended as though she'd never seen her before.

Mel couldn't help but observe white people, sometimes with heavy bags, standing on a crowded bus, rather than choosing to sit in the vacant seat beside her.

"That's extraordinary!" Robeson remarked thoughtfully. "Your views were almost a mirror image of white people's prejudices. They think all blacks are dirty, oversexed, untrustworthy, and dishonest!"

"Yes." Mel said. "We're far too ready to arrive at foolish generalisations based on our own limited experience. But it doesn't explain why our opinions of others are so negative."

Mel had felt lonely living in Nottingham by herself and, after a year working for the authority that had sponsored her training, she returned to the West Midlands to take a job with Warley Borough Council in what is now Sandwell. Here, as a health visitor, she looked after mothers and babies in Black Heath, Oldbury, and Smethwick.

She had her own car and could pop round after work to visit Aunt Epsi, Mr Son, and her little sister Carmelita, who lived near by in Birmingham. By this time, Aunt Epsi and Mr Son had bought a Victorian terraced house in an alley off Taunton Road in Sparkbrook, about 100 metres away from where they'd been living in Stoney Lane. Frank featured the house in one of his poems:

> Formerly of Jamaica, now
> Resident, Birmingham, England.
> Address: 1 Clent Villas, red brick
> Victorian terraced dwelling
> Opening on to a car-choked street
> On a gloom-grey December day.

Chapter 17

A quick word in the kitchen

When applying for university, I was invited to attend an open day at the Law School at the University of Lancaster. Dad offered to drive me there. On the 17 March 1999, we drove from Wolverhampton along the M6 to arrive in good time at the Bailrigg Campus. The journey gave me an opportunity to quiz Dad about the university he attended for three years from 1964 to 1967. Dad applied to Lancaster deliberately to be part of its first intake of 300 students, admitted in September 1964. The university was housed temporarily in the disused Waring and Gillow furniture factory at St Leonard Gate in the City, with the nearby Grand Theatre serving as the lecture theatre. Only in his third year was Dad able to use the newly-built facilities on the current site at Bailrigg. I also chose to go to Lancaster, arriving on campus almost exactly 35 years after my father studied there.

"So what did coming here do for you?" I asked Dad, as we eventually found somewhere to park on the periphery of the Lancaster campus.

"Ah!" Dad declared grandiloquently, "It was here that I tasted the essence of education and experienced enlightenment."

Misquoting President John Kennedy, he went on: "Ask not what your university did for you – ask what you did for your university – ask what together we can do for the freedom of man!"

"And woman!" I interrupted.

Dad was familiar with Kennedy's speeches, having been in the sixth form at the time of his assassination in 1963.

"My three years at university liberated me intellectually," he explained. "The blinkers of home and school fell from my eyes. I began for the first time to interpret the world for myself and to realise the need to change it, starting here at the university itself."

"Was it at Lancaster that you became a communist?" I inquired.

"Yes", he replied. "In the first year, I followed a course in the philosophy of religion, argued endlessly with a member of the humanist society, and began to realise that I'd been deceived and indoctrinated at school. They'd taught me only the argument for the existence of God and none of those against."

He went on enthusiastically: "I joined all the Left-wing societies: the Labour Students, the Socialist Union, and the Marxist Discussion Group. I learned about the great Libertarian and Socialist thinkers: people like Tom Paine, Robert Owen, William Morris, Karl Marx, Friedrich Engels, Vladimir Lenin, Mao Tse-tung, Frantz Fanon, Kwame Nkrumah, and Herbert Marcuse. I could rattle on and on.
I remember that *The Communist Manifesto* and Lenin's writings on imperialism got me terribly excited. Apart from Marx and Mao, I don't think I'd ever heard of these people, let alone read them, until I went to university.

By my second year, I had joined the Communist Party and persuaded myself I was going to dedicate my life to revolution, like Fidel Castro and Che Guevara."

His parents were devastated by his decision, blaming the atheists and communists at the University for undermining his Catholic faith.

"Did they give you a party card?" his mother had asked. "Give it to me. I'll burn it! Don't you realise you'll never be able to join the Civil Service?"

Lancaster University was set up to be different. It was to be a campus and collegiate university with a uniquely-balanced curriculum. Students were required to take three subjects of equal weight in their first year and then to choose one of them in which to major for the rest of the three-year course. In addition, students of arts subjects had to study a science, and science students an arts subject. These complementary subjects were known as 'distant minors'. Dad opted for physics. In his first year, he read English, philosophy, and politics.

The English foundation course was taught by David Craig, a Marxist, who insisted on explaining literature within its historical social context. Dr Roger Bell tutored the other module in linguistics. Frank's philosophy teacher was Professor Frank Sibley, formerly chair of the Philosophy Department at Cornell in the United States. Politics lecturers included Professor Philip Reynolds, who specialised in international affairs, and Mr Stanley Henig, who became the Labour MP for Lancaster.

By Christmas, Frank knew he wanted to major in English, by Easter it was politics and, by the end of the summer term, he had opted for philosophy. Frank never paid much attention to career planning, preferring immediate intellectual gratification, with the result that he left university with a philosophy degree and a grounding in the theories of social change.

Frank found himself a member of a lively first-year politics set, with none more lively and argumentative than Yusifu Usman, known simply as 'Joe'. Tall and thin, about 190cm in height, he came from Northern Nigeria and was one of the very few overseas students attending the university at the time. An admirer of Kwame Nkrumah, the first president of Ghana, Yusifu would introduce a Maoist point of view into the seminars, with a predictably incendiary effect.

On learning that because of the distance and cost of travel, Yusif would have to remain by himself in Lancaster over the Christmas break, Frank contacted his parents and persuaded them to invite Yusifu home to Bournville for the holiday. Yusifu settled in well, until it emerged one day at the dinner table that he was the child of a polygamous family. Frank's mother was horrified to discover that Yusifu's father had four wives.

"How can they put up with it?" she asked. "Why do they let a man treat them like that?

When Yusifu tried to explain that his mother counted herself fortunate to be married to an important man like his father, Phyllis exploded with feminist indignation. With further pointed probing, she soon became aware that Yusifu's father was a Muslim, and Yusifu himself, a communist. This left her in no doubt that he wasn't a suitable companion for her son. He was never invited again.

Meanwhile, Frank took Yusifu to visit his old school friends, including John Murphy, who lived near Rednal. John's dad was a shop steward at the Austin car factory. He had previously commissioned Frank to paint a picture of his prize Kerry Blue dog. John's mom was always kind, and Frank considered himself a family friend.

On arriving at the house, Yusifu and Frank sat in the living room talking to John and his mom. John went out to make everyone a cup of tea, but suddenly returned looking crestfallen.

"Frank," he said in a hushed voice, "my dad would like a quick word with you in the kitchen."

Thinking nothing of it, Frank went to the kitchen to speak with Mr Murphy.

"How are you, Mr Murphy?" he inquired, realising that there was something wrong. John's father was puffed up and red in the face, and his fists were clenched.

"Get that fucking nigger out of my house," he roared, "before I chuck him out myself."

Seeing that there was no point in arguing, Frank returned to the living room.

"Yusifu, we're leaving immediately!" he declared.

Later that evening, as arranged, they met John in the pub. He was most apologetic, explaining to Frank that his dad had been caught on a bad day, and hadn't wanted Frank to leave so suddenly.

Dad still has a book on African sculpture in his possession, inscribed: 'To Frank from Yusif, Christmas 1964'.

Most of Frank's time at university seemed to be taken up by his extra-curricular activities. Apart from joining a range of newly-formed clubs and interest groups, he founded a number of his own, starting with the Art Society, for which he served as secretary.

He arranged life drawing classes for the students at the Storey Institute (the local art school) and later exhibited their work in the Junior Common Room. He wrote and illustrated a series of articles for one of the student newspapers on the historic architecture of Lancaster, campaigning for the preservation of old buildings, such as the Custom House and the Music Pavilion, which had been allowed to fall into decay and were in danger of being bulldozed. But his artistic activities were soon displaced by his political campaigning, locally and nationally. In this, he was assisted by his membership of the editorial boards of two of the University's first newspapers: *John o Gauntlet,* and *Lancaster Red*, both of which he wrote for.

Many years later, when clearing the loft, Dad located ancient copies of the *Gauntlet*, carrying the mailed-glove logo which he'd designed. There were editions of *Lancaster Red*, too, the newsletter of the University's Socialist Union, whose advertisement for membership read:

'If you are in favour of public schools, South African apartheid, Ian Smith, hanging, private profit, America's war in Vietnam, Britain's massive arms burden, NATO, the Stock Exchange, Ascot, *The Daily Express*, racial discrimination, legislation against strikes, Edward Heath, Salazar, Franco, and the Monday Club, then DON'T JOIN THE SOCIALIST UNION. If, however, you oppose all or most of the above, you are becoming dangerously progressive! Tell your troubles to one of our Executive Committee members and we'll fix you up with a Socialist Union membership card.'

Frank had arrived at university on the eve of the October 1964 General Election. Harold Wilson's Labour Party scraped home to victory with a tiny overall majority of four seats. Frank watched the results on his landlady's tiny black and white television screen.

Frank was particularly interested in the outcome of the contest in Smethwick between the Labour candidate, Patrick Gordon Walker, and the Tory, Peter Griffiths. Frank's father (our granddad) worked at Smethwick's Chance Technical College. He was provoked to complain, most unusually for him, about the 'unchristian' nature of the Conservative campaign, which deliberately set out to vilify the local immigrant population. Mick Moran, a fellow student at the university and keen Labour supporter (who, like Frank, had been a pupil in the sixth form at St Philip's) and had been brought up in Smethwick, was also enraged by Peter Griffiths' tactics, and used the columns of *John O Gauntlet* to condemn the anti-immigrant campaign.

The normally safe Labour seat fell to the Conservatives. Shortly after the election, Harold Wilson, the new Prime Minister, denounced Peter Griffiths as a 'parliamentary leper'.

Early in 1965, the political spotlight focussed again on Smethwick, when the American Black Power leader, Malcolm X, visited the town to assess for himself the effect of Peter Griffiths' campaign on local race relations.

"I have come here," he told the media, "because I'm disturbed by reports that coloured people in Smethwick are being badly treated. I've heard they've been treated like the Jews under Hitler."

Malcolm X was condemned by most commentators for this provocative hyperbole, but Frank recalls sharing his sentiments exactly.

The *Gauntlet*'s attacks on Griffiths, and on Tory policy generally, spurred the Lancaster University Conservative Association ('filthy LUCA' - the largest political society on campus) to invite Peter Griffiths to the University to speak on his own behalf. As soon as the meeting was announced, the Socialist Union and Labour students joined forces to research Tory tactics in Smethwick, produce information leaflets, and protest against the visit. Frank prepared a huge 'Griffiths – parliamentary leper' banner for the occasion.

On 21 May 1965, the packed meeting was addressed in person by Peter Griffiths, who was greeted by waves of aggressive heckling.

The *Gauntlet* reported the occasion under the headline, 'Peter Griffiths: Genius or Madman?' It answered rhetorically: 'Neither, unfortunately: he's just a rather rude second-rate demagogue'. The article described Griffiths' delivery as hesitant and his content dull. Predictably, Griffiths focused on 'the immigrant problem' as it applied to Smethwick. When speaking of his proposals to repatriate unemployed immigrants, Griffiths provoked uproar by remarking that they would be 'happier in their sunny climate'. He concluded by threatening legal action over the leaflets that Frank had been handing out.

In March 1966, the Prime Minister, Harold Wilson, called another General Election which, this time, Labour won with a decisive majority of 97 seats. In the run-up to Election day, Frank went to Smethwick to lend his support for the Labour candidate, the actor, Andrew Faulds, and participated in a pre-election rally at which the television star, Harry Corbett (the younger member of the Steptoe and Son team) endorsed the Labour ticket. With the help of the Labour swing nationally, Griffiths and his anti-immigrant policies were roundly beaten at the ballot box.

Another event with a lasting impact on Frank's political development was Rhodesia's Unilateral Declaration of Independence (UDI) on 11 November 1965. Learning of Frank's interest, a white Rhodesian student gave him a copy of the UDI edition of *The Rhodesia Herald*, carrying the headline: 'Rhodesia goes it alone – censorship is imposed, price control introduced – tougher curbs on imports'.

Censors had already been allocated to the Herald, but it was allowed to report that, immediately after the Prime Minister, Ian Smith, declared Rhodesia independent, '…the Governor, Sir Humphrey Gibbs, announced that he had been instructed by the Queen to suspend Mr Smith and the Government… Britain has declared that Rhodesia's independence has been taken illegally and economic sanctions have been imposed'.

A Lancaster Rhodesia Action Committee was immediately established, with Frank as secretary. Within a week, it organised a protest march through Lancaster against Rhodesian UDI, denouncing it as a means of preserving white supremacy and disrupting the transition to majority rule. A picture in the *Gauntlet* shows Yusifu briefing the demonstrators. A further march and rally were held soon afterwards in Dalton Square, but a request for a public meeting in Morecombe was refused by councillors there, on the grounds that they didn't want 'a typical student demonstration' parading 'up and down the seafront'.

Under the heading, 'Not banned in Lancaster', *The Lancaster Guardian* carried a photograph of the protestors being addressed by Gerry Fowler (shortly to become Labour MP for the Wrekin), Dr David Craig, Dr Keith Bell, and Fr Matthew Shaw, the University chaplain, all describing conditions in Rhodesia, and the action being taken by the British government to end UDI.

The Rhodesia Action Committee established contact subsequently with groups with similar aims in other universities and participated in a nationwide campaign 'to spread information and encourage action to bring about democratic government in Rhodesia'. It was eventually merged into a Committee for Racial Equality, along with the University's Anti-Apartheid Movement, the Immigrant Education Project, and the Campaign Against Racial Discrimination. The same small nucleus of students formed the backbone of all these initiatives.

One bizarre consequence of being secretary of the ambiguously-named Rhodesia Action Committee was that Frank found himself on the mailing list of the Rhodesian Front, and in regular receipt of its propaganda letters. One received in 1965 reads:

'This Christmas is particularly dear to us in Rhodesia. It is our first independent Christmas. Yet although we are independent, we feel just as closely bound to you as before...... How can anyone with fellow feeling hack asunder the bonds which bind us together?'

The chief concern of all Left-wing students throughout the 1960s was the continuing war in Vietnam between the National Liberation Movement and the United States military and its puppet regime in Saigon. By 1966, the country was under constant bombardment by American planes, using explosives, anti-personnel weapons, and chemicals.

Julian Holt, the lanky saxophone-playing chairman of the Socialist Union, and Frank, who was its vice-chairman, used the columns of *Lancaster Red* to denounce the war and the war crimes being committed. The Left was particularly irked by the Labour government's refusal to condemn the conflict and destruction wreaked on the Vietnamese people by the indiscriminate use of American weaponry.

In 1966, as representatives of the University's Socialist Union, Julian and Frank travelled to London to a conference of the Vietnam Solidarity Campaign. It was addressed by the frail 94-year-old philosopher, Bertrand Russell, who had played a central role in the Campaign for Nuclear Disarmament. Supported by his personal assistant, Ralph Schoenman, Russell denounced the actions of the United States in Vietnam as a crime against humanity and called for the setting up of an International War Crimes Tribunal.

Julian and Frank managed to shake the old man's hand and congratulate him. They bought copies of his book on war crimes in Vietnam, and met Ralph Schoenman who, a demonstration or so later, showed them the contents of a 'lazy dog' anti-personnel bomb, full of razor-sharp metal blades.

The Tribunal, made up of notable people drawn from eighteen different countries, such as Russell himself, Jean Paul Sartre, Simone de Beauvoir, James Baldwin (the black American writer) and Stokely Carmichael (American Black-Power leader), met eventually in 1967, holding sessions in Stockholm and Copenhagen. Its deliberations were largely ignored in Britain and the United States.

"Is it true," I asked Dad, "that you were arrested when you were a student here?"

My English grandmother had already warned me about applying to Lancaster, with dire tales of how my father had been corrupted and criminalised there, but this had merely added to the allure of the place.

"Yes," he admitted, "I was."

"What happened?" I probed.

"It was over Vietnam," he explained. "The Socialist Union and the Labour Club decided to hold a 'Peace in Vietnam' march along the promenade at Morecambe. We all believed we had a right to peaceful protest, whether the Morecambe Council approved our requests to march or not. This was related to its earlier refusal to allow our public meeting on the Rhodesia situation. We did our best to avoid unnecessary provocation by banning partisan slogans like 'Victory to Ho Chi Minh'."

On Whit Sunday 29 May 1966, the students gathered near the Battery Hotel and made their way along the promenade, past groups of curious holidaymakers, towards the Central Pier, where they held a meeting near the Tourist Information Bureau. They carried banners reading: 'Withdraw all Americans from Vietnam', 'Stop bombing the Vietnamese', 'Houses not bombs', and 'Peace in Vietnam'.

Three people addressed the marchers, of which Frank was the last to speak. He was interrupted by a Police Chief Inspector with the words: "Your bit of fun is over. Your march was unlawful and was held without Corporation consent. You are now required to give your names and addresses to my police officers". The police took down the details of nineteen of the demonstrators, but many of them simply disappeared into the crowd of holidaymakers.

Frank and a fellow student, John Turley, were arrested because they refused to give their names to the police. Not until they had been locked up separately in cells for five hours at the police station did they change their minds, only to be kept there overnight to appear before the magistrate on Monday morning. The cell was cold, Dad said, and the single blanket covered in vomit and excrement.

They were charged on three counts: obstructing the police, obstructing the footpath, and unlawful assembly under common law – offences Frank was reminded he'd committed when he applied for a Criminal Record Check some forty years later. He was fined £4 on each count. The other demonstrators' lesser offence of obstruction found its way to court later, with each of them being fined £4. Julian Holt refused to pay his £4 fine and was eventually arrested four months later, in the Tramway Pub, when he was having a pint. For failing to pay, he was sentenced to one month's imprisonment.

"What did you all hope to achieve by walking down the promenade in Morecambe?" I remarked. "How was it meant to affect the war in Vietnam? It all seems completely pointless."

"I suppose," Dad said, "that most of us had been on the Easter CND peace marches and were inspired by Mahatma Ghandi's principles of non-violent civil disobedience as a means of stopping the war in Vietnam. We believed we were setting an example for others to follow."

"Who were you trying to persuade?" I persisted. "Was it the Morecambe councillors, the tourists, the British government, or the United States military?"

"We were part of a world-wide mass movement," he replied. "Our individual actions might seem trivial to you in hindsight but, collectively, they had an impact on public opinion and the US's resolve to go on fighting the war."

"Do you really think the authorities took any notice?" I asked.

"Have you heard of the Kent State University massacre?" he quizzed. "In 1970, in America, the Ohio National Guard opened fire on a student protest on the university campus, killing and wounding the demonstrators. Why did the authorities resort to such violence if they weren't rattled? That incident turned American public opinion against the war."

"You should count yourself lucky," I quipped, "that the police in Morecambe weren't armed. If you'd studied at Kent State University, it is unlikely that you and I would now be around to debate the issue!"

Quite by accident, Dad had also initiated a far more practical local campaign on another issue. With the campus still at the planning stage, the new undergraduates had to be accommodated in suitable lodgings, with resident landladies to provide them with meals on Sundays. The University had compiled a list of approved addresses, most of them hotels and boarding houses, in the nearby seaside resort of Morecambe, which had vacancies outside of the summer holiday season.

Mrs Boismaison was Frank's first landlady. She allowed him and a fellow student to have one bath a week each, run to a measured six inches of hot water. She also imposed an 11 pm curfew. When her students failed to get back from an event in Lancaster by the 11 pm deadline she'd imposed, she locked them out for the night, adding insult to injury the next morning by throwing their belongings into the garden where they got wet in the rain.

The University found Frank alternative accommodation, this time in a small hotel near Morecambe Promenade. All went well, until the landlady pointed out that she still had some vacant rooms and could take in more students.

Frank, to oblige her, brought round his friend Yusifu, to view the place. The landlady was discomfited and made it abundantly clear that she drew the line at taking in black students. As she explained later, her other guests wouldn't have wanted to stay there if they thought black people had slept in the beds.

Frank was furious at the humiliation suffered by his friend and decided he would quit the digs in protest, doing his best to persuade his housemates to follow his example, in order to 'hit her in the pocket'. Much to his disgust, only one of them agreed to join him, the others pointing out that the hotel provided some of the best digs in Morecambe.

With friends in the Socialist Union, and the Anti-Apartheid Society, Frank proposed a motion in the Junior Common Room that the names of landladies who practised discrimination against students, because of race, colour, or creed, should be deleted from the lodging list. With the motion carried, Frank approached the accommodation office to persuade it to implement the decision.

The University accommodation officer, while professing himself sympathetic, pointed out that, with more students arriving each year, there was shortage of reasonably-priced accommodation and he couldn't afford to be choosy. Besides, the landladies had a legal right to decide on whom they wished to accept as tenants.

Alerted to the need for a change in the law, Frank joined the nascent Campaign Against Racial Discrimination (CARD), set up, following the visit to Britain by the Reverend Martin Luther King early in 1965, by, among others, the Anti-Apartheid Movement, the Campaign for Nuclear Disarmament, the Indian Workers' Association, and the Standing Conference of West Indian Organisations.

He has retained to this day the information that CARD sent him on 'how to expose discrimination', with advice on collecting information on specific cases, and situational testing: sending a white person to apply for a job or flat which had just been refused to a 'coloured person'. CARD's aim was to build a case-by-case exposure of discrimination, so that parliament couldn't pretend it didn't exist.

Frank was disgusted at the feebleness of the new Labour Government's efforts in 1965 to introduce legislation that dealt only with racial discrimination in public places and incitement to racial hatred – to be achieved through conciliation, rather than criminal prosecution. CARD was absolutely right: the legislation should have made it unlawful to discriminate in housing and employment, and given the courts the power to impose fines for infringement. Evidence of discrimination by Morecambe landladies was subsequently submitted to CARD.

The students' longstanding campaign to improve their lodging conditions took on different guises. *The Lancaster Guardian* carried a picture of students, Frank among them, picketing the University's Finance Office with placards protesting at lodging rent increases which they claimed were unfair. Another undergraduate demand to be allowed to rent flats and bed-sitters was eventually granted, despite fears for the students' moral welfare. Until this point, approved boarding accommodation was for either men or women, but never for both on the same premises. Frank found it ironic that landladies were expected to police the sexual behaviour of their students, yet were permitted to discriminate against them on racial grounds.

A fellow student activist in CARD and anti-discrimination campaigning, was Sue Wallis, who Frank remembers appreciatively for her insistence on political self-help, and her aversion to gesture politics. It was Sue who organised classes in English and sociology for immigrants, raised money for famine relief from 'bread and cheese' lunches, and proposed the purchase of a disused property on a mortgage to house overseas students.

On her suggestion, she and Frank arranged a conference in May 1966 on the genetic and sociological aspects of race and racialism. Dr Paxman, from the University's Department of Biology emphasised that the concept of a 'pure' race was a biological nonsense. Dr Coxon from the Department of Social Studies at Leeds argued that legislation against discrimination should be based on sociological research. Gordon Lishman from Manchester spoke on racialist political groups, such as the Racial Preservation Society (formed eighteen months previously).

The conference was declared the most ambitious venture so far to be organised by a University society. Sue, however, was peeved by the refusal of the University's Conservative Association to support the event and said so publicly. LUCA's spokesman, Martin Fell, defended its boycott on the grounds that the organisers had raised a problem that scarcely existed in Lancaster, describing Sue as 'such a silly girl – just an inverted racialist', a gratuitous insult that Frank never forgot.

Chapter 18

Disembowel Enoch Powell !

Who was Enoch Powell? Most people of my generation seem never to have heard of him. At our family house in Wolverhampton, he was the bogeyman who lived just round the corner. His infamous Birmingham speech made headlines well over forty years ago in April 1968, but my parents have never forgotten the impact it had on their lives. Drawing a lurid comparison between British cities and the violent race riots sweeping the United States, Enoch Powell compared himself with 'the Roman', who thought he saw 'the River Tiber foaming with much blood'.

Enoch Powell declared that Commonwealth immigrants should be induced to go home and that there should be an immediate end to their children's right to join their parents and settle in the United Kingdom. He denounced legislation proposed by the Labour Party to make it unlawful to discriminate on grounds of race or colour in employment and housing.

It wasn't just Enoch Powell's anti-immigrant policies that caused the ensuing controversy, but the deliberately inflammatory way that he drew attention to them. He described a conversation he'd had with 'a middle aged quite ordinary man', who had wanted to emigrate with his children because, in Britain 'in fifteen or twenty years time', the black man would 'have the whip hand over the white man'. He told how, within an eight-year period, a widow in his Wolverhampton constituency had become the only white resident in her street, which had become 'a place of noise and confusion'. She was verbally abused by negroes, her windows had been broken, excreta pushed through her letter box and, when she went out, she was followed by 'charming wide-eyed grinning piccaninnies', chanting the word 'racialist'.

Powell suggested that the proposed race relations legislation would result in special privileges being granted to black immigrants and their descendants, and ordinary citizens being denied the right to discriminate in their own affairs. It wasn't the immigrants who were being discriminated against, but the local people among whom they had come to live. To enact the legislation would be 'exactly and diametrically wrong', and 'risk throwing a match on gunpowder'.

People were being made strangers in their own country. Indeed, the weapon of race relations legislation might soon be used by immigrants to overawe and dominate the indigenous population.

His rhetoric was carefully devised. He portrayed a country undergoing a black alien occupation, which was resulting in the persecution of ordinary white people, who had been betrayed by their politicians, leaving him alone with the courage to speak the truth.

Conscious that Powell's Wolverhampton constituency had been at the epicentre of this particular political earthquake, I asked Dad how he had ended up living there in the first place.

"I came to train as a teacher at the Wolverhampton Technical Teachers' College," he explained. "I got a job as a lecturer at Bilston College of Further Education and I ended up staying there."

On completing university, he had wanted to do Voluntary Service Overseas (VSO) in Africa, but was turned down following interview, perhaps because of his political views, or his degree in the impractical subject of philosophy. Aware that there were no job vacancies for revolutionaries, he realised that he would have to earn his living some other way and, on the advice of his father, decided to follow him into further education. The quest for employment was made more urgent by Frank's decision to marry Fraciszka, the girl he'd been courting from his sixth-form days.

Wolverhampton Technical Teachers' College, long since merged into the University of Wolverhampton, was one of the four colleges in England which specialised in the preparation of teachers for work in technical or further education. In the late 1960s, apprentices in technical subjects, such as engineering, construction, catering, and hairdressing, were sent on day or block release to a local college to study the theoretical aspects of their chosen trade. To ensure they acquired a broader outlook beyond what was immediately applicable to the job, they were required in their time at college to undertake additional 'general', or 'liberal', education classes.

Frank was offered a place at the Technical Teachers' College to train as a general, or liberal, education lecturer. While the job of educating working-class young people to appreciate high culture, literature and the arts held no appeal for him, he believed there were opportunities for building on their natural class-consciousness, to encourage them to reach a critical understanding of their place and function in society.

"Forty years ago, Wolverhampton must have been a very different place from how it is now," I remarked.

"Quite so," Dad said. "It was a busy and prosperous manufacturing town, with large factories and foundries providing work for many thousands of people. That's why people from the British West Indies, and then India, were drawn to the place. There were vacancies everywhere and a shortage of people to fill them. I found a job very easily, because the colleges were expanding to meet the training needs of the local manufacturing industries."

Frank and Franciszka first had to look for somewhere to live. Suitable accommodation wasn't easy to come by. After paying an agency, they managed to find and rent an upstairs flat in Oaklands road, off the Lea Road in Pennfields. It helped to be married and white. Landlords took a dim view of cohabiting couples and discriminated against black and Asian people, although the colour bar manifested itself in unexpected ways.

Areas were covertly zoned and houses designated along racial lines. For example, the roads to the north and west of the Lea Road were considered suitable for black and Asian tenants, while the roads to the south and east were reserved for whites. Houses, divided into bed-sits, would be allocated to either black or white tenants, but rarely to both.

Landlords with property portfolios were known to say to white, black or Asian clients: "This property isn't available, but you might like to look at a flat that's just become vacant in such-and-such street." Nevertheless, it was far more difficult for black and Asian people to find accommodation than for whites, with the obstacles for some groups, for example, young single black women, almost insurmountable.

"Were there many black and Asian people living in Wolverhampton when you arrived?" I asked.

"Judge for yourself," Dad said. "In 1967, less than 20,000 people, in a population of more than a quarter of a million, had been born abroad in what was then called the New Commonwealth. About 6,000 came from the British West Indies – mostly from Jamaica, 12,000 from the Indian subcontinent, and 1,000 from East Africa. In total, they made up roughly 7 per cent of the population. That compares with an estimated 25 per cent, or 1 in 4, from black and Asian minorities living in Wolverhampton today." He was always keen on the empirical data.

On arriving in Wolverhampton, Dad made contact with the local branch of the Communist Party, run by a caucus of older comrades, including its secretary, George Barnsby. Frank and Sam Spittle, a charismatic young silk-screen printer from a working-class background, were given the job of organising the Wolverhampton branch of the Young Communist League (YCL), a task they undertook with enthusiasm. The League met once a week at Frank and Franciszka's flat, until its membership grew so large that it had to move to a more spacious venue.

As soon as they arrived in Wolverhampton, Frank and Franciszka found themselves in the thick of its politics. In the Autumn of 1967, the Sikhs were campaigning for the right of bus workers to be able to wear a turban and beard as part of their uniform. Wolverhampton Council's Transport Committee resolutely refused to change the rules prohibiting turbans, even when faced with the prospect of mass protest and industrial action.

Early in 1968, over 5,000 Sikhs, from all over the country, marched from the gurdwara in Cannock Road to the town hall to deliver a protest letter. They were supported by the Indian Workers' Association, the Wolverhampton Council of Churches, the Communist Party, and the YCL. Dignified elderly Sikhs, in long white shirts and turbans, led the demonstration as it slowly wound its way to the town hall. No one from the council was there to take their letter or to receive a deputation.

The Transport Committee eventually lifted the turban ban in 1969 when a Sikh member of the Alkali Dal, Sohan Singh Jolly, threatened to burn himself to death. The West Midland Passenger Transport Authority, which was about to assume responsibility for the Wolverhampton bus service, had made it clear that it intended to scrap the regulation.

The campaign lasted twenty-one months, becoming ever more polarised and embittered, It served to provide Enoch Powell, MP for Wolverhampton South West, with his much-quoted example of the danger of communalism, 'the curse of India', which immigrants had imported into the country.

Frank and fellow student, Raj Mitra, were sent for teaching practice to Bilston College of Further Education in the former borough of Bilston, which had recently been absorbed into Wolverhampton.

Under the leadership of its Principal, Harry Lamb, the college had acquired a markedly liberal arts ethos, despite the fact that one of its main functions was to provide day release for large numbers of craft and technical apprentices from nearby factories and the Bilston steel works. The college had a sizeable engineering department, but the Principal had encouraged the growth of the liberal arts by splitting general education into two sections and putting a young, dynamic and radical member of staff, Ryman Reece Roper, in charge of a new department of Social Studies and Art.

While on teaching practice, Frank came to know Reece Roper, who encouraged him, along with Raj Mitra, to apply for posts teaching liberal studies that had been created for the forthcoming academic year. Both applicants were successful and took up full-time positions at Bilston in September 1968.

Frank had met Raj at the Technical Teachers' College and they remained close friends until Raj's untimely death from a brain tumour. Raj was a highly educated Bengali, born in Calcutta, who had been employed as a manager at Rubery Owen, until he decided to make a career in further education as a lecturer in liberal studies. He was an excellent cricketer and batted over many seasons for Castlecroft Cricket Club. A devout Hindu, he used to organise Wolverhampton's annual Durga Puja festivals. He also cooked excellent fish or boiled-egg curries for his friends: regular feasts that Frank had to forego when Raj got married.

Frank and Raj were practising to teach liberal studies under supervision at Bilston College at the time that Enoch Powell's 20 April 1968 'river of blood' speech made headlines. It had an immense impact on the nation as a whole, in Wolverhampton especially, and in the classrooms at the College. Edward Heath, the Conservative Leader, reacted swiftly by calling the speech 'racialist in tone' and announcing that Powell was dismissed from the Shadow Cabinet. Powell responded by suggesting that Heath secretly shared his views but was too fearful of public opinion to say so. Powell's speech and removal from the Shadow Cabinet generated widespread and intense public emotion.

People everywhere were excited and stirred by the speech, whether or not they'd actually heard or read it. They spoke about it on the buses, in public houses, on the streets, at work, and in the college staff room. Almost everyone agreed that Enoch Powell was right and Edward Heath was insane to dismiss such a great man.

Frank reports that in the weeks that followed, local people would knock on the door almost every night, collecting signatures in support of 'our Enoch'. They were immensely proud that such an important statesman represented their town at a national level and had placed them – probably for the first time ever – at the very centre of the political map. Civic pride and a sense of self-esteem, deriving from their assumed local expertise in the field of race relations, provided the foundation of their new political awakening.

For an isolated internationalist like Frank, aiming to unite the working class, but particularly, for black and Asian families, the situation was truly terrifying. Wulfrunians were barely able to contain their new-found political passion within the normal routines of daily life.

Frank saw black people being jostled, spat upon, and insulted by school children in bus queues. Two Jamaicans who attended YCL meetings were beaten up outside a fish and chip shop by a gang, shouting 'kill the niggers', and 'Enoch for Prime Minister'. The police showed little interest in investigating the offence.

At the college, students would break into a chant of ' Enoch, Enoch' whenever Raj entered the room, some refusing to be taught by a 'wog', until the Head of Department was summoned to restore order. In Frank's own classes, the same chant would break out whenever a black or Asian student dared to respond to his questions. Even taking the class register was a challenge. When the lecturer called out the name 'Singh', the students would stand up and sing obscene verses.

Frank soon learned that while racially-abusive students could be subdued to silence, they could not be engaged in rational debate about the issues that Powell had raised. Any attempt to do so would result in uproar, as they simultaneously expressed their wholehearted support for Enoch Powell. What was it Mr Powell had said? "To send them all back, stupid!"

Attitudes in the college staff room were much the same. Most of the lecturers supported Enoch Powell and thought there were far too many 'coloured' students at the college. They were regarded as posing a severe threat to the College's reputation and academic standards. Frank made himself unpopular by challenging the widely-shared view that negroes were innately less intelligent than white people. Hadn't he been taught at university that it was a scientific fact that they had a lower IQ?

The lecturers showed no embarrassment whatsoever at making known their opinions on the intellectual inferiority of 'coloured' people in front of Raj and the other Asian member of staff, who had a PhD. Most of the staff shared the view that the College needed to introduce tougher entrance tests in literacy and reasoning to screen out unsuitable students. Frank's bitter memories of the college in the 1960s made him even more determined to transform in totality the institution that succeeded it.

"Why were people so opposed to the immigrants?" I inquired, realising, as I spoke, that the topic of immigration was still a hot potato some forty years later.

"There's no simple explanation," Dad replied, "But it never had much to do with numbers."

He thought for a moment and continued. "The West Indian immigrants began to arrive in the late 1950s, the Asians throughout the 60s, all in search of paid work to send money home to improve life for themselves in the countries they came from. The longer they stayed, though, the more they underwent a transformation from being temporary workers into permanent settlers, with the same needs as the rest of the population for family life, housing, hospitals, and schools. But, in the daily struggle for these scarce resources, white residents thought they should be given priority. Enoch Powell summed it up conveniently for them with the image of a third world war: a foreign invasion threatening the British way of life."

This explanation differed from the one Frank would have offered in 1968. The Young Communist League produced notes to assist its officers in leading discussion groups on the perils of racialism. It recognised that some of the young people joining the YCL would be prejudiced, like those in the population as a whole. If racialism was allowed to go unchecked, it declared, the consequences for white, black and Asian people, alike, would be disastrous.

According to the Communist Party and its Youth League, racialism was an ideological tool which facilitated capitalist exploitation at home and imperialist plunder abroad. When capitalism was in difficulties, Britain's 'coloured citizens', as 'an easily identified section', were able to serve as a convenient scapegoat.

The theory of white racial superiority wasn't something new. It had developed to justify the slave trade and the rape of India. 'Woggism' had proved a useful mindset for the British imperialist armies. 'The sons of the working class, serving in the lower ranks, had to be persuaded to shoot down colonial people for demanding the same rights for which their fathers had fought back home.' The YCL briefing notes tried to answer questions such as: 'Do coloured workers threaten British wages and conditions?' 'Are immigrants holding back our children's education?', and 'Do immigrants sponge on the social services?' The person leading the discussion was advised not to talk too much, to address questions at 'less developed' comrades, to encourage thinking, and to resist the temptation to shout down any prejudice that showed itself.

An anti-Powell letter which Frank sent at the time on behalf of the YCL to the *Express & Star*, clearly reflects the official line. The YCL's letter set off an avalanche of anonymous abusive replies to the sending address. Dad kept a few examples as teaching aids, from which I'll quote:

'Your letter was tripe. Mr Powell was right in everything he said. The blacks are sure to make 20 per cent less demand on our social services because there are less of them, but they shouldn't get anything at all. How much do you suppose the Asians have paid who came from Kenya with seven, eight, or nine children? They pick up all the plums as soon as they arrive.'

'Personally, I prefer apes. They are at least fairly clean. Most of the blacks round here are a stinking lot of filthy pigs living off immoral earnings and mongrelising the country with half-caste kids. I wouldn't live near them and I would burn my home to the ground before I'd sell it to a black.'

Workers felt so strongly about Edward Heath's decision to drop Enoch Powell from the Shadow Cabinet that many decided to go on marches and strikes. Frank was in Wolverhampton when workers at Banks's Brewery (now Marstons) stopped work for half a day and marched to the town hall to deliver a petition to the mayor protesting at Powell's dismissal. Other pro-Powell marchers, carrying Union Jacks emblazoned with the name 'Enoch', walked six miles to join a further 700 demonstrators outside Dudley Town Hall, where Edward Heath was due to speak. They shouted, 'Heath out', and booed a black bus conductor as he left the meeting.

The Young Communist League joined a hastily convened umbrella group of those opposed to Enoch Powell. Known as the Wolverhampton Front Against Racialism, it managed to organise a protest march on the Saturday immediately following the speech. About 250 people, white, black, and Asian, set out to deliver letters denouncing the part Powell and the press had played in inflaming racial prejudice. They called at the local Conservative Party Office, Mr Powell's house in Merridale Road, and at the *Express & Star*, Wolverhampton's evening newspaper. Speakers pointed out that, in the week since the speech was made, every immigrant in Britain had gone in fear of safety for his home and family. Demonstrators wore yellow badges of shame as a reminder of the way Hitler had forced Jews to identify themselves. A leaflet explained that Powell was clearing 'the way for black-shirted thugs to jump on the bandwagon of racialist filth'. A photogaph exists of a young-looking Dad wearing a yellow star on that march.

Powell's new popularity had a profound effect on the local election results in May 1968, described in the press as a 'Tory H bomb'. In Wolverhampton, the Labour vote fell to 28 per cent, its lowest-ever proportion since the Second World War, while the Tory vote rose to 66 per cent, its highest point, giving the Conservatives a majority on the council of 20 seats.

Despite Powell's impassioned onslaught against the legislation, the Labour government pressed ahead with the Race Relations Act

1968, making it unlawful for the first time to discriminate on grounds of colour or race in employment and the provision of goods, facilities, housing, trade union membership, and advertising. Unfortunately, it exempted small residential dwellings, where the landlord or family members lived on the premises, and businesses with fewer than twenty-five employees. Many of the Morecambe and Wolverhampton landlords that Frank had had to deal with were still able to operate a colour bar.

At the Technical Teachers' College, the General Studies group was required to undertake a joint project, involving the preparation of innovative teaching lesson plans and materials on a subject of its choice. The group settled unanimously on the topic of the moment: immigration, with a focus on the contribution that Commonwealth immigrants made to the economy.

Graphs were prepared showing the youthful age of the migrant workforce, its tax contribution, and its disproportionately smaller need for welfare and health, compared with that of the general population with its more elderly age profile. Maps were drawn showing the parts of the world from which the immigrants came, with arrows representing the so-called pull and push factors. But at the heart of the student teachers' project was a proposal to shoot a short 16mm film, using general studies students at West Midlands College as actors and extras.

The story centred on the assassination of a Far-Right politician with extreme racist ideas. He is gunned down on the steps of his constituency office by a revolutionary student called 'Rudi'. The politician's death leads to an outbreak of race rioting, in which white people chase blacks through the streets, before lynching them. Blood flows, before reason and harmony prevail.

The project was well under way before the Principal and Head of Department at the college began to receive complaints. By then, one of Frank's colleagues – a wealthy solicitor bent on a change of career – had grown a moustache, donned a dark jacket and pinstripes, and been filmed feigning death on the steps of the Conservative Office on Tettenhall Road. The camera had also caught the students at Walsall College of Technology participating in a realistic, but mock, race riot. Rudi, the gunman, had been disarmed of his starter pistol, handcuffed, and led away by trainee teachers dresses as policemen.

As the Enoch Powell look-a-like collapsed on the office steps, Conservative Party officials came out and ordered the group to stop filming, to which the solicitor was heard to reply: "There is no copyright in people or places". Despite pressure from authority, the film was completed, and shown, to much applause, to an audience of student teachers, friends and sympathisers.

At the end of the course, the Teachers' College held its annual open day at which all the project materials were put on show. Officials from Wolverhampton's Conservative-controlled Education Committee and Department were invited to a preview. Soon after, Frank and fellow students were summoned to meet the Principal and Head of Department. Would they please withdraw their tasteless film and the charts showing the disproportionate contribution immigrants were making to the economy? The film had been judged unsuitable as teaching material and would bring the college into disrepute, while the graphs were deemed to be inaccurate political propaganda. Rather than comply, the students dismantled their exhibition and staged a walk-out, leaving an empty room for the open day.

The Young Communist League kept up its campaign against Enoch Powell, picketing most of the local public meetings he attended, and heckling him if its members gained access. Prior to the General Election in June 1970, the Conservatives held a public meeting at the Wolverhampton Grammar School at which Powell addressed a capacity audience.

Frank and Pete Carter, the Communist Party candidate for the South West Constituency, both managed to find seats at the back of the hall, and took advantage of the opportunity to ask the speaker questions, making their views of Mr Powell known at the same time. They were immediately surrounded by bouncers who hauled them over metal chairs and threw them out of the building onto concrete slabs. Pete was kicked in the stomach, and lodged a formal complaint, but Frank merely acquired a few bruises. Outside, a large crowd of mainly Asian young people, organised by the Indian Workers' Association, were chanting politically-inappropriate slogans, such as 'Disembowel Enoch Powell'! Powell went on to increase his majority in the constituency to a massive 14,467 votes.

To the despair of local Conservatives who identified with him so closely, Enoch Powell remained steadfast in his opposition to the policies of Edward Heath. In 1974, he announced he would not be seeking re-election in his Wolverhampton South West Constituency, and urged his supporters to vote Labour if they wanted to preserve British sovereignty in the face of the threat from the European Economic Community. He went on to represent the Ulster Unionists as an MP from 1974 to 1987.

When Powell died in 1998, Dad became infuriated at the glowing tributes paid to the man's statesmanship by politicians of both Right and Left, including the hitherto-respected Tony Benn. Dad's anger inspired him to write one of his poems for us. It's too long to quote in full, but the following lines left me with an insight into what it was like to live in Wolverhampton in 1968:

'… Identified as enemies,
We felt it then, our kristallnacht:
The children spat upon at school,
A turban taken from a Sikh,
Black people beaten in the street.
Such small personal matters, these,
Of no consequence to a man
Who believed the driving purpose
Of a politician was the
Dramatic presentation of
A polarised predicament.
You'd have been to him just one more
'Wide-eyed grinning piccaninny',
A number whose arrival meant
Destruction for his way of life…'

Chapter 19

An unconventional cure for asthma

Bilston College's foremost exponent of liberal studies was John Williams, who conceived of education as a giant logistical or military exercise. Classroom activity, in his view, had to be varied at least every ten minutes. The key to success in liberal studies teaching was to mobilise large numbers of students simultaneously - the whole college if possible - in pursuit of a wide choice of different expressive educational activities. Thus, he succeeded in organising a college-wide liberal studies hour, and then an entire afternoon dedicated to liberal studies options. One such choice was a regular weekly midday film show held in the College hall, at which short educational 16mm movies were shown. This occasion provided the stage for one of Frank's greatest political humiliations.

As part of the film series, Frank ordered a film on the South African apartheid system from the Anti-Apartheid Movement. As the film was being shown to the various classes assembled in the hall, one of Frank's colleagues, a senior member of staff in the department, rose to his feet and bellowed: "You don't have to watch this communist propaganda. These people are terrorists. If you want, you can leave now to have your lunch." Most of the students got up and left.

During the week that followed, in a desperate effort to restore political balance, the College contacted the South African Embassy which agreed to send it a film about a pedigree dog show in Cape Town. The manicured pooches provoked much mirth and proved far more popular than the movie on apartheid.

In Autumn 1968, when Frank took up his post as a lecturer at Bilston College of Further Education, he was given a full weekly timetable of twenty-two hours of class contact teaching liberal studies. The Construction Department, in particular, was hostile to any subject that wasn't immediately relevant to the building trade, and timetabled the liberal studies hour at 4 to 5 pm in the afternoon, Fridays included. Construction and engineering students took their cue from their subject lecturers, and gave liberal studies teachers a tough time.

Frank managed, nevertheless, to engage with the technicians and apprentices, whom he regarded respectfully at the time as the potential vanguard of the proletariat. His success and popularity with the students led to a request for his services at the Wolverhampton College of Technology, where the printing students - compositor and machine apprentices - were also required to take lessons in liberal studies.

Along with other liberal studies staff, Frank became a member of the West Midlands Branch of the Association for Liberal Education, and took on the editorship of its magazine, which was soon renamed, *Adlib*. Three editions were produced, each more radical in content than the last, before the Association terminated the arrangement on the spurious grounds that it didn't have the money to pay for the publication. It wasn't so much the content, as the brightly covered comic art covers, designed and screen printed by Sam Spittle, which scuppered *Adlib*. The first showed a purple super-hero described as 'Engineer man, *Adlib*'s mighty foe!'

Some of the articles also led to complaints. Phyllis, a black woman teacher at a Wolverhampton secondary school, wrote an account of her experience of listening on a daily basis to racially-prejudiced staff-room chatter: 'the Indian child can only learn by rote', 'The West Indian has no sense of urgency', and 'They expect to be smacked as at home'. Phyllis went on to claim that black school children were perceptive enough to realise that their teachers thought they were 'unpleasant, unattractive, ill-mannered, and stupid' and were responding predictably: 'You dislike me, so I don't see why I should be ordered around by you'.

Another article dealt with the contribution of the education system to oppressive gender stereotyping, and male lecturers' patronising and sexist attitudes. Colleges' entrance and aptitude testing was also called into question. *The Little Red School Book*, which had just been withdrawn from public circulation, was given a positive review for instructing its readers to question authority. Did we want to continue turning out 'mindless, unthinking sheep'?

Ryman Reece Roper was determined that the Department of Social Studies, Art and General Education, of which he was head, would become more than a liberal studies service provider by developing new subject areas and courses of its own. The department already offered subjects such as English, art, history and geography.

Science and mathematics fell within the realm of engineering. The new department, however, could lay claim to any GCE subject not allocated elsewhere, providing a member of staff could be found to teach it. Reece and Frank came up with GCE sociology, political studies, economics, psychology, and logic, all of which Frank was, at some stage, expected to teach, until subject specialists were appointed. He remained in charge of sociology and logic, although the latter was never sufficiently popular to make it a market leader.

Reece and Frank's next innovation was to make contact with the nascent Open University, due to take its first undergraduates in 1971, and to offer to run preparation courses to equip students with the skills to succeed in the arts and social science foundation modules. While the preparation courses were run successfully for a couple of years, it eventually became obvious that the 'open' in the university's title contradicted, or at least undermined, the opportunity for developing pre-entry study. In 1971, as a consequence of this initiative, Frank applied for part-time work as an Open University Tutor Counsellor, an evening commitment he retained for the next fourteen years.

Greater potential for expansion lay in applied social studies, with the department pioneering courses for teachers of children and adults with special needs, social workers, youth workers, health visitors, and health visitor fieldwork teachers. Frank led the way in setting up these courses and developing a new practical approach to teaching sociology that came to be described as 'society as a resource'.

From Reece and Frank's point of view, the department's expansion into the field of social studies had two other important consequences. It broadened the range and intake of students to include many more young people from black Caribbean and Asian backgrounds, attracted to the possibilities of employment in youth and social work. It also provided opportunities for the study of comparative social systems, cultures, communities, and family life. While there were never many takers, in 1973, the college put on a course in cross-cultural studies, which aimed to provide a knowledge of the history, political systems, and social and cultural patterns, of the West Indies, Africa, African America, and the Indian subcontinent. Aspects of cross-cultural studies were already integrated into most of the department's courses.

Teachers were needed to cover the range of new classes in social science and applied social studies. The college recruited a number of enthusiastic full and part-time staff with diverse and fascinating talents and personalities.

Perhaps the most complex was the gifted, highly qualified, but perverse, Dr Doojen Napal, who had come to Britain in 1965 from Mauritius, where he had studied and passed external London BA Honours and Masters degrees in history and political thought. He had also gained a teacher's certificate there, and served as a member of the Mauritian parliament.

He had experienced great difficulty on arrival in finding suitable employment, having to make do with a series of part-time or temporary jobs teaching English to immigrants, working as a university research assistant, and filling in as a history master at a girls' grammar school, until he was offered a post by Harry Lamb and Ryman Reece Roper as a lecturer in liberal studies at Bilston. While he had undoubtedly experienced appalling discrimination in applying for jobs, he had a high opinion of his intellectual worth and was haughty in his dealings with those he considered his intellectual inferiors, who included the majority of engineering and construction lecturers who didn't have university degrees.

They responded predictably to his airs and graces, by trying to 'take him down a peg or two'. They refused to use his title, referring to him as a 'wily oriental gentleman' when introducing him to their classes, and taking no action when their students misbehaved in his presence. Any residual respect shown to him by students disappeared rapidly when Powellism swept the college.

Doojen was allocated a work station close to Frank's in the staff room and regarded Frank as an intellectual equal, sympathetic friend, and ally, in his daily struggle with increasingly hostile staff and students. On finding Doojen sitting at the back of the classroom, holding his head, as his students ran riot, Frank had intervened to restore a semblance of order.

Doojen was a shrewd and sophisticated individual who could readily detect the political and psychological dynamics of a situation and encapsulate them in a damaging satirical phrase. (Frank hadn't found it amusing when Doojen described him publicly as 'a walking penis with the brain of Plato'.) Nevertheless, he soon came to realise that the reaction that Doojen provoked in his colleagues constituted an infallible test of their racial prejudice. Doojen was infuriating, often deliberately, but he didn't deserve the demeaning abuse that was levelled at him.

Frank, himself, found Doojen's intellectual snobbery and pronounced Rght-wing political sympathies extremely trying. Doojen's AWAAM was the only black or Asian association in the town to declare its wholehearted support for Enoch Powell and his policy of repatriation. Doojen had also written to Prime Minister Edward Heath urging him not to impose sanctions on, or to support a boycott of, South Africa.

It was Doojen's admiration for Enoch Powell that eventually led to his downfall. Doojen failed to turn up for work at the start of the 1974 Autumn term. It turned out that he had travelled to the South Down Constituency in Northern Ireland, where Enoch Powell was standing in the October General Election. He claimed he'd gone there to seek a cure for his asthma, but it was widely believed that he'd been campaigning for his hero, or at least, covering, or researching, the election campaign. The occasion provided the college authorities with the opportunity they'd been waiting for. Doojen never returned to the college.

Instead, he spent his time writing the first and only volume of a book, entitled *Enoch Powell, A Study in Personality and Politics*. Doojen's thesis was that Mr Powell was a tragic figure of Sophoclean proportions, whose personality was stunted by an over-possessive mother. In the chapter 'Mother's boy', Enoch's mother chooses a drawing room décor of silver (a symbol of faith and purity) and black (grief and patience) and insists on painting her rosewood piano black to match. Despite their political differences and Frank's impatience with this mumbo jumbo, Doojen gratefully dedicated a copy of his book 'to Frank Reeves, who often restored my faith in humanity in my darkest moments'. We also have a second copy dedicated 'to Melhado, for looking so well after my spiritual son'.

Another of Frank's colleagues was the aptly-named David Warm. He took charge of the full-time general education classes provided for black and Asian children of school leaving age who were without qualifications, often because they had only just arrived in the country. A large mild-mannered fellow, with a benign and sympathetic personality, he was immensely popular with his often severely troubled and disadvantaged students. They loved him almost to the point of worship. Dave's own Jewishness helped him to understand the mindset of the Hindu, Sikh, Moslem, and Christian Pentecostal young people in his charge, and to persuade them to tolerate and resolve the differences that arose between them.

Frank recalled Dave summarising the argument one class had been having about their respective approaches to marriage and family life: "The Indians marry, fall in love, and have children; the Jamaicans have children, fall in love, and marry; and the English fall in love, marry, and have children, and then perhaps do it again." Dave left in pursuit of his roots to work in a Jewish Youth Club in Manchester.

To run a Health Visitor Training Course, the College had to employ a team of qualified Health Visitor Tutors. The College appointed Ms Betty Simms as course leader. She was a capable older woman who had worked for many years in Libya and knew Colonel Gaddafi. Betty's upbringing and time spent abroad had made her politically radical, and her ambition was to turn out health visitors who were socially and politically committed to the communities and families they were appointed to serve. She allied herself with Frank and insisted that he teach the sociology and neighbourhood study to her classes.

To enhance their understanding of the economic realities confronting their clients, the students were timetabled to visit factories, foundries, coal mines, and other places of work. Frank remembers helping the health visitors, clad in their overalls and hard hats, to jump on conveyor belts deep below ground to travel to the coalface at the Cannock Number 5 Mine.

All the students were women qualified and experienced in nursing and midwifery or obstetrics. Their discipline, rigour, and intelligence made them ideal students. Betty expanded her portfolio to run courses for fieldwork teachers and school nurses. It was while teaching on a fieldwork teachers' course, that Frank encountered Mel as a student.

The proportion of black and Asian students at the college increased, partly as a result of the department's policy of putting on courses suited to their needs. In recognition of this trend, Frank sought to attract more teachers from black and Asian backgrounds to contribute to the courses for which he was responsible. He became friendly with a Sri Lankan sociology graduate, Sadun Perera, whom he persuaded to teach GCE sociology. Sadun continued to teach sociology at the College of Further Education until it was absorbed into the new Bilston Community College some eleven years later.

Frank also prevailed upon his friend Raj Mitra, who was in charge of courses teaching English to immigrants, to employ Phyllis, one of the new black secondary school teachers, to help on a part-time basis with the growing number of evening classes. Through his ally, Betty Simms, he also helped to create a trainee Health Visitor Tutor post, for which Mel was able to apply successfully.

At the same time as working hard to grow the department, Ryman Reece Roper and Frank were both deeply involved in party politics and the trade union movement. Reece stood as a Labour Party parliamentary candidate in South Staffordshire, and Frank ran as a communist in the West Midland County Council elections - neither successfully. Later, when Frank had joined the Labour Party, Dennis Turner, then an MP, would joke how Frank was the only member of the Labour Party who (as a communist) had run against him. (This was in the first County Council election for the Ettingshall and Springvale Ward in 1973.)

Frank and Reece spent very little time at home performing domestic duties, with predictable consequences for their marriages and family life. Frank taught evening classes three nights a week: Open University prep on Monday, logic on Tuesday, and sociology on Thursday. On Wednesday, he attended Communist Party meetings and, on Friday, the Young Communist League. On other occasions, it was the trade union, or the Council for Community Relations.

Frank and Reece were delegates from the college and the Schoolmasters' Union to the Executive of the Wolverhampton Council for Community Relations (WCCR), a body that had recently replaced the town's Council for Racial Harmony. Its aim was to improve the life of the inhabitants of Wolverhampton, 'without distinction of sex or race', and to raise awareness about 'the requirements, advantages, duties and responsibilities of living in a multi-racial society'. The WCCR employed a full-time community relations officer, Aaron Haynes, who quickly earned his reputation in Wolverhampton as the black person's answer to Enoch Powell.

Aaron was born in Barbados in 1927 and educated at Combermere School, before graduating in the United States. He had served as a teacher in the Caribbean and London. As an educationalist, he was keen to promote projects involving young people and their problems, and to work closely with like-minded people, such as Reece and Frank at Bilston College of Further Education.

Frank attended a series of WCCR residential youth training conferences held at Easter in Rhyl, North Wales, and Pendrell Hall, Staffordshire. Young people from different racial backgrounds explored the difficulties that they might encounter in employment, housing, and education, and what action they should take if they encountered discrimination. Sessions were popular and stimulating and led to the development of lasting cross-cultural friendships.

The WCCR also organised an annual essay competition for children in the local secondary schools on themes relating to race relations, for example, 'my dream for Wolverhampton'. Aaron had the winning entries published under the title, *How Black?* One story told of how parents had reacted to the news that their daughter had a black boy friend. Other essays dealt with the disadvantage of becoming engaged to a person of different racial origins, and the consequences of a 'coloured' family moving in next door.

The stories had meaning for many of the young people attending school or college in Wolverhampton at the time. Students would approach lecturers whom they considered sympathetic to discuss relational problems and to ask for help. The increasing number of black and Asian youngsters at the College, made it inevitable that some would develop emotional attachments to a boy or girl from a different race, religion, or a caste, from themselves.

The consequences, however, could be very serious, in some cases leading to violence or death. Frank and Dave Warm had to refer some of the more threatening incidents to the police, who appointed a senior officer, Alan Leivesley, to deal with cases of this nature. They usually involved Sikh or Hindu girls refusing to comply with their parents' plans for an arranged marriage and leaving home to be with a boy they had met at college. White girls with black boyfriends encountered a great deal of unpleasantness, too.

Trevor, a black Jamaican, and Jackie, a white girl from the Lunt in Bilston, met as students at the college. They developed a deep affection for one another, despite the implacable opposition of Trevor's mother and Jackie's father to their increasingly passionate relationship. With both families united in hunting them down and ending the affair, they sought shelter, first staying at Frank's house and then, when their cover was blown, with Reece Roper in Wombourne. They married and went on to have two children together at around the same time that we were born. Trevor and Jackie are clearly visible in our parents' wedding photographs, and Trevor remains a family friend to this day.

The WCCR gave evidence on the experiences of 'coloured' young people to the Parliamentary Select Committee on Race Relations, and fully endorsed many of its recommendations to government, such as 'schools should prepare all their children for adult life in a multi-racial society'. It is no accident that the Select Committee thought there should be 'more courses specially designed for immigrants in colleges of further education'. By 1970, Bilston College was already running full-time general education classes for older and recently-arrived children of New Commonwealth immigrants.

The WCCR also kept up its opposition to its local MP, Enoch Powell, who by now was expressing his ambition to become minister of repatriation. On one memorable occasion at a public meeting in Wombourne, Powell recognised hecklers Reece, Frank and George Barnsby in the audience and announced:

"I know the Community Relations Council is here, carrying on their Maoist work, organised and directed from overseas for the purpose of subverting and destroying the institutions of this country. An increasing number of people are aware of it and will not allow it" (13 June 1970).

To help him in the business of teaching sociology, Frank joined the Association for Teachers of Social Science. The West Midlands branch was chaired by Roland Meighan, a lecturer at the University of Birmingham, who became a life-long friend. Frank became regional secretary and then, in 1974, the national conference organiser. With the help of friends from the Bilston social studies section, Frank staged the ambitious 'Society as a Resource' conference at Compton Park, Wolverhampton.

Speakers included Professor A H Halsey from Nuffield College, Oxford, Peter Leonard, Director of Education at the National Institute of Social Work Training, Vivien Stern, Education Officer at the Community Relations Commission, and Aaron Haynes from the Wolverhampton Council for Community Relations. But what made the event unique were the visits to experience at first hand what life was like in industry, social institutions, sport, and leisure.

Delegates were taken down a mine to the coalface, to the assembly line at British Leyland's Longbridge factory, and to the furnaces and rolling mill at the Bilston Steel Works. They were ferried to old people's homes, sheltered workshops, adventure playgrounds and nightclubs, with an invitation to engage in ethnographic observation. They returned with amazing stories of their sociological adventures. At British Leyland, managers had forbidden them all from talking to the workers for fear that an unwitting remark might trigger a strike.

As an evening event, Frank and Dave Warm arranged for small groups of delegates to dine out with a family from another culture. They saw this as one means of understanding concepts such as 'culture' and 'ethnicity' but, just as importantly, of appreciating the worth of others' culture in a social climate of misrepresentation, prejudice and intolerance. Some delegates wriggled at the prospect, suggesting the proposal treated 'immigrants as objects' but, at the prior 'matching and dispatching' session, the hosts made clear that they were delighted at the interest being shown in their culture and country of origin. Mel drove one group to Sparkbrook to visit Aunt Epsi, where they were introduced to Jamaican food and culture.

When the affable Harry Lamb retired, a new principal, John Inch, was appointed to replace him. It soon became apparent to Reece and Frank that the latitude they'd been granted for radical educational innovation had come to an end. Over 190cms tall, the unsuitably-named John Inch had been a teacher of geography at the Wulfrun College, and was considered by the Local Authority to be a safe pair of hands. He was also a member of the Conservative Party and served for many years as a councillor and Chair of Seisdon Rural District Council. Unsurprisingly, he wasn't fond of Left-wing lecturers who drove cars with stickers supporting the National

Union of Miners' strike and who worked to oust the Conservative government.

When Bilston Girls' High School was reorganised as a Sixth Form Centre to serve the secondary schools of Bilston, Ryman Reece Roper applied successfully to become its head teacher. Frank was now aged 30 and had taught at the College for seven years. Thinking it time for a sabbatical to recharge his intellectual batteries, he decided to study full-time for a master's degree in education at the University of Birmingham and asked to be seconded with, or without, pay.

As expected, the Principal denied his request and Frank was obliged to resign his post to take up the place, in the expectation that he would still be able to support himself, working as a part-time lecturer on health visiting and other specialist courses. He hadn't calculated on Mr Inch's determination to see the back of him. All heads of department were instructed that Frank was not to be re-employed at the College under any circumstances.

"Why was the Principal so vindictive?" I inquired.

"I'm really not sure," Dad replied, "but it was very personal. I was the only one leaving that year who he refused to allow back as a part-timer, and a timetable had already been drawn up for me. But no contract was ever issued."

"You must have done something to upset him," I said.

"It could have been my membership of the Communist Party," he suggested, "Or the way I challenged his authority in staff meetings, or even my outspoken opposition to Enoch Powell. Some of the satirical verse – the samizdat –might have been attributed to me, although Doojen was responsible for most of it."

"What verse would that be?" I probed.

"Oh, there was a lot of it circulating," he said. "I remember one rhyme that went:

I do not like thee, six-foot John,
The reason why I think upon.
I think your great size signifies

It's to your brain that 'Inch' applies."

"Sizism of the worst kind!" I remarked. "I'm appalled! I hope you didn't write it. It manages to insult the poor man's physical and mental characteristics simultaneously."

"I know," Dad said. "Totally unacceptable! I didn't write it, but it explains a lot if he thought I had!"

I wondered why he'd remembered the lines, but chose to move on. "What did you do when you realised you weren't going to be given part-time work?" I asked. "You must have been worried."

"I was," Dad said. "I thought I might have to sell my house."

As luck would have it, Frank's friend at the Open University came to the rescue. He was offered employment for as many days as he chose to accept, working as Assistant Senior Counsellor with responsibility for assessing the extra help needed by disabled students. The counselling turned out to be better paid than the part-time teaching at Bilston.

Chapter 20

Message on a windscreen

As teenagers, we were curious to know how and at what age our parents learned about sex.

"When did you first learn the facts of life?" I asked them in turn and was surprised by their answers.

Mom thought long and hard. "It was not something you talked about either at home or with your mother or with girls at school," she said. "I believe I was thirteen or thereabouts. I was out riding my bike and noticed dark marks on my clothing. I thought it was bicycle oil. When I got back I told my mom. All she said was "I'll sort it out." She didn't explain that I was having my first period and that the bleeding would go on occurring at regular monthly intervals. She gave me some cloth to tie round myself and told me to change it, wash the cloth, and to do that until the bleeding stopped. We didn't use purpose-made disposable sanitary towels in those days."

"How did you find out it was likely to happen again?" Toussaint persisted.

"I don't really recall," she replied, "but I think I compared notes with other girls in my class at school in Spanish Town."

"But when did you know how babies came about?" I quizzed.

"Not until much later," Mom admitted. "I was probably fifteen. We were studying human anatomy in the biology class at school, and it all started to fall into place. There was also a girl who had to change school. I think because she'd become pregnant. We thought this was very shocking and dirty."

We interrogated our father in the same way. He remembered the occasion very clearly.

"I was eleven and in the first form at grammar school. A small group of us were making our way back from a swimming lesson. One boy told us how babies were made. We thought he was mad.

We punched and kicked him for suggesting our moms and dads could ever do a thing as shocking as that."

"Were you ever taught at school about sex?" Toussaint asked.

"Not that I can remember," he replied. "It might have been dealt with in biology lessons, but biology was an optional subject chosen by those who weren't doing well at physics and chemistry."

According to Dad, no attempt was ever made to discuss the facts of sexuality, although the Oratorian fathers, who gave them religious instruction, operated on the understanding that even the younger boys had a basic knowledge.

"We were always being urged," Dad recalled, "to avoid 'impure thoughts', 'occasions of temptation', and 'playing with ourselves'."

This last expression, he explained, was a euphemism for masturbation.

"When did you know that women had periods?" I inquired.

"Not until at least seventeen," he said, "and I learned that from other boys. Looking back on it, it's extraordinary that I grew up in a household with three sisters and knew nothing whatsoever about such regular events."

We soon moved on from the facts of life to questions about friendships with members of the opposite sex. We wanted to know when our parents first had sexual intercourse, but were not in the least surprised when they told us to mind our own business.

"We've never asked you that question!" they said in their defence.

They were reticent in answering any questions about personal relations and intimacy, regarding our inquisitiveness as unacceptably precocious. We persevered, eventually piecing together accounts of their love lives, or at least what they were prepared to admit to, which, in Dad's case, was probably the bare minimum. Mom, we concluded, had very little to tell.

"Who was your first boy friend?" Toussaint asked Mom.

"I was friendly with a young man called Errol," she eventually admitted. "We used to go out to nightclubs and the cinema together."

"In England or Jamaica?" Toussaint persisted, realising from the name that, in all likelihood, Errol was a Jamaican.

"He was staying in Birmingham," she said. "He was a Jamaican who had won a scholarship to study engineering in England."

"Were you in love?" I asked.

"I'm not sure what you are driving at," Mom replied. "We were fond of each other, but that's as far as it went."

We knew we weren't going to learn any more. We threw in the towel with a reluctant: "What happened to Errol, then?"

"When his course finished, he returned to Jamaica. We wrote to each other occasionally. I stopped writing to him when I met Frank."

By comparison, our father's love life was sensational. We had long since suspected that he had a secret and disreputable history. We'd had the benefit of seeing a photograph of a little white boy on Grandma Reeves's dressing table. When we asked who it was, she had said in a hushed voice: "That's Billy. He's your older brother." She'd seemed embarrassed, or ashamed, and avoided answering further questions.

With this in mind, it was with cautious determination that we approached the issue of Dad's previous relationships with women other than our mother.

"Who was your first girlfriend?" I asked, "And how did you get to know her?"

Unexpectedly, Dad was quite open with us. He could recall in remarkable detail his first encounter with members of the opposite sex, possibly because he attended a boys-only grammar school and didn't have the chance to meet many girls of his age.

In 1963, when he was eighteen and in the sixth form, the school's dramatic society staged Shakespeare's *The Tempest*, a set text for that year's Advanced Level English Literature. The cast was drawn from the boys at St Philip's and the girls of St Paul's, the nearby girls' Catholic Grammar School. Frank's initial involvement was through his art, by helping to design and paint the stage set, but the producer was short of a Ferdinand to play next to Prospero's daughter, Miranda, a part already filled by an attractive girl called Helen.

He agreed to play Ferdinand and took Helen out on a date, but she made clear she wasn't interested in him and had a career in acting to pursue. At this point, he noticed a tall well-developed blonde called Franciszka, who was playing the part of the goddess, Iris. She wore her hair in pigtails which, on important occasions, she rolled up and pinned into a golden crown. She was half Polish, her father having served in the Polish air force in Scotland during the war. Franciszka became Frank's first proper girlfriend, and the relationship lasted for the three years they spent apart studying, she at teacher training college and he at university.

They were married immediately after completing their courses in July 1967, at the Sutton Coldfield Register Office. Once married, they moved to Wolverhampton and rented a flat in Graiseley, near the town centre, a location convenient for the Technical Teachers' College, where Frank had enrolled, and the Prestwood Road Infant School, where Franciszka had been appointed as a teacher. Soon afterwards, when Frank became a lecturer at Bilston College, they took out a mortgage to buy a newly-built terraced house next to an old chapel in Bath Street, Sedgley. The house was situated high up on the Beacon with splendid panoramic views across the industrial landscape of the Black Country.

Frank's college lay down the hill in Bilston, a couple of miles away. This encouraged him to take driving lessons. He passed his driving test in 1969 and bought his first car, a second-hand Triumph Herald. He used it to take Franciszka and himself to work and back.

"Did you have to get married?" Toussaint asked knowingly.

"No," Dad said, "There wasn't a baby on the way, but in the 60s, family and society took a very dim view of unmarried couples."

"You became a father soon afterwards, didn't you?" I remarked.

"Yes," Dad admitted. "Franciszka didn't enjoy her work and wanted to start a family. I think she liked the idea of becoming a housewife".

"So when was the baby born?" I persisted.

"Billy was born in March 1970," Dad said, "nearly three years after we were married. Franciszka had a miscarriage a year earlier, so we were pleased he was a full-term healthy boy, 9 lbs in weight".

"What's that in metric?" Toussaint wanted to know.

We were edging our way towards the question that we really wanted answering. What had happened to Franciszka and Billy? We would never admit to thinking it but, if Dad had walked out on them, wasn't he capable of doing the same to us?

Toussaint was determined to find out the truth: "What happened to your first marriage?" she demanded.

"I became emotionally involved with someone else," Dad said simply. "Franciszka returned with Billy to live with her parents in Sutton Coldfield, and our home in Sedgley was sold three years after we moved in."

"Your marriage didn't last long then, did it?" Toussaint observed dryly.

"Did you go on seeing Billy?" I wanted to know.

"Of course I did. I was very fond of him," he replied defensively. "I used to go across to Sutton every two weeks as arranged with Franciszka. But, as time went on, things became more and more difficult. When I went over there I was not allowed into the house and had to take Billy for walks even in cold or rainy weather. He used to cry when I took him from his mom and, according to Franciszka, he cried for days after I took him back to her. She wouldn't allow me to drive him over to Wolverhampton in case Phyllis made friends with him."

Franciszka met a PE teacher whom she agreed to marry. She pointed out to Frank that having two father figures was confusing and upsetting to Billy and suggested it would be better for all concerned if Frank allowed her and her new husband to adopt the child. After much heart searching, Frank eventually agreed to her proposal on the understanding that Franciszka wrote to him at least once a year to tell him about Billy's progress.

Soon after the adoption in May 1975, Franciszka moved house and Frank lost contact with her. The promised letters never arrived.

Dad claims to this day that he regrets agreeing to the adoption and that he was insufficiently aware of its legal implications. Leaving, and then losing, Billy, upset him a great deal, although he is reluctant to mention it in the knowledge of the emotional distress that he must have caused Billy.

In 1989, Dad received a letter addressed to 'Dear FW Reeves', from a university student claiming to be reading philosophy and to be strongly influenced by Marxist and feminist thought. Initially, Dad thought it was a sick joke. It turned out to be from Billy, now aged nineteen, professing an "unrelenting curiosity to know for better or worse" whether the name he'd discovered in the telephone directory was that of his father. Subsequent correspondence revealed he knew nothing whatsoever about Frank's personal circumstances. He was unaware of how Frank had met his mother, what or where Frank had studied, Frank's occupation, and Frank's new family. He hadn't asked his mother because "whenever I attempt to approach her on the subject she is visibly disturbed and I don't wish to upset her. I think she feels a little guilty about the fact that I was never allowed to see you…"

Both Frank and Billy found the similarity between their early lives extraordinary, particularly their decision to study the unusual subject of philosophy at university, and their mutual interest in Marxism and Left-wing politics.

As Billy put it in one of his letters: "This is uncanny. I have always believed that factors such as intelligence and belief are socially determined and vehemently contested the view that mental characteristics are inherited. This coincidence casts doubt on one of my strongest convictions."

The parallels didn't stop there. Billy went on to become a lecturer specialising in teaching English as a foreign language in a college of further education. He gained rapid promotion as a college manager. Frank was amazed to meet him over ten years later attending the annual general meeting of the East Staffordshire Race Equality Council, of which he was a member.

Toussaint was ten, Robeson six, and I eight years old when we first met Billy. At 180cm, the same height as Dad, he towered over us. He was clearly pleased to see his half-sisters and brother. Dad took him to Leominster to visit his grandparents and, for a time, the family reconciliation seemed complete. But the clock could not be wound back quite so easily. From our point of view, Billy and Frank, despite common interests, showed little overt affection towards each other when they met, and Billy's visits became less and less frequent.

Having satisfied his curiosity about his father, Billy may all the time have been asking himself: "What kind of a man abandons a two-year-old child?" Frank, for his part, began to realise that in coping with the total emotional break brought about by the adoption, he had succeeded in stifling once and for all the natural affection he had once felt for his son. I believe Frank and Billy may still be in contact.

"Now, tell us about the woman you ran off with," I quizzed.

"You mean Phyllis?"

"The same name as Grandma!" I exclaimed in horror.

"Yes," Dad said. "My mother blamed her for everything: the breakdown of my marriage and the loss of her beloved grandson, for a start. She called her a 'whore' and a 'Jezebel'. Once, when we were passing through Leominster, your grandparents refused to allow her into their house. The fact that she shared the name, 'Phyllis', was the final straw."

"Where did you meet her?" Toussaint asked.

"I was teaching evening classes at the college," he replied. "She used to attend all three of my classes: sociology, logic, and Open

University preparation. One night, the weather was very bad and only one student - Phyllis - turned up. I had to give her a lift home."

"Had to?" we chorused.

Phyllis had trained at St Peter's College in Saltley, Birmingham, as a secondary school teacher, and worked at Graiseley Secondary Modern School in Wolverhampton. She had won a scholarship to Alpha Girls' High School in Kingston Jamaica, where she had taken her GCEs, before joining her parents in England in 1964. The family bought a house on the Willenhall Road, Bilston, and worshipped regularly at the New Testament Church of God, a black Pentecostal Church.

When Frank got to know her, she was already active in campaigning against racial discrimination and a member of the Wolverhampton Community Relations Council, taking her cue from the recently assassinated American black civil rights leader, Martin Luther King. Phyllis was a vivacious fun-loving head-strong Jamaican woman, and Frank sensed in her a kindred spirit. She was his first black girlfriend.

When they met, she was still living with her parents. She had experienced great difficulty in finding herself a flat. Frank prevailed on a friend who owned property on the Tettenhall Road, Wolverhampton, to rent her a bed sitter. She and Frank lived together there for a couple of years until Frank bought another house in nearby Oak Street.

Phyllis was an inveterate student, for ever enrolling on courses. She also liked dancing, partying, and visiting nightclubs. Every weekend, she and Frank went out to the Jamaican Club 67 in Piper's Row, where rock steady and reggae music were played non-stop until the place closed at about three o'clock in the morning. They also used to visit the cinema. Frank recalled going with Phyllis to see the first feature-length film about Jamaica: 'The Harder They Come'. The level of the Jamaican audience's participation was such that the cinema manager had to plead for calm.

On Sundays, by way of contrast, Phyllis would spend many hours in church, always inviting Frank to accompany her. He claims to have attended the services reluctantly and only for the sociological experience. It was the first time he'd seen members of a congregation apparently possessed by spirits and speaking in tongues. If religious fervour took a grip and the service ran on for more than three hours, Frank would creep out for a pint at the pub on the other side of the road.

"How did people react in those days to your dating a black woman?" I inquired.

"Some people disapproved," Dad admitted, "And they made their feelings known. But I think most people weren't used to seeing mixed couples and were just curious. People certainly noticed us. On more than one occasion we were mistaken for Madeline Bell and Roger Cook of the Blue Mink and asked for our autographs."

"Who were the Blue Mink?" Toussaint asked inevitably.

"They were a pop group in the early seventies," Dad said, "chiefly remembered for their hit 'Melting Pot'. You must have heard it! It's one of the only songs I know about race mixing."

"How does it go?" Toussaint probed.

Dad sang the chorus:

"What we need is a great big melting pot
Big enough, enough, enough to take
The world and all it's got
And keep it stirring for a hundred years or more
And turn out coffee-coloured people by the score."

"That's not very nice!" I remarked.

"The point I'm trying to make," Dad said, "was that people thought we looked like the lead singers from the Blue Mink. Phyllis was black and had an Afro hair style like Madeline, and I was white and had a beard like Roger Cook."

"Perhaps it was the association in people's minds of a black and white couple with the Melting Pot song," Toussaint added thoughtfully. I myself had had a similar experience recently in London, where I'd been stopped in the street on a couple of occasions and asked whether I was the actress, Halle Berry.

When Frank and Phyllis walked past a bus queue, heads would always turn and they would become the focus of attention. Occasionally, a car window would be wound down for a passenger to shout, "Why can't you find one of your own?" This remark was usually directed at Phyllis by black men.

At the college, knowing that Frank was dating a black woman, colleagues from other departments would sidle up and ask him "What's it like with 'a bit of black'?"

Dad believes that white women who dated black men had a far more unpleasant time, particularly when their partners were absent and they were accompanied by mixed-race children. White men and older women would openly abuse them in the street, swearing at them and calling them 'slags' and 'whores'. Dad uses their experience to contradict the view that white people can never truly understand what it is like to be on the receiving end of racial prejudice.

"Why didn't you marry Phyllis?" Toussaint asked.

"Because I met somebody else, I suppose," he replied sheepishly.

In Autumn 1972, a young African woman named Bridget Tlou turned up to enrol on a two-year full-time GCE A level course at the college. She had been a student nurse at a hospital in South Wales and it was something of a mystery as to why she decided to change career and relocate to Wolverhampton. She was born near Beitbridge in what was then Southern Rhodesia.

As her sociology tutor, Frank soon discovered they shared a radical political perspective. They both hated colonialism, and wanted to see a rapid end to apartheid in South Africa, as well as to the illegal regime in Southern Rhodesia which, they both agreed, could only be brought down by armed struggle.

To this day, Dad can't decide whether he fell in love with Bridget or her politics. She took full advantage of his help and admiration to further the Rhodesian freedom struggle – as well as her own educational prospects. More of this story can be found in Chapter 25. As soon as she completed her studies at the college, she put an abrupt end to the relationship and left to attend university in the East Midlands.

We were most curious to discover the circumstances in which our parents had met. Mom and Dad agreed on the facts, but not on the way they should be interpreted.

While working as a health visitor in Sandwell, Mel agreed to become a field work teacher, a community practitioner who takes on the day-to-day supervision of health visitor students. To prepare her for this extra responsibility she had to attend the fieldwork teachers' course at Bilston College.

Frank was timetabled to explain the importance of social research to a lively and intelligent class of experienced health visitors. The most lively and challenging of all the students was a slender young black woman who asked awkward questions and showed a great deal of interest in his subject matter. Frank was impressed and asked the course tutor the name of the student.

When the course finished at the end of the week, Frank found a note stuck to the windscreen of his car. It read: 'Found your lecture very interesting. Would you like to carry on the discussion?' followed by the name, 'Mel Chevannes', and a telephone number. Like any other red-blooded man given such encouragement, Frank made the telephone call and their friendship developed from there.

"So it was you who chased after him!" Toussaint said to Mom. "Phew! You must have fancied him pretty badly."

Mom was embarrassed. "It wasn't like that at all. I was interested only in what he'd been teaching us, not in him personally."

"That's not how I saw it," Dad observed. "She was the first and only woman ever to leave me her telephone number in that way. How did she know which car I drove?"

Sensing how inexperienced our mother was in the protocols of courtship, we remained inclined to believe her story.

By this time, Phyllis had moved out, Bridget had left the scene, and Frank was sharing the house in Oak Street with Mark, a lecturer friend from the college, with whom he later parted company over an unpaid telephone bill.

Mel and Frank's relationship continued to develop, growing in intensity when Mel took up a post at Bilston College as a trainee health visitor tutor under Betty Simms, the course leader. Mel worked there for a year, until leaving in 1975 to study at Bolton Technical Teachers' College for her health visitor teaching certificate. Frank resigned at the same time from his job as a social studies lecturer at the college to take a Master's degree in education at the University of Birmingham.

During the week, he would stay with Mel's mom, Aunt Epsi, and stepfather, Mr Son, in Sparkbrook, near the university, to save him from travelling back to Wolverhampton every night. Aunt Epsi used to feed him on mountains of rice and peas, yam and green banana, which he had to eat till fit to burst for fear of upsetting her. We've never been able to decide whether Dad's first love is for Jamaican food or Jamaican women.

Mel and Frank's enforced absence from each other during the week for the duration of the year's study may have helped to consolidate their relationship and to lead them to marry when their courses finished.

"Given your track record," I said to Dad cheekily, "how could you be sure that Mom was right for you?"

"By that time, with all my experience," he joked, "I'd discovered the KISS test."

In our age of the computer, we understood KISS to mean 'Keep It Simple Stupid'. It was apparent that Dad's relationships had never been simple. "What do you mean?" Toussaint demanded.

"Relational compatibility can be judged on the KISS test," he explained in a mock academic manner. "K is for kindness, I for ideas and intellect, and the Ss for Sexuality, and Style. Couples have to be compatible on all four dimensions. Your mother and I were matched exactly, whereas my previous relationships were more asymmetrical."

"Sexist crap!" we retorted. "You're just trying to excuse your appalling behaviour."

PART III WHEN WE MEET NOW

Chapter 21

De higher monkey climb!

My Mom's favourite saying is the Jamaican proverb: 'De higher monkey climb de more him expose behind'. For Mel, this is advice to ambitious people who acquire power to remain sensitive to the conditions and needs of the common people, and to steer clear of the opportunities for abuse and corruption afforded by high office. It also hints at pride before a fall, a risk faced by every successful politician.

I was just about to sit my GCSE exams when the May 1997 General Election took place. Despite my parents' determination to secure a Labour victory, education still trumped politics at home, and I was directed to concentrate on revision, rather than on pushing innumerable leaflets through letterboxes on behalf of Jenny Jones, our Labour candidate for the constituency of Wolverhampton South West, where we lived. Even without my youthful assistance, the Labour Party romped home.

At local level, Jenny won a majority of 5,118 votes over the Conservative candidate. The seat had been Tory since 1950, represented by Enoch Powell for 24 years and then, on his resignation, for a further 23 years by Nicholas Budgen, both MPs earning notoriety for their consistent opposition to New Commonwealth immigration. For me, that had meant that they wanted to repatriate my mother and Aunt Epsi!

Nationally, the Labour Party, under Tony Blair, achieved a landslide victory of 418 seats compared to the Conservatives' 165. Our family and friends were elated at the prospect of having a new government committed to rebuilding and renewing the welfare state, and especially the National Health Service.

Mom, in particular, was aware of the growing problems faced by a badly under-resourced health service, and of Labour's manifesto pledge to rid it of top-down management, root out unnecessary administrative costs, and spend more money on front-line patient care. For my parents, the election outcome marked not just the triumph of New Labour, but an opportunity once more to manifest a new socialist morality.

I should explain that from an early age, we children had been taught that there was no such thing as sin - only inconsiderate, unkind, damaging, cruel, oppressive, and exploitative behaviour towards other human beings. Whereas what was right and wrong might well depend on our intentions, what really mattered were the long-term consequences or outcomes of our behaviour towards others. Our parents believed that we could progressively improve the way we related to our fellow human beings by adopting disciplined habits, routines, procedures, laws, institutions, and expectations, which guaranteed people's basic needs, irrespective of their standing in society, their health, their ability to find work, or their capacity to pay for goods and services.

Traditional religions made much of individuals' responsibility for their neighbours' wellbeing, and the importance of personal goodness, kindness, and generosity. These virtues, however, did not manifest themselves automatically in a collective scheme of welfare, provided for all, whose success could be judged on outcomes of inclusivity and equality. Indeed, my parents' main complaint about the Old Testament commandments, and organised religions generally, was their utter inadequacy in dealing with the uneven distribution and abuse of power. People's ability to contribute to the common good, or to cause immense harm, depended self-evidently on their standing in society: their command of force, their control over resources and possession of wealth, their gender status, their membership of a dominant race, ethnicity or religion, or some other factor.

For Mel and Frank, a practical example of the socialist morality that they advocated was the British National Health Service, funded through taxation and provided free when people were ill and needed treatment, irrespective of their ability to pay. For them, the NHS was the crowning achievement to date of the socialist movement and something worth devoting their lives to defend.

Frank had a similar mindset in regard to the right to universal education, which he felt could never be achieved while wealthy families continued to purchase superior and privileged schooling for their children. Realistically, he never expected that New Labour under Tony Blair would bring about any significant change, despite education being trailed as its number-one priority, with smaller class sizes and nursery places for four-year-olds. What he didn't envisage was that Labour would take the country in the opposite direction by introducing tuition fees and abolishing grants for students in higher education. (It was at this point as a student that I lost my faith in the Labour Party. Dad lost it in 2003 when Tony Blair took the country illegally to war in Iraq.)

A longstanding member of the Socialist Health Association, Mel resolved after the 1997 election to make greater use of her professional knowledge and skills to promote and improve the service she regarded as the beacon of socialist morality and achievement. Recognising that the health service was badly in need of a leadership that was committed to its founding principles, she applied to the National Appointments Committee to become a non-executive director of a National Health Service Trust. As a member of the Leicestershire Health Authority and of the NHS Trent Research and Development Council, she was already well prepared to take on the role.

In 1998, she received a letter appointing her to chair the Royal Wolverhampton Hospitals NHS Trust. The Royal Wolverhampton Trust, with its New Cross Hospital, based at Heath Town near Wednesfield, is a major acute facility of 700 beds, employing 5,000 staff, and treating over 600,000 patients a year, on a budget of £250 million. Provision includes specialist cardiac, stroke, bowel cancer, renal and neo-natal services. It is the largest teaching hospital in the Black Country area, providing placements for Birmingham University medical students and for nursing, midwifery and other health professionals from Wolverhampton University.

The Board, which Mel was appointed to chair, consisted of independent Non-Executive Directors (publicly-appointed members), such as herself, expected to provide independent scrutiny of the Hospital's affairs, together with Executive Directors (senior employees of the Trust), such as the Chief Executive and the Directors of Finance, Hospital Services, Medical Services, and Nursing. Collectively, the Directors are required to provide strategic direction for the hospital and to make sure it met patients' needs through maintaining high standards of clinical care and financial management.

The role of hospital trust chair was by no means ceremonial. To fulfil her duties to a standard that satisfied her as a health professional, my mother found it necessary to devote the equivalent of at least two days a week to the task. As she was still holding down a full time job as Head of Nursing and Midwifery at De Montfort University in Leicester, she had to work the equivalent of a seven-day week, putting in time in the evenings, during holidays, and at weekends, and with the additional chore of having to commute on a regular basis between her workplace in Leicester and the Hospital and her home in Wolverhampton. I was studying for my GCE A levels at the time and could see how busy she was. Nevertheless, she served as a model for me, my sister and brother, of what dedication and hard work might achieve. Her excessive efforts provided us with no option but to emulate her determination to succeed.

"Was there any reaction to you, as a black woman, being appointed to such a prestigious position?" I asked.

"When my appointment was first announced," Mom said, "the Board members, senior managers and doctors at the hospital seemed very surprised. When individuals came to congratulate me, I was invariably quizzed as to how I'd manage to pull it off. Despite my background in the health service, they were curious to discover my political connections. I was even asked, in jest, which lodge I belonged to."

"Lodge!" I exclaimed.

"The Freemasons," Mom explained, "are rumoured to exercise undue influence over the health service. Although I have never found any direct evidence of this, there were odd occasions when I couldn't fathom out, however hard I tried, how a particular decision had been reached, or how a person with no knowledge of the health service had come to be appointed to an important post. I hasten to add that I'm not talking specifically about the Wolverhampton Trust."

"What I was driving at," I persisted, "was whether people were willing to accept your authority as Chair."

"You mean because I was black?" she clarified. "I had a lot of experience of chairing committees, both on the Council, in the voluntary sector and in the course of my various jobs as a manager. I think the members could sense that I knew what I was doing, and that I had a vision for the Hospital. I also put in the hours and carefully planned and prepared what I wanted to achieve. Once I'd become Chair, the question, to my mind, became one of competence - not colour."

Shortly after she took up her position, Mel was involved in the selection and appointment of a new Chief Executive for the hospital, following the departure of the previous post holder. The appointment panel selected Mark Hackett, an NHS career manager, who had studied at the LSE on a National Graduate Management Training Scheme and had previously headed up the Birmingham Women's Hospitals Trust.

Mel and Mark, both new appointees, shared an enthusiasm for improving and expanding National Health Service facilities at New Cross. They immediately embarked on a campaign, approved by the Board, to rebuild and re-equip dilapidated parts of the Hospital, with its miles of dowdy-looking corridors, Nightingale wards, and wooden huts. Other key issues that had to be tackled were the unacceptable waiting times before ambulances could discharge sick patients into the care of hospital staff, and before patients could be admitted for treatment because of the shortage of beds. New Cross was not performing well compared with similar hospitals elsewhere. Mel recalls Frank Dobson, the Secretary of State for Health at the time, telling her: "when you're at basement level, the only way is up". The snag to hospital development was that money for providing the much-needed facilities could only be obtained by establishing Public-Private Partnerships (PPP), thus handing over to the private sector a significant role in the operation of public services.

Plans for a £90 million redevelopment of the New Cross site were announced in 2000. A spectacular two-storey hotel-style glass reception area, with a plaza of shops, banks, seating areas, restaurant and crèche, and escalators to take staff and visitors to medical departments and laboratories, was proposed. This grand scheme included a new haematology unit, a women and children hospital, a regional cardiac centre, and purpose-built renal facilities. Mel, as the Chair of the Trust, was reported in the press as saying:

"We are all keen to improve the standard of care for patients, and the care environment. These plans will help us achieve the best for our patients, support the work of our staff, and bring services together to speed up treatment times."

The first new facility to be developed at a cost of £1.2 million was the Medical Admissions Unit of 32 beds, with a throughput of 45 patients a day. Alan Milburn, the new Secretary of State for Health, toured the facility with Mel and the Chief Executive and talked to patients.

Shortly afterwards, a much-needed £44 million Regional Cardiac and Cardiology Centre was approved for completion in May 2004. Prior to its coming into service, local patients were required to wait for up to eighteen months for treatment at other Midlands hospitals. Alan Milburn returned to Wolverhampton in January 2003 to lay the foundation stone for the Centre, by then described as costing £60 million and having seven wards, four operating theatres, two catheterisation suites, a critical care unit, and an outpatient department dedicated to providing cardiac and thoracic surgery, secondary and tertiary cardiology, rehabilitation, clinical measurement, and day procedures.

Mel and Mark were elated by the Labour Government's success in investing in the National Health Service and the impact that this was having on the quality of hospital care. Mel had considerable reservations, however, about the likely long-term effects of Private Finance Initiatives on the NHS and its public service ethos. Nevertheless, the only available means of obtaining money for developing the facilities on the New Cross site was by attracting investment from the private sector which looked to see a generous return. Surely, PFI had to cost more than direct funding from the public purse? The government, after all, could borrow money at a lower interest rate than the private sector and didn't need to make a profit. Wasn't PFI really about opening up the state monopoly on health provision to market forces and competition?

For six years, Mel and Mark, with the Board's backing, spearheaded the transformation of the hospital at New Cross into a dynamic modern health service, with significantly-reduced waiting times, improved patient care, and greatly improved performance. For much of this period, the building cranes on the site could be seen from miles away.

In 2004, however, Mark was appointed to a new post as Chief Executive of the NHS Trust Hospital in Southampton. Prior to his leaving, the managerial culture of the NHS underwent a sudden transformation, with a new insistence on spending restrictions and fiscal control, with an inevitable negative impact on Labour's original promise to improve the quality of patient services. Management consultants were sent in to hospitals which weren't immediately able to balance their budgets, uncooperative non-executive board members were removed, and chief executives and finance directors dismissed. These actions were justified spuriously, without reference to local health needs, on the basis of 'independent financial reviews', paid for, of course, by the Strategic Health Authorities. Hospital Trusts, at the time, found themselves exposed to a most unpleasant climate of fear and intimidation.

The West Midlands Strategic Health Authority feigned alarm at the shortfall in the budget of the Wolverhampton Trust, despite the fact that it had for some time been receiving frequent and detailed reports on the Hospital's financial health and was fully aware that more patients were being treated month on month. The Authority had itself published data showing Wolverhampton to be one of the eighty-eight most disadvantaged areas for heart disease, cancer, and diabetes. And it readily agreed that the health needs of the area were under-funded to the tune of £18 million. Mel believed that unenthusiastic bureaucrats at the Strategic Health Authority were using the shortfall in the Hospital budget as an excuse to impose greater control over the Chief Executive and Hospital Board, to rein in the Hospital's success in developing and improving services, and ultimately, to replace Board members with their 'preferred' people.

With Mark's departure, Mel guessed correctly that a deliberately-engineered austerity budget would be imposed on the Hospital and, rather than agree to cuts which she regarded as unnecessary and indefensible, chose instead to submit her resignation.

"Cutting jobs and services to recoup artificial losses conjured up by contrived accountancy is against my principles", she told the press. "The drastic action proposed for saving money by cutting services is in direct conflict with the need to care for patients and to support staff in the NHS. After blame has been apportioned, heads have rolled, and bureaucrats have been appeased, extra money will still have to be found to spend on the health care of Wolverhampton people."

She made it clear that she was leaving the Trust in a much better shape than she had found it in 1998, when money, merely to improve service levels, had been in short supply. Since 1998, funding for new projects had increased by over 40 per cent, the quality of service was now judged to merit two out of a possible three stars, and the workforce was at last beginning to reflect the ethnic diversity of Wolverhampton and surrounding districts.

Despite the fact that she and Mark had wrestled successfully with the Department of Health and the Strategic Health Authority to win resources for the Hospital, Mel arrived at the opinion from her experience as Chair that the management structure designed to deliver the health service was overly bureaucratic, unnecessarily complex, wasteful, and insensitive to local health need. Apart from the Department of Health in London, for example, there was a regional tier in the form of the Strategic Health Authority, and in Wolverhampton, an acute Hospital Trust operating alongside a Primary Care Trust, each with its chief executive, finance department, payroll, human resource and other management units. In the final analysis, accountants, rather than clinicians, called the shots, taking decisions with little or no reference to the health needs of the local population.

As staff wages constituted the main costs, attempts to reduce expenditure at the Trust meant fewer nurses, the premature discharge of patients (some living alone), the closure of wards, and greater pressure on care in the community.

Mel had been a popular Chair, and the news of her resignation brought with it a flood of letters of support and commiseration, some correspondents inquiring as to how she was coping with the prospect of unemployment. Of course, she had performed her role as Chair of the Trust in addition to her academic post and was still in a full-time job.

In June 2002, she applied successfully for the post of Dean of the School of Health at the University of Wolverhampton. Her new appointment was a considerable promotion from Head of Department and allowed her to live at home in Wolverhampton during the week, thus bringing to an end her regular commuting to

Leicester, which, in the four years she had chaired the Hospital Trust, had proved an exhausting extra burden.

Mel had never wanted to work away from her family but had been forced to leave the West Midlands to find work suited to her talents and experience. She was delighted, if not emotionally overwhelmed, at the change in her circumstances. Unfortunately, by the time she returned, I was the only one of us children still living at home. Toussaint was in Manchester researching for her PhD and Robeson had just started his undergraduate studies at University College London. The chief beneficiary of Mom's company, of course, was Dad. He was no longer dependent on take-away meals and relished the prospect of more Jamaican home cooking during the week.

Mel's first task in her new post was to consolidate the University's health courses by bringing staff and students, scattered at various NHS locations across the Black Country, onto the University's campuses, and rationalising the diverse range of nursing and health programmes. She found herself leading on ambitious plans for coordinating and integrating the health education curriculum in new purpose-built teaching facilities, together with a clinical skills centre and offices for staff, to be situated on the Wolverhampton City Campus. The School of Health's base on the Walsall Campus was also designated for extensive modernisation and refurbishment.

In November 2005, the new three-storey block in Wolverhampton was officially opened and named - the reader has already guessed - the Mary Seacole Building. Mel commissioned an interior décor based on pictures of Mary Seacole, and donated a framed reproduction of the bronze bust of the Crimean nurse veteran kept at the British Museum.

In addition to the gargantuan construction, refurbishment, and relocation exercise, Mel pushed through a comprehensive updating and revalidation of the pre-registration nursing curriculum, community specialist programmes, awards for qualified staff, taught masters' degrees, and courses in health studies, complementary therapies, and non-medical prescribing. A major review by NHS Healthcare Education confirmed that all courses on offer in the School met academic and professional standards.

To ensure the continued relevance of the provision on offer, Mel and her management team sought to strengthen links with NHS and non-NHS health organisations and collaboration with other universities, colleges, and professional networks. Mel was also insistent on developing an equality and diversity action plan for the School, based on two interrelated themes: the students' educational journey and staff members' experience, with targets for improvement set annually.

Between 2002 and 2007, fifteen additional teaching staff were recruited and a further thee people taken on to deliver externally-funded projects. The School now had approximately 4,000 full and part-time students on roll and over 100 academic staff and researchers. Under Mel's leadership, the School began to develop a specialist research function, establishing a dedicated team of researchers to work on the specific health themes of clinical development, ethnicity, mental health practice, public health, and primary care. This growing nucleus of research led Mel to create the University's Centre for Health and Social Care Improvement, officially opened by the Vice-Chancellor, Professor Caroline Gipps, in September 2006.

Mel retired from her post as Dean in August 2007, shortly after her sixty-third birthday, leaving to her successor the legacy of a modern integrated high-quality nursing and health education facility, housed in state-of-the-art accommodation. Considerable progress had also been made on the equalities front, with a far more racially-balanced staffing profile and a set of procedures aimed at ensuring sensitivity and fairness in the treatment of students.

Mel's two high-profile roles in Wolverhampton inevitably attracted media attention, and she was frequently asked to comment on health issues, or to defend the record of the NHS, particularly when medical intervention had gone wrong.

Recently, I came across an article about my mother that had appeared in the *Wolverhampton Ad News*. It was entitled 'Caribbean cuisine, a clever cuckoo, and that CBE!' and was one in a series on 'movers and shakers' in which a local reporter 'grills some of the city's names to find out what makes them tick'. Mel, as Dean of the School of Health and Chair of the Hospital, is asked a standard set of questions about her 'favourite things'.

Quizzed about her favourite music, she reveals that she loves George Gershwin's Porgy and Bess, as well as Paul Robeson's spirituals, mentioning, as an example, 'We are climbing Jacob's ladder'. She explains that she interprets the song to mean that we must always struggle to improve ourselves.

As to be expected, her favourite place is Jamaica, and her favourite food the cuisine of the Caribbean (in particular, curried chicken and rice and peas, with freshly-cooked spinach).

Her favourite book is *The Black Jacobins*, by CLR James, which tells the story of the first successful black slave revolt in St Domingue led by Toussaint L'Ouverture. "This is a wonderful and inspiring account," Mel explains, "representing leadership and determination against overwhelming odds."

Her favourite film is 'One flew over the cuckoo's nest', from the novel written by Ken Kesey, and directed by Miles Forman. She points out that it shows the way institutions can crush individuals, as well as the destructive effect of labelling and stereotyping. This picture should serve as a warning to those, like herself, in charge of large organisations which are ostensibly set up to serve the interests of clients, but don't always live up to their objectives.

Mel's favourite heroine, of course, is Mary Seacole, who she describes as "a mixed-race Jamaican woman who, despite prejudice, made her way to the Crimea during the Crimean War, where she devoted herself to nursing sick and injured British soldiers."

Mel claims that her best moment occurred when she received a letter from the Queen telling her that she was to be made a Commander of the British Empire for her contribution to multi-cultural nursing. I think she said this for the benefit of the media, as she had always told us that she had been ecstatically happy at the birth of her first child following her earlier miscarriages. The giveaway is when she tells her interviewer that she considers the worst moment in her life too private to mention.

Asked to write her obituary by completing the sentence: 'She was a woman', Mel adds 'who never gave up'.

Chapter 22

Capacity! What capacity?

In 2001, serious civil disturbances broke out in the northern towns of Bradford, Oldham, Leeds, and Burnley. Violence flared between Muslim young men and white youths, with the police intervening to restore law and order. An investigation chaired by Lord Herman Ouseley into race relations in Bradford was already in progress as the conflict took place. This led the government and local authority policy makers to take an intense interest in the report when it was published shortly afterwards.

Community Pride, not Prejudice, or the Ouseley report, as it came to be known, was based on the assumption that communities in Bradford were experiencing increasing 'polarisation', 'segregation' and 'fragmentation', along ethnic lines. The report was preoccupied with how to bring about greater integration between ethnic groups, especially between Muslims and the local white population. White people apparently thought that their needs were neglected in favour of Muslims who were being given preferential treatment, while members of the Muslim community believed that the racism and Islamophobia of white people were blighting their lives.

According to the Ouseley report, different communities were seeking to protect their identities and cultures by discouraging contact with other groups and institutions. 'Self-segregation' of this kind was said to be driven by fear of others, the need for safety from harassment and violent crime, and the belief that the only way to retain cultural identity and religious faith was to 'stick to one's own'.

After the disturbances, local reports were produced on inter-ethnic relations in Burnley and Oldham, followed by two further national reports by government-initiated committees, chaired respectively by Ted Cantle and John Denham. They adopted the same analysis of the situation as the original report written about Bradford. They all concluded, on the basis of extremely flimsy anecdotal evidence, that communities were breaking apart like Humpty Dumpty, and that what was needed to put them back together again was a new policy and programme of action that soon came to be known as 'community cohesion'.

I went up to read law at the University of Lancaster in the autumn of 1999, at the same time as Dad eventually found work as a race equality officer at Worcester Racial Equality Council. After six months of unemployment, he was mightily relieved, and pleased to be doing something useful with his time. I'd heard of race equality councils but wasn't sure about what they were or did.

"What do race equality councils do?" I asked over the phone. "And what's your job at Worcester?"

"It's easy to tell you what they've been set up to do," Dad replied, "but far more difficult to explain how they operate in practice."

"So what are you hoping to do?"

"We're trying to reduce the incidents of racial discrimination, make sure everyone is treated fairly, and that local ethnic and racial groups get on well together."

"Pretty ambitious then! I remarked sardonically. "And how do you propose to go about that?"

He explained: "We do casework with individuals who come to us complaining of discrimination or harassment. We help other organisations develop equal opportunities to ensure fair treatment. We develop projects that bring different sections of the community together. And we provide information about ethnic and race relations."

"You've been in the race equality business in one way or another for most of your adult life," I thought to myself. "You ought to be good at this kind of work by now."

Dad drove over thirty miles every day from Wolverhampton to an office in central Worcester next door to the Race Equality Council, or 'REC', as he usually called it. The REC was accommodated in Queen Elizabeth House, a quaint oak-framed black-and-white building in the Shambles. Whenever I visited his place of work, Dad took me up the creaking wooden stairs onto the balcony to the spot where Queen Elizabeth I was said to have addressed the people of Worcester. I could never resist a surreptitious wave in regal fashion to the passers-by below!

The REC in Worcester gave information and advice to people who had experienced obstacles in gaining access to employment, housing, education, health facilities, and other services, because of their colour, race, or national origins. The organisations helped clients who had experienced discrimination to take their cases to employment tribunal or county court. This anti-discrimination casework not only provided a much-appreciated service for individuals, but also informed the REC's approach to policy and community development.

Dad was impressed by the variety and complexity of the issues brought to the REC by clients. Often desperate for help, they knew they had been on the receiving end of the unpleasantness, even if they didn't always express their problem in the language of discrimination. Much of the time, they were just relieved to discuss their experience and to get the matter of their chest. When race equality officers read back to them their account, now set out formally in legal language, they often admitted that the scales had fallen from their eyes. Usually, it was the first time they'd encountered the framework of discrimination law and the concepts of formal evidence or comparative treatment.

As well as acting as a port of call for people who had suffered discrimination as defined by the civil legislation of the Race Relations Act 1976, the REC also gave help to those on the receiving end of criminal behaviour. Dad confessed himself to be shocked by the cases of racially-motivated harassment that he came across on the course of his work. It wasn't just the range of the verbal and physical abuse and damage to property that appalled him, but its scale and frequency, and the inadequacy of the measures available for dealing with it. Most people had no idea of the torment being routinely inflicted on the innocent victims. Frank had only been dimly aware of it himself, until he started work as a race equality officer.

Those on the receiving end - perhaps an ethnic minority family moving into a house on a white estate, or refugees accommodated in a block of high-rise flats - might be subjected to a constant barrage of anti-social behaviour. This took a variety of forms: repeated door-knocking, verbal abuse, children bullied on journeys to and from school, rubbish dumped outside the house, excrement poked through the letter box, cars tampered with or damaged, driveways blocked, windows smashed, property stolen or vandalised, sprayed graffiti, arson attempts, threatening behaviour, abusive notes or letter, persistent noise or banging, and malicious complaints. Sometimes, the victims developed severe depression, or other forms of mental illness.

The REC employed Frank, together with Tahir and Debbie, to work on a project funded by money from the National Lottery to improve, or 'build', the capacity of the thirteen or so race equality councils that existed at that time in the region. The project had been initiated by Waqar Azmi, the Chief Executive of the Worcestershire REC, and was supported by the Boards and Executives of all the RECs in the West Midlands.

The first task of the project - soon retitled Race Equality West Midlands (REWM) - was to establish the needs of the RECs by conducting an audit and then developing a work programme based on its findings. The race equality movement's requirements turned out to be extensive. As a consequence, the team adopted and embarked upon an ambitious programme to develop race equality strategy, improve services, increase funding, encourage collaborative ventures, modernise communications, undertake further needs analyses and research, and provide a relevant management and officer training scheme.

In 1999, the RECs believed that the importance of their work was recognised and they were optimistic about their future prospects. The CRE, too, seemed keen to see an improvement in the way RECs did business and, as a condition of grant aid, introduced a quality assurance scheme, known as 'core standards'.

One of the capacity-building project's first tasks was to help the RECs comply with the CRE's quality of service requirements. It did this by producing a series of standard policies and procedures for most of the RECs' routine activities. The strategy and services of most racial equality councils had not altered much since they adopted their constitutions some ten years previously, but the social environment was changing rapidly.

By 2000, black and Asian minorities made up 1 in 10 of the population of England and Wales and constituted nearly a third of the population of Birmingham. RECs had to think carefully about the services they should continue to provide for these established minority communities and work out what to offer new and potential user groups, such as the growing number of asylum seekers and refugees, migrant workers from central and eastern Europe, Gypsies and Travellers, people of mixed race, and white communities complaining about neglect and the privileges of others.

Frank found the working environment in the middle of Worcester very amenable and soon made lasting friends with his much-younger colleagues there, in particular, Waqar Azmi, Tahir Abbas, and Zahoor (Zak) Ahmad. They all happened to be Muslims. Despite Frank's professed atheism, they welcomed him with warmth, respect and kindness. He, in return, did his best to accommodate their unshakable belief in Allah and Mohammed, his prophet, and to fit into their world of halal food, orange juice or coca cola, and fasting at Ramadan.

For Frank, a great admirer of Charles Darwin, the most problematic aspect of Islam was its literal interpretation of the creation story which seemed to rule out the immensely important scientific significance of evolution and natural selection. Nevertheless, the religious and cultural differences between staff at the REC appeared superficial and insignificant in the light of their mutual liking for one another and their common purpose of tackling prejudice and discrimination against people from different ethnic groups.

As well as the regional capacity-building project, Waqar embarked on a national initiative: the British Federation of Race Equality Councils, or BFoREC. Waqar and Frank travelled the country – London, Edinburgh and Cardiff – to persuade race equality directors and their chairs to commit to a new national body representing the collective interests of race equality councils and similar bodies, and able to speak on their behalf to government, the Home Office, the Commission for Racial Equality, and other key policy makers.

Shortly after BFoREC was established, Waqar left Worcestershire REC. Out of necessity, Frank stepped in as convener and secretary of the new body, while Milton Crosdale, the veteran Chief Executive of Nottingham REC, took over the Chair from Waqar. It was not an auspicious time for building the capacity of the race equality movement, either at a national or a local level.

The Labour government showed no inclination to involve RECs in any of its various community initiatives, conspicuously managing to avoid mentioning them in most of its key policy documents relating to regeneration, community development, crime prevention, conflict resolution, and the voluntary sector. The Commission for Racial Equality was in the process of moving from directly funding race equality officer posts to a system of grant aid based on making applications to deliver approved outcomes, a regime known as 'Getting Results'. The new competitive process resulted in an uneven allocation of funding, with some RECs receiving what they applied for and others ending up with nothing. Without a regular and predictable funding stream, many RECs were forced to lay off staff or, when funding also dried up from alternative sources, to close down completely.

The climate became even bleaker when the Equality Act 2006 abolished the Commission for Racial Equality and subsumed its powers into the Equality and Human Rights Commission. While the new Commission inherited the CRE's grant-making powers, it now had responsibility for promoting equality and diversity in relation to age, disability, gender, gender reassignment, religion and belief, and sexual orientation, as well as to race. Inevitably, the already limited grant aid was spread more thinly to support voluntary groups promoting other kinds of equality. By 2010, not a single race equality organisation in the West Midlands had been allocated an EHRC community development grant, and any case work for individual victims of discrimination was being undertaken by Citizens' Advice Bureaux. Subsequent cuts by the Coalition government put the final nail in the race equality coffin.

Jack Straw, the Home Secretary, had appeared to signal a golden age of race equality with his decision in 1997 to hold an inquiry into Stephen Lawrence's death. More than a decade later, despite the best efforts of Race Equality West Midlands and BFoREC, the once-proud race equality movement had been decimated, if not totally obliterated, in the course of the Labour Government's three terms in power. When Frank started his job in race equality in 1999, there was a country-wide network of more than one hundred race equality councils and partnerships. Ten years later, approximately forty remained, of which only a tiny proportion continued to receive grants from the CRE's successor, the EHRC.

"Would you describe your capacity-building project as a success?" I asked disparagingly.

Dad laughed. "Capacity! What capacity?" he snorted. "I think we made a critical contribution to the debate. We never sold out to the superficial rhetoric of powerful people looking for instant solutions."

"That didn't get you very far," I persisted.

"No," he agreed. "But eventually people will come to accept the need for specialist services to support victims of racial harassment and attack, and for independent professional local agencies to resolve conflicts between communities. I also believe that disinterested, independent policy research will come to be valued in preference to the dishonest 'tell me what I want to hear' exercises of recent years."

When Waqar left his job at Worcester to work for the consultancy firm, TMP Worldwide, Frank became Acting Chief Executive of the REC until a replacement was appointed nearly a year later. Meanwhile, he continued to work for Race Equality West Midlands, now chaired by Amir Kabal, the Director of East Staffordshire Race Equality Council, who took over when Waqar left. Soon after the newly-appointed Chief Executive of Worcestershire REC assumed the reins, Race Equality West Midlands became a fully-autonomous charitable company and, to signal its regional role, relocated to the Aston Science Park near the centre of Birmingham.

Frank's colleague, Tahir, left for a job in research at the Home Office in London, later returning as a lecturer and research fellow in the Sociology Department at the University of Birmingham. In his new role at the University, Tahir soon established a reputation as an expert in the sociology of Islam and Muslim community relations, an academic field of growing importance following the 9/11 attack by Al Qaida on the World Trade Centre. When he became head of the newly-formed Centre for the Study of Ethnicity and Culture at the university, he was instrumental in forming a partnership with Race Equality West Midlands to run a joint programme of topical race equality and community relations seminars.

These lunch-time sessions, open to the public, proved a great success. Guest speakers included Frank and Tahir's old acquaintances, John Rex, Sally Tomlinson, Marian Fitzgerald, John Eade, Bishop Joe Aldred, Salma Yaqoob, and Trevor Philips, Chair of the CRE. The lunchtime lectures that I managed to attend were concluded sociably enough in the University's Sociology House with an impromptu feast of samosas and pakora washed down with fruit juice.

Following outbreaks of inter-communal violence in various urban locations in the north of England in 2001, the government began to develop a new initiative that soon came to be known as 'community cohesion'. It intended this to replace its previous policy of multi-culturalism which it now regarded as a mistake. The trouble with both terms was that they were never sufficiently well defined or worked through for their implications or effects to be understood.

"Community cohesion? Getting people to stick together?" I queried.

Dad nodded: "That's the sum total of it," he said. "The politicians, and ex-local government officers wheeled out to chair these communities didn't seem to be aware of the legacy of political literature relating to social order or, indeed, to see the sociological necessity of grounding their ideas on actual demographical data or social research. At the many conferences I attended on the subject, 'community cohesion' was interpreted in the broadest possible way to include any example of good relations between neighbours."

Community cohesion policy sounded very similar to the RECs' third aim of promoting good relations, but was concerned merely with issues of integration and intermixing, rather than with the RECs' primary focus on racial equality. While RECs were anxious to convince the government that they had a role in resolving the kinds of ethnic conflict that had occurred in northern England, many people working in the race relations field, including Frank, were deeply sceptical of the suggestion that communities were living parallel lives and choosing to live apart, and also that the remedy to this problem lay in efforts to improve contact, and inculcate shared British values.

By this time, of course, the government had begun to promote its community cohesion policy with rhetorical vigour and was dismissive of counter-argument. Projects that continued to emphasise economic inequality as a major contributing factor to ethnic division, simply went out of fashion in Blairite Britain.

Worse, it became clear that the RECs were seen as part of the problem, rather than the solution, to issues of community cohesion, and were being largely ignored or sidelined as the new cohesion programmes were rolled out across the country. Indeed, the policy of multi-culturalism that the RECs had long fostered was increasingly blamed by politicians and media commentators for separating communities by the active encouragement of cultural distinctiveness.

Frank thought this assumption absurd. As long as he had been in the business of promoting multiculturalism, it had meant bringing together communities, originating from different places and with different traditions, to explore what they shared in common: most usually, of course, identical social and economic needs. He felt that after centuries of British imperial domination, it was ridiculous to assume that Asian, Caribbean and British cultures remained discrete and separate from one another. Quite spontaneously, communities adopted from others what they saw to be of use or benefit. In places, such as Wolverhampton, a modified synthesised vibrant integrated multi-cultural way of life was already very much in evidence. Most local people found the emergent forms of music, dance, fashion, diet, public celebrations, and youth culture, to be stimulating and exciting.

Frank also regarded the suggestion that minority groups were consciously and actively rejecting British values and opportunities for integration, and seeking to keep themselves separate and exclusive, as a dangerous and un-evidenced over-generalisation. It transferred the responsibility for rejection and segregation away from the white community and its decision-makers to relatively powerless ethnic minorities, who usually found themselves on the receiving end of social processes over which they had no control.

All Frank's considerable personal experience of living in Wolverhampton and participating fully in a multi-racial local community convinced him that people - black, Indian, Pakistani and white - were becoming more integrated and at ease in each other's company and were mostly constrained in where they chose to live by what they could afford. There was a fair degree of social intermixing, too, with a small, but significant, proportion of Pakistani men marrying white women (as humorously portrayed in the film, *East is East,* made in 1999).

Frank and Jameel Malik, a consultant at REWM, began to examine data on ethnic clustering in Sandwell. Areas with a mainly-white population, as well as areas with a high ethnic minority concentration, were closely associated with poverty and deprivation, whereas more ethnically-integrated neighbourhoods tended to be more prosperous. The evidence seemed to show that people living in poor areas hadn't always chosen to live there to be next to members of their own ethnic group, but because they did not have the means to buy property or live in more affluent areas. It was quite obvious to Frank that the government had deliberately chosen to ignore the ghettoisation of poor people, both white and ethnic minority, caused by the rising cost of housing and had opted instead for a set of ineffectual social, relational and attitudinal solutions.

"Unmitigated Blairite New Labour!" Dad remarked. "The government simply airbrushed out the basic economic or social class dimension that divides communities."

On the 7th July 2005, four Muslim men, three of British Pakistani and one of British Jamaican descent, blew themselves up in a coordinated attack on London tube trains and a double-decker bus, killing 52 and injuring a further 70 members of the public. On hearing the news, Mom, Dad, Toussaint and I tried separately to contact Robeson, who lived in central London, only to find the mobile phone network had failed, as other anxious people made similar calls to relatives and friends. When we got through eventually, Robeson was unaffected, but had been breathtakingly close to the action. Being early for work on that day, he had chosen to walk, rather than to take his usual bus along the fated route through Tavistock Square. If he'd got on the bus at his usual time and the bomb had been synchronised with the three other attacks on the tube at 8.50am, he might well have been caught in the blast.

Two weeks later, four more attacks were mounted on the transport system but, on this occasion, only the detonators went off. On the following day, however, a young Brazilian man, Jean Charles de Menezes, suspected of being a terrorist, was shot seven times in the head by the London Metropolitan Police as he boarded a train at Stockwell Tube Station. It turned out that he had no terrorist links whatsoever, and had been the innocent victim of a police shoot-to-kill policy introduced to deal with the bombing threat.

Dad and I were shaken not only by the sudden and arbitrary nature of Jean Charles de Menezes' death, but by his uncanny resemblance in appearance to Robeson, although other members of the family couldn't see the connection. Even so, in the weeks that followed, Robeson was stopped and searched by the London police on at least five different occasions, although it was impossible to tell whether this was on suspicion of being a terrorist, or of being in possession of drugs. I asked him whether he was worried about being mistaken for a terrorist. He reassured me that he had, as a statistician, calculated the odds to be far less than those of being hit by a car, and was not in the least perturbed.

That September, Trevor Phillips, then Chair of the Commission for Racial Equality (CRE), made a well-publicised speech entitled: 'After 7/7: Sleepwalking into Segregation'. The headline suggested that Britain was rapidly descending into a racially-segregated society. His assertion caused alarm and dissent in government circles, the press, and the wider society. Trevor claimed that schools were becoming more exclusive and that some districts were becoming fully-fledged ghettoes: 'black holes into which no-one goes without fear and trepidation, and from which no-one ever escapes undamaged'.

Concerned at the implied criticism of government policy, particularly after the recent bombings on London transport, the Department of Community and Local Government called an emergency meeting of demographers and policy-makers to discuss the truth of these claims. Trevor was summoned to attend. Aware, no doubt, that he was likely to be put in the hot seat, Trevor declined to go, but asked Frank to attend the meeting in his stead to represent the CRE.

Frank went along to what turned out to be a seminar attended by civil servants and senior academics, and chaired by David Miliband, then the Minister of Communities and Local Government. The academics systematically rubbished Trevor's claims about segregated neighbourhoods, but acknowledged that worrying ethnic concentrations were occurring in schools. Frank's contribution was to stress that black ghettoisation in the USA was entirely different to the emerging patterns of ethnic settlement in the United Kingdom.

As the meeting concluded, he exchanged a few friendly words with David Miliband, telling him that he'd known his father and admired his book, *The State in Capitalist Society*. Afterwards, Dad showed me a note signed by David Miliband expressing appreciation for the kind words he'd said about his father, Ralph. Little did Frank know at the time that David would go on to become Foreign Secretary and then an unsuccessful contender for the Labour Party leadership after Gordon Brown's departure.

Following the events of 9/11, but especially after the bombing of the transport network on 7 July 2005, the focus of race relations work across the country shifted inexorably to analyses of relations between the general population and Muslims living in Britain. Henceforth, interventions were aimed primarily at improving understanding and collaboration between communities in order to isolate potential terrorists. These government-backed initiatives were referred to collectively as 'Preventing Violent Extremism'. Ethnicity, until then defined chiefly in terms of broad cultural, national and racial identity, began to assume a distinctly religious dimension. Race equality officers found themselves dealing increasingly with issues relating not only to racial, but to religious difference.

The work of REWM was no exception. Encouraged by consultant Tahir's expertise in the sociology of Islam, the concerns of Amir Kabal, REWM's chair, and world events, such as the wars in Afghanistan, Iraq, and Lebanon, REWM began to explore the issues affecting the Muslim population, such as the growing Islamophobia that followed the 9/11 and 7/7 attacks. It set out to produce a detailed chronology of the main events, international, national and local, that had led to a deterioration of relationships with the Muslim community since 2001.

In autumn 2007, REWM, in appreciation of its growing reputation in the field of ethnic community relations and conflict resolution, was commissioned by the Dudley Preventing Violent Extremism Winning Hearts and Minds Project to investigate the state of ethnic and religious relations between Muslims and non-Muslims in the Black Country, against the background of a decision by Dudley Council to turn down planning permission for a new mosque and community centre. The research explored in some detail the attitude of the Muslim residents to the non-Muslim population and vice-versa, detailing each group's knowledge of local religious practices, and views on intermarriage, friendship with people from other ethnic groups, trust, equality, treatment of women, homosexuality, halal food, and much else besides. Of particular interest were the differences of attitude towards the proposed mosque, with three quarters of Muslims supporting the plan, and three fifths of non-Muslims opposing it.

The controversy over Dudley Muslims' planning application to build a new mosque and community centre was deliberately fanned by the British National Party and the United Kingdom Independence Party (UKIP), both of which managed to tap into a deep vein of religious and cultural traditionalism, to raise a reputedly 22,000-signature-strong petition against the proposal. This pressure resulted in Dudley Council's multi-party Development Control Committee voting unanimously to reject the plan, a decision later overturned by the Planning Inspectorate and again when appealed in the High Court. REWM found that the mosque issue had profoundly polarised the politics of relations between Muslims and non-Muslims in Dudley. Dudley Council wasn't keen for its dirty washing to be aired in public and showed little interest in the subsequent REWM report, for which payment was never made.

Political opposition to the mosque continued, delaying any start date for the building work. On the 3 April 2010, the Far-Right English Defence League (EDL) staged a mass protest in central Dudley against the proposed mosque, leading to the arrest of twelve protestors for attacking the barriers set up to control the demonstrators. The town's market was cancelled, shop fronts were boarded up, and streets cordoned off to prevent conflict between EDL supporters and a counter-demonstration by Unite Against Fascism in support of diversity and the right to worship.

As the new millennium unfolded, the race equality movement found itself faced with the resurgence of Right-wing extremism. The threat to relations came no longer from the National Front, but from the British National Party (BNP) led by Nick Griffin. The BNP made no secret of its racially-based nationalism, ruling out the possibility that black or Asian people could ever be truly part of 'our island race'. It wanted to put an immediate stop to any further immigration, resettle immigrants and their British-born children 'voluntarily' in their countries of ethnic origin, deport criminal and illegal immigrants, abolish the Race Relations Act, withdraw from a European Union, and restore flogging and the death penalty. Race mixing, of course, presented a serious practical challenge to this old-style racism.

In the local election of 2003, the BNP stood twenty-one candidates in the West Midlands, of whom four were elected as councillors, one in Dudley, two in Sandwell, and one in Stoke on Trent. In wards in urban areas, the BNP and other extreme Right-wing parties were polling, on average, a quarter of the votes cast.

Frank, together with colleagues in the RECs and at the Commission for Racial Equality (CRE), worked hard to counter the apparent rise in the electoral strength of extreme Right-wing racist parties, such as the BNP. Assisted by Eric Seward, a former regional director of the CRE, REWM produced a series of reports on the electoral performance of the racist Far-Right, including published guidance on what local authorities and organisations in the voluntary sector could do within the law to obstruct its racist activities. Trevor Phillips invited Frank and others to a meeting in London with Margaret Hodge, the MP for Barking and Dagenham, to discuss what could be done to thwart the activities of the BNP, which had won seats on the council, and was attracting increasing levels of support from the local electorate.

Frank and Eric compiled and published a book, entitled *From BUF to BNP, Chronology of Racist Extremism.* 'BUF', of course, stands for the British Union of Fascists. The book deliberately set out to show the historical continuity of racist, anti-Semitic, populist, authoritarian, corporate, and nationalist value systems, from those of the fascist groups of the 1920s and 30s to the BNP of 2000 plus. It also demonstrated how anti-racists, democrats, and minority communities had a long and honourable tradition of opposing the Extreme Right. The book stands out from others on my shelf as it has a bright blue cover superimposed with a distinctive picture of a union flag distorted to form a swastika.

For the most part, consultants, staff, and volunteers, contributing to the work of REWM, were a lively, vigorous, intelligent and committed bunch, although the intermittent nature of funding meant that all contracts were for a fixed-term, which resulted in a high turnover. The organisation could offer immense job satisfaction but no prospect of a career or promotion.

When I popped into the office or attended a REWM seminar at the University, Dad used to introduce me to members of his team. I was impressed by their age range and diversity of national, ethnic, and religious backgrounds.

Adele, Frank's deputy, was a whimsical middle-aged Jamaican woman with Rastafarian-style grey locks, who was in the habit of micro-waving odoriferous fish in the office for her lunch. She was also the mother of three mixed-race children. Yvonne, a white woman, married to Don, a Guyanese banker, served as REWM's finance officer, remaining with the organisation from the time it was first set up in Worcester. She was invaluable to Frank, providing stability in financial management, together with sound general advice.

Frank's personal assistant was Rukhsana, a slender young Muslim woman from a Kashmiri family background. She had a degree in business computing. When she left, her post was filled by Dulce Lempianem (or Pedroso), another graduate, with a master's degree in sociology, who had previously served as Frank's research assistant. Dulce was a strikingly attractive mixed-race woman, with a Cuban father and Finnish mother. Fluent in Finnish, Spanish and English - a rare and valuable combination of languages - Dulce was also intellectually curious about her Caribbean roots and her mixed-race experiences. She had a young daughter called Taika. We became friends and remain in correspondence through Facebook.

Another key member of the REWM team was the indefatigable Freda, a light-skinned Wolverhampton-born woman of Jamaican descent, and the proud mother of twins, Jade and Jordan. Freda occupied various roles in the office, gradually making herself indispensable to the organisation's smooth operation. It was she who helped organised the university seminar series and REWM's meticulously-planned conferences. Freda had other talents, too, as an interior designer, illustrator, photographer, and teaching assistant.

The team's self-evident diversity not only made REWM a stimulating place to work, but contributed greatly to the quality of the work it produced, with new and original perspectives being constantly generated. One of REWM's most innovative and successful projects was 'Multiple Heritage Voices'. It was initiated by Ayo Bakare, a graduate volunteer, who applied successfully to the Heritage Lottery Fund for a grant to record the history of Birmingham's mixed-race population, mount a summer project for young people to explore their mixed-race heritage, and create a lasting visual resource of Birmingham's racial mixing.

Ayo, an agreeable young woman from Bradford, with a Nigerian father and white mother, was ideally placed to head up the project that she had prepared and submitted. Working closely with the Ladywood Detached Youth Project, the Birmingham Inheritance Project, and various other volunteers, she brought young people together with the activities and space to learn about their own multiplicity of heritage and nationality. To conclude the year-long exercise, a beautifully-designed booklet was produced, published, and presented to the young people involved in the project, local schools, community groups, and libraries.

Ayo and I became friends. I was as surprised as Dad to learn that she was a member of the University of Birmingham women's rugby team. Although I turned down her invitation to take up the sport, we remain in regular touch via Facebook. I hope that one day she'll visit me while I'm living in Kenya.

Chapter 23

Under the shade of the family tree

As they tried to sleep that night, Mel and Frank realised that they had forgotten the nocturnal sounds of Linstead, which have to be heard to be believed. Soon after nightfall, the cacophony consists of the hooting of trucks summoning the higglers, or ordering other vehicles to make way. This is supplemented by the whistles of the pea-nut vendors, and sound systems blasting out from the numerous rum bars. Nearer to the bedroom, this background racket is augmented by snatches of singing and choruses escaping from the local chapel. Then there are the natural noises of croaking, or squeaking, frogs, and the whir of cicada-like creatures. It is far too hot to muffle the sound by closing windows or shutters.

As they struggle to sleep, a dog starts to bark, followed by another, and still another further away. By three or four in the morning, the local dogs are howling in chorus to be answered immediately by dogs in the near and far distance. Are they cast in an ancient Hammer House of Horror movie, with werewolves baying at the full moon? As dawn approaches, the barking dogs are joined by the fowl, a full range of raucous roosters, crowing at full throttle from every direction, accompanied by a synchronised choir of clucking hens. Gradually, the barking and the crowing become less intense and the rumble of mechanised traffic resumes, together with the claxons of trucks transporting the higglers and their wares back to early-morning market. Oh, for the silence of a cold damp night in Wolverhampton!

In 1979, three years after they married, Mel and Frank went on holiday to Jamaica. It was the first time since arriving in 1964 that Mel had returned to her country of birth – an absence of fifteen years. Frank was immensely excited at the prospect of visiting his wife's country of birth, whereas Mel was pleased at the opportunity to introduce her husband to relatives and friends.

Frank had read up on Jamaican geography, history, and politics, and was keen to make better sense of his newly-acquired knowledge in the course of his visit. He rapidly developed a deep affection for the island and its people, which has led to my parents returning repeatedly over the last thirty years to the same destination, provoking Mel to insist that it was high time they started to explore other parts of the world.

In August 1993, when all three of us children were judged old enough to appreciate our cultural heritage, we, too, were taken to visit Jamaica, where we were proudly presented to our relatives: great uncles and aunts, and numerous second and third cousins. We went to Mom's birthplace in 'country', as well as to Spanish Town and Kingston, to be shown our mother's old schools. Dad hired a car and drove us to many of the island's tourist attractions, such as Fort Charles at Port Royal, Navy island at Port Antonio, and Ocho Rios and the Dunn's River Falls. Light-skinned, well-behaved, and English born and educated, we were feted by relatives and had a very good time.

In 2004, on Frank's insistence, our parents made a valedictory journey to Jamaica, in the knowledge that many of Mel's aunts and uncles were now so old that this might indeed be the last chance to see them.

Mel and Frank flew to Montego Bay and then took the hotel bus to the Sandcastles Hotel near the centre of Ocho Rios, where they'd booked a self-catering suite. Later that week, they hired a car and set out in the pouring rain for Linstead, via Fern Gulley, Walker's Wood, Moneague, and Ewarton. The road had been greatly improved since they last drove that way, but they found the descent from Hollymount to Ewarton just as frightening, with trucks swinging out around the bends and much aggressive honking. They drew up outside the Worrell house at 3 Victoria Street, Linstead to be warmly greeted, first by the dogs, and then by Uncle Dada (Abraham) and his wife Cislyn, both looking much older and frailer than at their last visit.

Uncle Dada, or Dads, was Aunt Epsi's youngest brother, a tall kindly man, who in his youth had worked on farms in the United States, before returning to Jamaica as a builder. In his middle age, he had fallen from a roof and been forced to give up heavy construction work. He now made his living in business with his wife, baking and decorating wedding cakes to order. Frank and Dada got on well together and had long conversations about Jamaican politics and world events.

Cislyn, Dada's wife, was a retired domestic science teacher, with firm views on how to run her kitchen and household. Mel's uncle and aunt were always generous with their hospitality and had effortlessly accommodated the five of us when we stayed at Linstead in 1993.

After an initial exchange of family gossip, a snack of bun and cheese, and a Red Stripe beer, Frank, Mel, Dada and Cislyn set out by car for Content, the little village in the hills where Mel was born. Frank drove past cane fields and citrus groves towards Wakefield and Spring Vale, to turn left shortly afterwards onto a very minor road in the direction of Giblatore.

Twisting and turning, the narrow lane rose through a valley clothed in thick vegetation. The former cart track had a tarmacked surface now, but suffered from potholes and erosion on crucial bends. Along the lane, where the gradient permitted, various kinds of residence had been erected, their aspect self-evidently dependent on the wealth, or lack of it, of the residents. There were more homes than on past visits, ranging from large recently-painted bungalows constructed of concrete blocks, through small two-room concrete structures, to single wooden shacks or shelters. The well-appointed houses had usually been built with money sent home by family members working abroad in the USA, Canada, or Britain. Traditional wattle and daub buildings had all but disappeared. Content now had a piped water supply and electricity - provided that residents could afford to pay the bills.

Most buildings were surrounded by cultivated plots, with breadfruit, banana, coconut, and ackee trees, and an undergrowth of yam, citrus, and coffee. Frank had always been fascinated by the exotic Jamaican flora, attempting to identify the natural sources of the food and beverages with which he was familiar at home. As well as noticing the ever-present coffee bushes, he spent time examining the cacao trees, source of the chocolate that he had been fed on as a child. The cacao beans were contained in the large pods that sprouted from the tree's thick trunk and branches. Mel, who as a girl, had harvested cacao beans and made them into chocolate drinks, showed little interest, taking the pods' unusual positioning for granted.

With Dada and Cislyn's help, Mel and Frank located their few surviving relatives living in Content. They went first to visit Aunt

Zeta, the wife of Mel's maternal uncle, Andrew. Andrew had died some three years previously. Family news was exchanged, and Frank took a photograph of the old lady reading her prayer book.

Mel's Uncle Willy and his wife, Miss T, had also passed away recently, and so the party called next on Aunt Dine, Mel's father's sister. She lived in a small two-bedroom house made of plastered concrete blocks with a corrugated iron roof, which Frank described as a shed. There was no paved or stepped path from the road - just steeply-sloping compacted red earth. The rain from the roof was collected by means of a hollow bamboo to a butt, to provide water, and there was a pit latrine at the bottom of the garden. The house had access to electricity and there were signs of a former television aerial, but Aunt Dine, aged 83, claimed to prefer her kerosene lamp. She had no need for electricity and could not afford it, in any case. Her son paid the rent on her little house of J$ 700 per month.

When after some time, she realised who it was who had come to visit her, she lifted her hands to heaven and called out:

"Praise God, it Coolie! Give tanks to di Laad!"

She had cataracts and could barely see. She insisted on explaining at some length how she had lost her husband, Master George, some three years earlier.

The old lady sat on her bed, chatting away to Mel, and smiling broadly to show her bare gums and few remaining teeth. Like her brother Fitzroy (Mel's dad), she remained quarrelsome and cantankerous. She questioned Mel closely about her mother's health and our progress. She scolded Mel as to why she hadn't brought a photograph of us children to show her.

Aunt Dine's daughter, Jasmine (Mel's cousin), who lived close by, joined the party. She looked very like Mel. All three women had wasp-thin wrists and raised veins on the back of their hands. Jasmine must have been about twenty years younger than Mel, but her face was lined and she looked so much older. While the vivid colours and the surrounding exotic vegetation made Content look like the Garden of Eden, it was far from being a rural paradise. People who stayed on the land struggled hard just to survive.

It occurred to Frank that Jasmine was the Mel who had remained behind in the countryside, never making the transition to an urban setting, or migrating abroad in search of a better life. This was the Mel who had foregone the opportunity of fulfilling her educational potential and of reaping the benefits of an advanced industrial society, with modern health care, sick pay, and a pension scheme.

As Frank drove the party back to Linstead, he noticed the grimy and perspiring men, swinging their cutlasses on the road as they returned from their wearisome daily routine of cultivation. It was two years later that Mel and Frank received word of Aunt Dine's death.

Back in Linstead, Cislyn and Dada cooked them a tasty dinner of rice and gungo peas, spicy chicken and salad. They ate it with relish, washing it down with a fine rum punch. Later, they strolled along Victoria Street in the direction of Linstead market, made famous by the well-known Jamaican folk song of that name. It was about eight o'clock on a Friday night, but the streets were clogged with higglers sitting on the pavement, trolleys, vans, trucks, and other traffic, including donkeys and goats. The noise of commerce and of frustrated drivers sounding horns was deafening. The bright street lights silhouetted the crowds of people in what looked like a frantic scene from Dante's Inferno.

Next morning, showered and dressed, Mel and Frank partook of a tasty breakfast of mackerel and green bananas, followed by pawpaw, and then set out on a drive to visit Mel's friend, Claudette Blackwood, who lived in Mandeville in the Jamaican Parish of Manchester. Frank drove south towards Spanish Town, through the Rio Cobre gorge before joining the new toll road, Highway 2000, at Vineyards East in the direction of Clarendon, and on to Mandeville.

As he approached the gorge, he recognised that this must have been the route that Mel followed as a child in her move from Content to join her mother in Spanish Town. Frank never ceased to find the journey through the gorge spectacular and exhilarating. For approximately five miles, the road follows the winding course of the river between towering one-hundred-meter limestone cliffs, bedecked by tropical vegetation. Travellers find themselves in a fast-moving procession of traffic, speeding along the narrow winding highway, with reckless drivers attempting to overtake even on the blindest of bends. Occasionally, Frank glimpsed the gleaming ribbon of turquoise river far below and hoped that his hire car wouldn't be forced off the road and into the abyss by the madness of the other motorists.

Halfway down the gorge, the road crosses at right angles from one side of the river to the other over a narrow 'Flat Bridge', so called because it has no side walls, and has been deliberately constructed to allow the river to flow freely above and below it in times of flood. While functionally efficient, the bridge was not designed with the safety of drivers in mind. Over the years, vehicles have plunged off it to drown their passengers in the fast-moving current. Frank has been delayed for hours in traffic jams caused by stubborn individuals refusing to back up, and off the bridge, to give way to vehicles coming from the opposite direction.

Jamaican roads and, for that matter, Jamaican drivers have a poor safety record. On this occasion, Mel and Frank's journey to Mandeville was delayed by a multiple pile-up blocking the road with badly mangled cars, despite road-safety signs warning drivers that:

> 'Undertakers love careless overtakers.'
> 'Speed kills: Don't be in a hurry to enter eternity.'
> 'Drive right or you could be dead wrong.'

Arriving in Mandeville, Frank and Mel soon located Claudette, who was delighted to see them. They invariably identified Claudette to us children as the friend who made them a present of their wedding cake. Mel and Claudette first met on the wards at Selly Oak Hospital in Birmingham, where they both worked as nurses. My parents always praised Claudette's kindness and generosity, but were less polite about her efforts at keeping up appearances, comparing her in jest to Hyacinth Bucket. The pictures in her living room revealed her political orientation, as well as her taste in music. One was a portrait of the Queen in her state regalia, the other a poster of a youthful-looking Elvis Presley.

While working as a nurse in England, Claudette had been diagnosed with the debilitating and degenerative illness of systemic lupus, causing her to return in the early 1980s to live with her mother and brother in Mandeville. She had believed that the climate, altitude, and familiar environment would prolong her life. More than 600 meters above sea level, the town's main attraction was its cool fresh climate, in marked contrast to other parts of Jamaica. Almost 25 years later, Claudette was still alive, but confided in Mel that her condition was deteriorating and that she'd been told she hadn't long to live.

As a nurse who had worked in England, she had at first found part-time employment in the Mandeville Hospital, but had gradually reduced her commitment as her illness progressed. In later years, she relied almost entirely on the small pension she was granted on leaving the British National Health Service. This forced her to live frugally even by Jamaican standards.

Mel and Frank took Claudette out to eat at a restaurant in the shopping plaza. They sat in the shade, catching up on news and gossip. Claudette had learned from correspondence of Mel's visit to Buckingham Palace to receive her CBE and demanded a blow-by-blow description of the occasion and of her audience with Prince Charles. Claudette was clearly delighted at her friend's award, and glowed contentedly in the aura of Mel's success and the recognition she had received from royalty. She was also impressed by Mel's professorial title, choosing to address her on every possible occasion as 'professor'.

When her visitors informed her that the time had come for them to travel back to Linstead, Claudette began to weep and hugged Mel closely before they parted. After fond farewells, Mel and Frank drove slowly around Mandeville's picturesque town square or 'Green' to remind themselves of the enjoyable visits they had paid there in the past. The square had changed little since their last visit, but Mandeville seemed more prosperous than ever, and just as concrete, clean and modern. New mansions had been built and an opulent suburbia was much in evidence.

On their return to Linstead, Mel and Frank took the opportunity to visit Aunt Miriam's grave. Aunt Miriam - Aunt Epsi's younger sister - had passed away in Jamaica shortly after returning from London to retire there, and following the deaths of her husband, Alpheus, and son, Lionel. She was particularly affected by the death of her son, an event which was felt to have contributed to her own demise.

On the occasions that we had met her, our Great Aunt Miriam was warm and friendly, and overfed us with tasty Jamaican meals. Dad warned us, however, that, unlike Aunt Epsi, she was intensely superstitious and secretive, with a 'higgler mentality', which wasn't surprising, because she had indeed been a higgler before she came to live in England.

Aunt Miriam, of course, thought of herself as a Christian, but mentally, like others, she took out a triple insurance policy, relying in turn on Christianity, Obeah (withcraft), and scientific medicine to get a result. When her grandson, born an apparently healthy boy, developed paraplegia in early infancy, she was certain that Obeah had been worked on him. She caused him to be sent back to Jamaica to visit every notable guzuman (witch doctor) on the island, but to no avail. All her life, she believed firmly that malice could be inflicted on her and her family by the invocation of duppies (spirits) and curses (spells).

The cemetery was an unfenced area of land next to the highway between Bog Walk and Linstead. The many graves on the site were capped by concrete slabs impressed with the name of the deceased. Aunt Miriam was buried in a plot nearest the road, while the grave of her husband, Alpheus, was situated some way back near to a large cotton tree. This separation in death was explained by Aunt Miriam's preference for a 'clean' spot - unlike Alpheus's, with leaves already deposited on it from the cotton tree. Frank, who had studied Jamaican folklore, was of the view that she had been apprehensive about the duppies (spirits), who were traditionally believed to live in the cotton tree. The unfenced cemetery provided grazing opportunities for the goats which ate both the grass and the wreaths left by relatives. Mel and Frank witnessed these creatures resting, and occasionally mating, on the more comfortably-placed headstones.

Mel and Frank returned to Sandcastles Hotel after their tour of the island. Here, they were visited by Sonia, Mel's friend from Kingston Technical High School, and the Jamaica Telephone Company. She was chauffeured by her daughter, Tamika, now aged 28, and training to be a radiographer. The four of them drove to Harmony Hall and on to Shaw Park Botanical Gardens, finally ending up at the cruise liner mooring site. The visits served merely as a prop for Mel and Sonia to reminisce about their family members, old school friends, KT, Mel's visits to Sonia's house in Jamaica, and Sonia and Tamika's visit to Wolverhampton, many years earlier.

During their holidays spent there, my parents have explored Jamaica thoroughly and visited more of the sights than many of the island's permanent residents. Given the extent of their 2004 itinerary, I asked them to select just one of the highlights of their trip.

"It has to be our visit to Nine Mile," they said. "We'd never before been to the Bob Marley Mausoleum."

Bob Marley was the most famous of Jamaica's reggae stars. He had died of cancer in 1981 at the age of 36. His body had been brought back from Florida to Jamaica and buried at Nine Mile, his place of birth in the Parish of St Ann. His father was Captain Marley, a fifty-year-old white quartermaster attached to the British West India Regiment, while his mother was Cadella Booker, an eighteen-year-old black Jamaican woman.

With our white British father and black Jamaican mother, we could identify easily with Bob Marley. Our father's claim of affinity with him arose from the odd fact that Bob had preceded him into the world by exactly one day, on 6 February 1945. I was preoccupied more pertinently with how a person, so clearly of mixed race, had come to see himself as an 'Ethiopian', anticipating the collapse of a white 'Babylon' and a return to the promised land in Africa, forcefully expressed in his powerful song, 'Exodus'.

The Bob Marley Mausoleum is situated in a little village in the Jamaican hills beyond Browns Town. Along with other visitors, Mel and Frank were allocated a Rastafarian guide called Yoto, with locks and tam, who led them upwards along a cool passage cut into the limestone rock, to a fenced courtyard beyond. To one side, leaning over the fence, six young Rastafarian men dangled a ganja bush and shouted to the tourists to buy plastic bags full of weed or, alternatively, ready-rolled spliffs. Many of the tourists found the offer impossible to resist.

The air was soon filled with the sweet spicy smell of what the young men described as "the finest marijuana in the world". Mel, on this occasion wearing her medical hat, felt sufficiently angered by the behaviour around her to tell the marijuana vendors that the prolonged use of ganja would damage their health.

"I'm a nurse. I know what I'm talking about. I've seen the harm it causes."

"De erb is da true revelation," they insisted. "It heal de nation!…It give wisdom and overstanding!...It purify de bady!"

An ill-tempered slanging match developed, with the young men sinisterly muttering among themselves:

"She no lub Rastaman. She tan too long in a Babylan!"

It so happened that Mel was the only black person among the visitors. Yoto, anxious to avoid further drama, moved the party forward, explaining how he was going to conduct the tour:

"We don't drink and drive. We smoke and fly," ending each declaration with a slow and deliberate:

"Ha, ha, ha, ha!"

He explained how he was going to take the group up, "Like a lion," to Zion - a low hillock on which was situated a small wooden shack. The visitors were told that this had been Bob Marley's home from the time he was six to his thirteenth birthday.

Inside the shack was a single bed. Could it have been the original referred to in Marley's song 'Is this love?' Outside was a stone, painted red, yellow and green, on which, it was claimed, Marley rested his head before experiencing the ganja-inspired vision captured in the song, 'Talking blues'. The Rastafarian colours of red, yellow and green were everywhere in evidence. Red is thought to symbolise the blood of a common humanity, yellow the life-giving sun, and green the earth and plant life, especially the sacred ganja.

Yoto outlined the significant events in Marley's life, his complicated domestic relationships, and the issues that had arisen since his death from cancer in 1981, interspersing his comments with "ha, ha, ha, ha!", and snatches of Bob Marley songs, their refrain taken up by a party of young children leaning across a fence, further up the hill.

Yoto gave a graphic demonstration of how Bob had lit his spliffs, coughed and choked, and fallen asleep smoking. Still puffing at his gigantic spliff, he invited photographs of himself, and told his audience to send them to the inappropriately named President

George 'Bush' if they objected to his behaviour. By this time, most of the visitors were smoking, too, and the aroma of the pungent ganja wafted across the valley, like incense through a sanctuary.

A small concrete chapel nearby turned out to be the mausoleum containing Bob Marley's remains. Before entering, all visitors were expected to remove their footwear, while the men, including the Rastas, had to take off their hats. Inside, a two-meter-tall marble-tiled tomb, containing the bodies of Marley and one of his younger brothers, filled most of the space, only allowing people to walk in single file through the building. The stained glass in the windows threw red, yellow and green light onto the tomb, which was hung with various tapestries and a small Ethiopian Orthodox crucifix. Opposite the entrance was a large bronze bust of Marley. Staring down from another wall was another image of Marley resembling Christ, the good shepherd, with lamb in arm, herding a flock of sheep, only in this picture the shepherd wore a broad red, yellow and gold sash, and the face was distinctly that of Marley.

After the mausoleum, visitors were invited to take a collection for the unruly children singing snatches of Marley's songs on the far side of the fence, and to tip the guide. They were then taken to the bar. Crowds of tourists stood around drinking beer, smoking spliffs, and getting well and truly 'irie'. A video of Marley's performances and interviews played on a large television screen. Serving behind the bar was a young woman with a nasty black eye and facial bruising, a reminder that even at this hallowed spot, with its message of brotherly love, the 'sistren' were still subject to domestic violence.

Mel and Frank made their way out of the complex through the reception area, where Bob Marley tee shirts, CDs, Rastafarian belts, hemp candles, hemp soap, and a full range of paraphernalia for ganja smoking were on sale. The ganja itself could be bought outside from the many eager Rastafarian higglers.

Our parents have listened and danced to Caribbean music all their adult lives, progressing from mento and ska, through rock steady to reggae. They are fond, too, of steel bands and calypso. They are fully aware of Bob Marley's stature as a singer, song writer and guitarist, and appreciate his influence on the musical development of reggae, from a small island dance beat, to a globally-recognised cultural art form that has secured Jamaica a place on the world stage.

Knowing full well the answer he would receive, Robeson cheekily asked his mother: "Were you ever inspired by Bob Marley to think of becoming a Rastafarian?"

"Never!" Mom replied indignantly.

"Not even to celebrate your African roots?" he needled deliberately.

"I'm a Jamaican", she said, "and proud of my island's distinctive synthesis of culture and art. I don't need to pretend that I'm African to big-up my colour, or national origins".

While admiring Marley's contribution to music and culture, our parents are opposed to cultic practices, including those of Rastafarianism, with its use of ganja as a sacrament, and the elevation of Haile Selassie, the former despotic ruler of Ethiopa, to the status of a god. The question the visit forced them to ask was whether Marley's musical achievements would have been possible, were it not for his devotion to Rastafarianism and its drug-induced visions of African return.

Just as enigmatic was the spectacle at Nine Mile of a memorial to a person of mixed race, administered on a commercial footing by a sect of black Rastafarians catering, apparently, for the needs of an almost exclusively white population of tourists. This shrine to Rastafarians' most illustrious son was entirely given over (at least when my parents were there) to the tourist industry. The Marley Mausoleum had long since become the sole focus of business in the tiny hamlet of Nine Mile, a place that hardly featured on the map until Marley was interred there. All that was required now was for a miraculous cure to turn the place into a Jamaican Lourdes. But would pilgrims flooding to the Nine Mile Zion be mostly white, black, or even mixed race?

Chapter 24

The House of Terror

The 'House of Terror' on Andrassy Road in Budapest is a museum dedicated wholly to the victims of Hungary's two brutal twentieth-century dictatorships, those of the Arrow Cross fascists and the Soviet-backed communists. Telling parallels are drawn between the two regimes The museum is accommodated in a smart late-nineteenth-century neo-classical building with a terrible history. In 1937, the block was occupied by the Arrow Cross Party. When this national socialist party took power in the winter of 1944, it used the basement to beat and torture anyone suspected of opposing it.

After the Nazis were defeated at the hands of the Red Army, the building became the headquarters of the Communist AVO, or secret police. The cellars were then used to interrogate people suspected of being enemies of the new regime. The individual chambers of the basement and the cellars of adjacent properties were connected to form a sizeable underground detention centre. This subterranean rabbit warren has now been restored to show the conditions under which detainees were kept for interrogation and torture.

Below ground level is the solitary punishment cell with its 60x50cm floor space and eye level light bulbs, kept shining day and night. Nearby is the wet cell, where a prisoner was forced to sit for long periods in water, and the fox-hole, a dark cubby hole with a ceiling so low it prevented its occupant from straightening up. The so-called 'treatment room' displays an array of torture instruments, including equipment for administering electric shocks. One chamber is set out as an execution suite, complete with gallows and rope, last used in 1985. No official executions actually took place at 60 Andrassy Road. The occasional fatalities there were caused by excessive beatings, torture, and suicide. Mel and Frank are still left with the nightmare of the human suffering and degradation that took place in these premises.

Rooms elsewhere in the museum recorded the brutal 45-year history of the Hungarian state from 1944 to 1989. In 1944, recognising that Hungary's ally, Germany, was on the brink of losing the war, Miklos Horthy, the Hungarian regent, sought to extricate his country from the war by declaring a ceasefire. In response, Hitler sent in

German troops and installed a government of Hungarian fascists - the Arrow Cross - which began a total mobilisation of Hungary's resources and manpower to stop the Soviet westward advance. With the Nazi occupation came the National Socialist 'regulation of the Jewish question'. Many Hungarian Jews were transported to extermination camps before the Red Army drove out the Nazis and consolidated its hold on the country.

Our parents' old friends, such as Sam Spittle and his wife, Mary, called occasionally at our house. Frank and Sammy would reminisce about their adventures together in the Young Communist League, recalling, for example, the problems they had in controlling the behaviour of younger YCL members at the anti-Vietnam War demonstration in Grosvenor Square in 1968.

On one occasion, when Sammy and Mary had left, I quizzed Dad about his current political opinions.

"I know you're a member of the Labour Party", I began, "but are you still a communist at heart?"

"Your mother and I are democratic socialists," he replied, "committed to bringing about greater social and economic equality, and reining in the power of international capitalism before it lays the planet waste. But in regard to the communist parties of the Soviet Union, Eastern Europe, and Great Britain, the scales fell from our eyes a long time ago."

"What do you mean?" I probed.

"For a long time, I did think of myself as a Marxist-Leninist," he confessed, "but I don't think I ever properly understood the implications of expressions, such as the 'science of revolution', 'the dictatorship of the proletariat', or even 'state control of the means of production, distribution and exchange'. Revolutions are never 'scientific' in the sense that we apply the word to the physical sciences. 'The dictatorship of the proletariat', was never government by, and for, the working-class majority. On the contrary, it was a real dictatorship, first by a handful of top Soviet Communist Party members, and afterwards, for 24 years, by one man, Joseph Stalin, an intelligent, but genocidal, psychopath.

State control of the economy involved centralised planning and target setting as an alternative to laissez-faire market capitalism. In any case, it was a system that just didn't deliver the goods in sufficient quantity to raise the Soviet bloc's standards of living to compete with the West.

But the main fault of communism in Russia and Eastern Europe was the consolidation and abuse of power by a small number of self-serving party bureaucrats. The extent of the problem was slowly brought home to us by reading about life in Russia, talking with refugees from Eastern Europe and, more recently, visiting a nation which rebelled against the Russian forces occupying it."

"So do you now regret being in the Communist Party?" I queried.

"I agreed at the time," he insisted, "with the Party's policies on a wide range of issues. Unlike the Labour Party, for example, the CP was unwavering in its condemnation of colonial domination, the War in Vietnam, apartheid, and the illegal regime in Rhodesia. If the Party's principles on these issues had been adopted, the UK would never have become embroiled in unnecessary and costly wars in Iraq and Afghanistan. It had an excellent record, too, in opposing racism and anti-immigrant hysteria at home. Nevertheless, I fully accept that the CP was inexcusably remiss in its analysis of the human rights violations and abuse of democracy and free speech that occurred in the Soviet Union and Eastern Europe".

"But Dad," I interrupted, "you admitted to me that you stayed with the Communist Party even when the Warsaw Pact tanks rolled into Czechoslovakia in 1968 to halt the reforms of Alexander Dubcek."

"I accept that, too," he acknowledged regretfully, "and, what's more, all that Dubcek proposed was to decentralise the economy and to guarantee free speech, press freedom, and the right to travel – what came to be known as 'socialism with a human face'. The British Communist Party, incidentally, called for the troops to be withdrawn and for the Czechoslovakian government to be allowed to make its own reforms.

You're right to raise the question of how I could have ignored the fundamental question of why the so-called democratic socialist countries of Eastern Europe acquiesced so readily to the invasion of a fraternal neighbouring state. I suppose I interpreted the intervention as an inevitable consequence of the Cold War, the division of Europe, and the need to defend socialist states against Western encroachment. The Americans were carpet-bombing Vietnam at the time, which seemed far worse."

The Poles that Frank met, such as Franciszka's father, referred constantly to the 1939 non-aggression pact between Hitler and Stalin, in which the two leaders made a squalid deal to divide Poland between them. Stalin was also accused of ordering the Katyn Forest massacre, the murder by Soviet Secret police in 1940 of more than 21,000 Polish officers, civil servants and intellectuals, who had been rounded up in the Soviet-occupied half of the country.

Along with Party apologists before him, Frank had at first explained the pact as a strategy devised by Stalin to buy time and avoid a war with Germany in which Britain and France would stand aloof as the two ideological giants destroyed one another. The Katyn Forest massacre, he believed, was a Nazi atrocity blamed on the Soviets by Polish anti-communists. He was wrong on both counts.

A visiting professor from Finland told Frank of the Soviet invasion of her country in 1939, a campaign fiercely resisted by the Finns against an army with three times as many soldiers and a hundred times as many tanks. One tenth of Finnish territory, apparently, still remains in Russian hands. Had this been a pre-emptive strike by the Russians to prevent German ambitions, or just another of Stalin's aggrandising aberrations?

Frank was an avid reader, and studied Roy Medvedev's book on Stalinism, *Let History Judge,* when it first became available in the UK in 1972. This major Russian study of the Soviet leader was first conceived after the twentieth congress of the Soviet Communist Party at which Krushchev denounced Stalin and his policies, and caused a crisis in the world communist movement.

It describes the rise of Stalin, his seizure of power, and the consequences of his decisions for the Soviet Union and its brand of socialism. It advances the theory that Stalin was responsible for the emergence of a 'pseudo socialism', which violated human rights on a colossal scale, and showed indifference and nastiness to the plight of millions of ordinary people by acting in a bureaucratic, ignorant and brutal manner. As a Marxist, Medvedev retained his belief in the merits of the Soviet system, merely arguing for a purification of the Communist Movement by washing away an accumulation of 'Stalinist filth'. Frank admits to having been satisfied at the time with Medvedev's analysis.

Frank's unease over the condition of people living in Eastern Europe and the Soviet Union was reawakened by discussions he had with people he met in the course of his employment. For example, Ramaz Klimiashvili, a Georgian colleague at the Research Unit on Ethnic Relations, told him, over his vodka (and Frank's rum), of the difficulties he had experienced in marrying an English woman and being granted permission to leave the Soviet Union to live in England. The authorities had actively discouraged his relationship with a foreigner, interpreting it as an act of disloyalty to the regime. Ramaz also described the situation of surveillance at the university he attended in Tbilisi, where fellow students were rewarded for informing on their colleagues. Ramaz had no patience whatsoever with apologists for the oppressive system under which he'd grown up.

"In hindsight, Dad," I persisted, "aren't you ashamed of your association with communists and the Communist Party?" How could somebody as clever as you have bought into such ridiculous propaganda?"

"You're missing the point," he said. "I didn't join the Communist Party to defend the Soviet Union, but because the CP consistently lent its weight to the causes that I believed in. The CP and the world-wide socialist movement campaigned for, and brought about more of the changes I wanted to see in the world than I have ever managed to achieve through my membership of the Labour Party. I can assure you that it was rare to find a Labour Party branch actively mobilising against, for example, apartheid, racism, racist immigration controls, the fascism of the National Front, anti-trade union legislation, and nuclear weapons or, for that matter, declaring its support for the miners, firemen, or other trade unionists.

Besides, I was attracted to the social philosophy of Marxism. I think it is right to attach importance to the material basis of human relations. Economic forces are pre-eminent in fashioning our lives. Capitalism affects not just our behaviour as workers and consumers, but the way we think and express ourselves in art, literature and music. Marxism provides a far more fundamental insight into world affairs than the common-sense observations of statesman and politicians, whether from the Right or the Left."

Mom and Dad constantly encouraged us children to ask questions such as: Why are people behaving in this way? What are they hoping to achieve for themselves? How are they benefiting from the choices they make? Who benefits most from the rules? What stories do people invent to justify their self-interested behaviour? In later years, we began to recognise the systematic nature of this form of inquiry and to adopt its method for ourselves. We weren't aware at the time that we were absorbing a materialist interpretation of the natural world, human development, and world history.

Yet it seems that all three of us have come to believe that only science can provide us with answers to the origins and destiny of the universe, that the evidence for evolution through natural selection is overwhelming, and that human society is best understood by studying different groups' relations to the dominant economic conditions. As a result, we have been brought up as atheists, believing that the various gods we see around us have been given their distinguishing characteristics by the human communities who worship them. Put simply, god didn't create us: we created 'him' or, in the case of us feminists, 'her'. And we were also able to observe for ourselves that a person didn't have to be religious to behave in an ethical way, and vice versa, of course.

Nevertheless, it was apparent to us from an early age that many members of our extended family were deeply religious and intensely worried about our parents' lack of faith and the impact this might have on us. Our paternal grandparents, Norman and Phyllis, would have dearly loved to have had us baptised as Catholics and for us to attend mass with them. Our maternal grandmother, Aunt Epsi, used to take us with her to clean her local Pentecostalist church in Sparkbrook. She impressed on us the need to read the bible and taught us to sing choruses, tap tambourines, and clap hands. Like our father before us, however, we found the repetitive nature of religious ceremonies tedious and intellectually stultifying.

By way of contrast, one close member of the family took her religion so seriously that she became a missionary. At the age of 27, our Aunt Carmelita (Mel's step-sister) was sufficiently inspired by her religious faith to quit her job as a trainee draughtswoman at Birmingham City Council to join Youth with a Mission, or Y-

WAM. Y-WAM came into being out of a 'passion to know God and to make Him known'. It pursues this purpose through evangelism, charitable activity (referred to as 'mercy ministry'), training, and discipleship. As a Christian organisation, Y-WAM affirms the Bible as the authoritative word of God and, with the Holy Spirit's inspiration, the absolute reference point for every aspect of life and ministry'.

Since 1987, Carmelita has worked for Y-WAM as a missionary administrator in a number of different countries: short spells in Kenya and Tanzania, and a stay of nine years in Albania. In 2004, she became the director of Y-WAM's Central European regional division.

Operating in well over one hundred countries, the Y-WAM missionary network was founded in the 1960s by Loren Cunningham, a minister of the American-based Evangelical Pentecostal Assemblies of God, which is allied to the Evangelical Christian Community, and associated with the Christian Right. Y-WAM launched its mission to Central and Eastern Europe in the early 1990s, soon after the fall of the communist regimes, in the hope that its brand of feel-good religion might find a home there. After all, Karl Marx, nearly 150 years previously, had perceptively observed that religion 'is the sigh of the oppressed creature, and the heart of a heartless world'.

"Dad, hasn't it occurred to you," I remarked, "that most belief systems share the same characteristics - including communism?"

"Of course!" Dad replied, "I'm fully aware of the way communist and capitalist regimes have divided the world with their slogans. It's very well described in George Orwell's book, *Animal Farm.* You remember: 'four legs good and two legs bad'."

Despite the different positions they hold on matters of religious faith, metaphysical belief systems, and the role and status of science, my parents and Aunt Carmelita have regular contact and meet when possible. They share a deep affection and get on well together when they meet. Mel helped bring up her little sister when they lived together in Sparkbrook. Frank, who once wanted to be an artist, and Carmelita, who went to Bournville's Ruskin School of Art, are both interested in art and architecture and appreciate each other's taste in interior design.

My parents respect Carmelita's firmness of purpose, self-reliance, love of travel, and ability to relocate to distant and different places. I, too, have a great admiration for my aunt, whose determination to travel and work abroad I share, she with the spiritual development of others in mind, I with their social and economic. I am aware, nevertheless, that Dad has little patience for Y-WAM's anti-intellectual, touchy-feely theology and activities.

In the summer of 2007, Carmelita invited Mel and Frank to stay with her at her apartment in central Budapest. Her flat mate had returned to the United States, leaving a bedroom free. Mel and Frank spent much of their time exploring the city with Carmelita. The weather in August was warm and dry and ideal for their excursions.

On one occasion, they took the train to Visegrad and caught a boat along the Danube bend back to base. Another afternoon was spent at the Statue Park, deliberately situated in a rural setting some distance from the centre of the city. During their stay, Louis Hamilton, the mixed-race British Formula 1 driving ace, won the Hungarian Grand Prix, an occasion which filled the bars of Budapest for a short time with British supporters.

Mel and Frank thought Budapest to be a most beautiful place, full of historic, scenic, and architectural wonder. It helped to have Carmelita with her smattering of Hungarian to show them round and teach them how to use the underground and bus service. Carmelita took them to see many of the main tourist sites, the Old Town: the Matyas Church and the statue of St Stephen, the Castle District, the Chain Bridge, Heroes' Square, and City Park. But four places they visited served to remind them of Hungary's recent and terrible history, and affected them profoundly.

While walking along the east bank of the Danube, just south of the Hungarian Parliament Building, they saw what appeared to be a row of shoes at the river edge. On closer inspection, they realised that this was a carefully-crafted sculpture, made up of sixty pairs of men, women and children's footwear, cast in iron and set into the stone parapet. This monument commemorated the night of 8 January 1945 when an execution squad from the Arrow Cross (the Hungarian National Socialist Party) rounded up the Jewish inhabitants of Ulloi Street and marched them down to the Danube, where they were machine-gunned into the river.

My parents said that this monument, depicting the victims' shoes left behind on the bank, brought tears to their eyes and raised the temperature of their hatred for nationalist and racist ideologies to new heights. They resolved to explore the old Jewish Quarter of Budapest with its nineteenth-century synagogue - still the largest in Europe - and its holocaust memorial.

When the Arrow Cross seized power in 1944, it invited the German, Adolph Eichmann, to Budapest, to help organise the extermination of the 200,000-strong Jewish community. More than 60,000 Jews were force-marched to the west to dig trenches on the Austrian border, 30,000 managed to obtain passes issued by neutral countries, while 70,000 were kept imprisoned in the ghetto.

In a garden at the rear of the synagogue is a holocaust memorial unveiled in 1991, consisting of a sculpture of a weeping willow tree, each willow leaf bearing the name of one of the 600,000 Hungarian Jews killed by the Nazis. Mel and Frank were surprised to discover that Tony Curtis, the American actor, was of Hungarian-Jewish descent and had contributed to the cost of the memorial. A sobering experience, the mood chimed once more with my parents' life-time resolve to fight racism and fascism in all its manifestations.

Following the German defeat in the Second World War, 200,000 ethnic Germans were expelled from Hungary. The Czechoslovak government, in turn, got rid not only of its German population, but of all the Hungarians living within its borders. Under the Hungarian-Czechoslovak population exchange agreement of 1946, more than 100,000 ethnic Hungarians were forced to leave Czechoslovakia, in exchange for 60,000 ethnic Slovakians sent back to Slovakia. What a lesson in the role that extreme nationalist ideologies have played in ethnic and race relations! One in ten of the Hungarian population was killed in the Second World War, and the country left in ruins.

By 1947, the Hungarian Communist Party, while winning less than a fifth of the popular vote, managed to seize power and impose a totalitarian dictatorship, using all the instruments of the state to terrorise and assassinate those who stood in its way. By 1949, electors could vote only for candidates approved of by the

Communist Party, with the result that it achieved a 96 per cent victory. Only in 1990, did Hungary once more hold free elections.

The Communist Party's ideology - referred to either as 'Marxist-Leninism', or 'Stalinism' - was used to determine not only the form of the economy, but of culture, education, the arts, and social life. All the organs of the state were controlled by the Party, with the important decisions being taken by its political committee, led by Matyas Rakosi, who was sometimes styled 'Stalin's foremost Hungarian pupil'. Parliamentary government disappeared, the constitution was changed, and a system of councils was introduced along Soviet lines.

Private ownership of the means of production, distribution and exchange was abolished in favour of a centralised planned economy. The sudden, ill-thought-out nature of the changes led to economic shortages, queues for bread, empty shops, and national bankruptcy. Party members, meanwhile, received preferential treatment. To help introduce the new economic order, Soviet expert advisors were brought in to direct key sectors of industry, such as uranium mining, air transport, munitions, oil, and foreign exports.

None of these changes went unopposed. Backed by occupying Soviet troops garrisoned across the country, the regime developed all the paraphernalia of a police and surveillance state to deal with those it considered subversive. More than a thousand judges were dismissed and replaced by Party stalwarts, who put on show trials, replacing the principle of equality before the law with one of 'class justice'. The age for the imposition of the death penalty was reduced to 16. Between 1945 and 1956, around 1,500 people were accused of sedition, 400 executed, and the rest sentenced to life imprisonment.

Under the orders of the Party leaders, and their Soviet advisors, the secret police, based at 60 Andrassy Road – now 'the House of Terror' - arrested, tortured, or beat to death, anyone suspected of subversion, including their own parents, brothers, lovers, friends, and former comrades. Before long, substantial numbers of Communist Party activists followed them into the basement to be forced into making confessions. They were then imprisoned, or executed. The museum has on display 800 dossiers relating to investigations, political trials, indictments, sentences, and appeals, for the period 1945 to 1956.

In 1956, students in Budapest organised a protest demonstration in support of workers in Poland, demanding better working conditions and free elections. The Hungarian students made similar demands: the withdrawal from their country of Soviet troops, multi-party elections, independent courts, rehabilitation of political prisoners, and freedom of opinion and the press.

On the 23rd October, a vast crowd gathered on the streets and marched on parliament, to be addressed by Imré Nagy, one of the more moderate members of the Communist Party. Following armed clashes on the streets and the intervention of Soviet troops, the protest movement turned into a full-scale armed insurrection, resulting in Imré Nagy being swept into power. Nagy announced an immediate truce, the end of the one-party system, free elections, and the abolition of the hated State Security Department.

By November, Soviet tanks began to stream across the border. They encountered stiff resistance from the hastily set-up workers' councils and military committees, but soon put down the uprising. More than 2,500 people lost their lives, 20,000 were injured, and 200,000 fled to the West. A further 15,000 people were arrested, 860 deported to the Soviet Union as prisoners of war, and 229 executed. Imré Nagy was tried in camera on a charge of treason and sentenced to death.

One of the rooms in the museum is painted red. Records of executions and rejected appeals for clemency are shown on replica scaffolds, while the names of executed insurrectionists boom out from the loudspeakers.

Mindful that they once were willing to defend the Soviet Union, Mel and Frank still think about their visit to the House of Terror, and its political implications for them as socialists. If the British NHS embodied the loftiest principles of socialist morality, they could not avoid the conclusion, by way of contrast, that Hungary's experience of communist dictatorship represented the shameful depths of socialist depravity.

While in Hungary, Frank chose to read *The Undefeated*, a book by George Paloczi-Horvath, a Hungarian nobleman, who came to realise his family's wealth was based on the exploitation of the peasantry, and went on to become first an anti-Nazi, and then a communist. He returned from England after the Second World War to help build the new communist order. With his literary and journalistic skills, he was initially welcomed into the Party, but was later arrested, tortured and imprisoned under conditions of solitary confinement in underground prison cells, for reasons even he didn't fully understand. Released eventually in 1954, he fled in the aftermath of the Hungarian Uprising and sought political asylum in Britain. Frank found the author's analysis of what had gone wrong with communism and the Soviet Union of great interest.

Paloczi-Horvath and the other imprisoned communists were allowed to read the communist classics while they were incarcerated, and entered into earnest discussion with one another over why the system had failed them and the working class. Their key question was whether the inhuman and inefficient Soviet system was an inevitable consequence of Marxism-Leninism or not. A majority of the prisoners who participated in the debate believed that a decent, real communism was possible, but that Marxism-Leninism had been corrupted by Stalin and his henchmen. A minority shared Paloczi-Horvath's view that the concepts of class warfare, class enemies, proletarian dictatorship, and one-party rule, had led inevitably to the cruel bureaucratic despostism to which they had fallen victim.

Mel, Frank and Carmelita concluded their holiday with an excursion to the Statue Park, full of immense public statues, commissioned during the communist era and formerly erected around the city. The statues had been moved to the park following a majority decision of the residents living in the districts where they were originally situated.

Opened in 1993, the Statue Park - or Statue Cemetery - has gradually become a major tourist attraction. It provides a home for the gigantic icons of Karl Marx, Friedrich Engels, Vladimir Lenin, and the Hungarian revolutionary leader, Bela Kun.

It all seemed so dated: the lofty sentiment of a bygone age, captured in stone by the artists, now rendered ridiculous by the reality of the proponents' gross abuse of power. Frank found himself quoting Shelley:

'My name is Ozymandias, King of Kings:
Look on my works, ye Mighty, and despair!'
Nothing beside remains. Round the decay
Of that colossal wreck, boundless and bare
The lone and level sands stretch far away.

Chapter 25

Rhodes to Zim and back again

When exploring Cape Town, South Africa, Mel and Frank discovered two public benches outside the court building in Queen Victoria Street. They were marked 'whites only' and 'non-whites only' and had been left as a memorial to apartheid legislation. The accompanying plaque headed 'Race Classification Board 1959-1991' explained:

'In the 1960s, a room in this building was the scene of formal hearings of the most bizarre and humiliating kind, as ordinary people came before an appeal panel to argue about what 'race' they should be labelled. Between 1950 and 1991, apartheid's Population Registration Act classified every South African as belonging to one of at least seven 'races' - and accordingly, granted, or denied them, citizenship rights on a sliding scale from white (full rights) to Bantu (with the fewest). The classification was subjective and families were split apart when paler or darker-skinned children or parents - or those with curlier hair, or different features - were placed in separate categories.'

In 1984, 518 coloured people had been reclassified as white and one white person had been reclassified as coloured. The Population Registration Act No 30 of 1950 ruled that: 'A White person is in appearance white and not coloured' and 'A Coloured is a person who is not White or a Bantu.'

Photos were taken of Mel sitting on the Whites Only bench and of Frank sitting on the Non-Whites Only bench. Both parents looked relaxed and happy, although they later claimed to be seething with internal rage at the dehumanising cruelty that had reduced people's worth to the superficiality of their physical appearance.

Mom and Dad were particularly incensed by those aspects of apartheid legislation, which prohibited inter-racial relationships such as their own. Mixed marriages had been forbidden in 1948. Soon afterwards, sexual relations between black and white were also criminalised. South African police actively investigated mixed couples suspected of violating the Immorality Act. They would break into homes to arrest people found in bed together, using their underwear as forensic evidence in court. Couples found guilty were sent to jail, but the black partner was nearly always given a heavier sentence.

In October 2005, I gave up my job and went back to university to study for an MSc in the Management of Poverty Reduction and International Development. As part of my course, I had to produce a dissertation. I chose to explore the relationship between truth, reconciliation and justice. Did truth commissions set up in former conflict situations have the ability to contribute to social justice and reconciliation as well as to bring out the truth? I decided to go to South Africa to study the impact of the post-apartheid Truth and Reconciliation Commission.

Mom and Dad were thrilled with the idea and suggested I stay with their friends the Mpofus, a Zimbabwean family, who had settled in Cape Town. I hadn't been aware that they had friends in South Africa. My parents took out their wedding photographs once more to point out two of their African guests: Joshu Mpofu, a muscular grey-suited man, with a black beard, and Nonhlanhla, his young daughter, in white socks and a pink dress.

Frank was introduced to Ratie Mpofu in 1973 by Bridget, his Zimbabwean girlfriend at the time. Ratie arrived in England in 1969 at the age of 24 to study physiotherapy in Birmingham. She passed the three-and-a-half year course, to become a member of the Chartered Society of Physiotherapy. She then took a job as a physio in Birmingham, renting a flat with a Kenyan friend. In 1974, she was joined by her husband, Joshua, who enrolled as a student at Fircroft College in Birmingham and then went on to read sociology at the University of York.

Frank and Mel used to visit Ratie and Josh in Birmingham and at York. Mel still recalls taking the Mpofu family out for the day to the seaside. This was the first time their child, Nonhlanhla, had ever seen the sea. She gazed at the water and asked: "Where does it end?" Nonhlanhla now lives near the coast in Cape Town and can look at the ocean everyday. Ratie and Josh returned in 1982 to the newly-liberated Zimbabwe, but had since relocated with their family to South Africa.

When I arrived in Cape Town, Ratie and Joshua collected me from the airport and welcomed me into their home. I met their three children, Nonhlanhla, Vela, and Veronica, all now grown up. We discussed the politics of Africa animatedly for the next four weeks, until I left for Johannesburg.

In Cape Town, my appearance led people to think I was a South African Coloured – a member of one of the three original apartheid-era racial groupings. I was repeatedly addressed in Afrikaans, the language that most Coloureds spoke. When I replied in English, it was assumed that I was pretending to be a white person – a status to which, self-evidently, I wasn't entitled.

Neither were Coloured women expected to demean themselves by consorting with black men, which in my case was unavoidable as I was staying with the Mpofus. When Vela and I strolled through the shopping precinct one day, he pointed out that my "Coloured brothers" were giving him menacing stares for, as he put it, "stealing one of their girls". I didn't believe him at first, but soon noticed the angry glares of the Coloured men.

While in South Africa, I managed to collect plenty of data for my dissertation. I was also fortunate to be among a group granted an audience with Nelson Mandela. I returned to complete my masters at Birmingham University and, afterwards, to land a job working for Oxfam. In 2008, I was transferred to Oxfam's Horn, East, and Central Africa Office in Nairobi, to take up the post of international diversity officer on a one-year contract.

Although six storeys up, my Oxfam billet in Almond Court, a gated compound some two kilometres from State House, was airy and spacious. Making full use of the location and accommodation, provided for me, I decided to invite Mom and Dad to visit, enticing them not only with the promise of a holiday in Kenya, but with the suggestion, readily accepted, that they use the opportunity to fly on to South Africa to visit their old friends, the Mpofus.

It was fortunate that South Africa had by then become a rainbow nation and was under black majority rule. My parents would never have agreed to visit that country under the apartheid regime, with its policy of legally-enforced separate racial development, segregation, and disenfranchisement of the majority African population. Even at their wedding reception in 1976, Mom and Dad held a minute's silence for the 500 students shot down by the South African authorities at Soweto in the June of that year.

As members of the Anti-Apartheid movement since before I was born, they were enthusiastic supporters of the travel, trade and sports boycotts of the old regime. Whenever we visited a fruit stall or off-licence, we were made to examine brands and labels to ensure the family never bought goods produced in the apartheid state.

In 2009, my parents met me in the Java Café at Jomo Kenyatta International Airport, stayed overnight at my flat, and then left in the morning on a short safari to the Masai Mara. When they returned a few days later, I took them to my place of work, Shelter Afrique house, the Eastern Africa offices of Oxfam GB, where they chatted with some of my colleagues. As regular donors to Oxfam GB, Mom and Dad were interested in their work and questioned them closely. A friend, who was responsible for water and sewage on the humanitarian programme, informed them jokingly that they had 'graduated', because they demonstrated to him a knowledge of the two fundamental principles of his work: that water flows down hill and that it has to be kept separate from shit!

Mom and Dad were keen to see as much of Kenya as possible. Dad, with his longstanding interest in African history, culture and art, wanted to explore the ruins of the Swahili civilisation that once flourished along the east coast. We flew to Mombasa and drove north along the coast towards Malindi.

In the following days, we visited the impressive ancient Swahili sites at Gede, Mnarani, and Jumba la Mtwana, which date back at least to the 13th century. We were all impressed by the extensive complexes of mosques, palaces, courtyards, madrassahs, houses, and wells, long abandoned, but recently rediscovered under the matted vegetation of the coastal forests. Frank said that the layout of the settlements reminded him of the Arab cities he'd seen in Morocco. During the excavation, items of Ming porcelain and Venetian glass had been discovered, proving these towns had served as trading posts for Arabian, Chinese, Persian, and Venetian merchants.

While we found our excursion to the east coast informative and convivial, Dad and I were more interested in Kenya's recent colonial and post-colonial history. It turned out that we had both just read Caroline Elkins' book, *Britain's Gulag*, an account of the Mau Mau uprising in Kenya and its brutal suppression by the British colonial government. Almost the entire Kikuyu tribe - 1,500,000 strong - was detained in camps, or confined to villages by barbed wire fences, before the British government was persuaded to grant Kenya its independence.

Elkins documents, in sickening detail, the widespread killing, torture, beatings, rape, forced labour, and starvation inflicted on the local tribespeople. This overwhelming indictment of imperialism, the brutal force maintaining it, and the racist ideology it spawned, left both of us wondering whether, from the point of view of the people they ruled, there had been any substantial difference between the British and the Soviet Empires in their abuse of power.

Back in Nairobi, Mel and Frank chose to visit the Memorial Garden that now occupies the site of the former American Embassy, destroyed on the 7 August 1998, by an Al Qaida-placed bomb. Frank recognised the relevance of this attack to Race Equality West Midlands' work on violent extremism. Simultaneous explosions had wrecked American embassies in Nairobi and Dar es Salaam. A yellow Mitsubishi van, containing 800kg of TNT, exploded in the parking bay of the embassy in Haile Selassie Avenue in Nairobi. Forty people were killed at the embassy, twelve of them American. But the nearby Ufundu Co-operative House took the brunt of the blast, which left 263 dead and more than 5,000 injured, most of the Kenyan, with damage estimated at US $500 million.

Beyond the turnstile is a small garden, neatly laid out with seats and shelter from the sun. The names of the victims of the explosion are inscribed on a stone wall, similar in style to the memorial in Washington DC to the Americans who died in Vietnam, but not as extensive. Mel and Frank found the garden a simple and sombre monument to those who had been so pointlessly blown to bits. Three years before 9/11, this had been Al Qaida's first successful atrocity and a harbinger of the form that warfare would take in the 21st century.

I organised a reception for my parents at my flat during their stay and introduced them to some of my friends, who asked them politely whether they were enjoying their visit. Mel recounted how the Kenyans she had spoken to were curious to discover her nationality. She told them: "I'm from Jamaica."

"Which tribe in Jamaica?" they would quiz.

When Mel explained that there weren't any tribes in Jamaica, they would look astonished and inquire: "How does your country manage without tribes?"

She would retort: "And how does your country cope with them?"

Most Kenyans seemed to be aware that Usain Bolt was from Jamaica. "Kenya is a big country," they would say, "so we have the fastest long-distance runners. Jamaica is a little island. That's why you have the fastest man over a short distance."

Kenyans also listened to reggae and were familiar with Bob Marley. There were, indeed, Kenyan Rastafarians. Most of the time, however, local people assumed Mel to be an African, and more specifically, a Kikuyu.

"We thought you were a Kikuyu," they would say. "You look like a Kikuyu."

From the knowing glances of hotel staff and waiters at seeing a mixed couple, Mel sensed that they assumed she was a Kikuyu woman who had attached herself to a white man as a gold-digging exercise, and that my white father had come to enjoy the experience of a black woman.

Most of the friends my parents met at the reception worked for NGOs on some aspect of international development. After they had left, I asked Mom and Dad what they thought of them.

"They were all very pleasant," Mom said, "and we had a most interesting afternoon discussing where they were from, and their jobs with different NGOs."

"Development workers talk only about one issue," Dad observed. "The abuse of power by senior African politicians."

"Or the failure of the state to take on their welfare projects," Mom added incisively.

One Kenyan minister had recently sold off the country's entire strategic grain reserve while people were on the verge of starvation in the Turkana region. Kenyan politicians were not only well paid but had voted themselves, alone among their fellow citizens, tax-free status. In this context, we international development workers were constantly questioning our role - however minor - in propping up members of a self-seeking and corrupt elite, who were contributing to the impoverishment of their own people, rather than working to alleviate their hardship.

On another occasion, Hazel, a bubbly intelligent Zimbabwean, accompanied by her cousin's child, Zvidzai, popped in from her flat downstairs. Mom and Dad talked to her at length about the deteriorating situation in Zimbabwe, the Mugabe terror, and the collapse of the economy. Some people's total pension entitlement in Zimbabwean dollars was less than the price of the bus fare across Harare to collect it. We decided to make my parents multi-millionaires by gifting them a Zimbabwe bank note bearing a face value of five hundred million (500,000,000) Zimbabwean dollars. It was, of course, worthless. The Zimbabwean government had already replaced its super-inflated currency with US dollars and SA rands. Dad recalled a pre-war photograph he'd seen of a German citizen going to shop with a wheel-barrow-full of marks.

I was sad when the time came for Mom and Dad to fly on to South Africa to visit Ratie and Joshua Mpofu. On arrival in Cape Town, they were made very welcome by their old friends and introduced to the other residents of the house in Sanatorium Road, Claremont, where I'd stayed three years before. They met Vela (Ratie and Joshua's son), Sibonakaliso (Joshua's brother's wife), and her son, Arthur. When Mel helped out in the kitchen, the Mpofus would always mention how much they had appreciated my cooking when I'd stayed with them.

In the days of apartheid, Claremont had been an exclusively white British suburb of Cape Town, but anyone who could afford the price could now buy a house there. Joshua and Ratie had lived in Sanatorium Road - still a mainly-white area - for about ten years. All the houses in the road had security gates and burglar bars, but these hadn't prevented the Mpofus from being burgled five times since they'd moved in.

The Mpofus took Mel and Frank sightseeing. They went to Signal Hill, a promontory rising high above Cape Town with panoramic views of the bay, the docks, and the great office blocks of the city. Below them, Frank could see a green patch in the townscape and inquired of an Indian couple whether it was a park.

"That's District Six", they told him, "That's where we used to live before we were forced to move."

Afterwards, Joshua drove the party to Albertus Street to visit the District Six Museum, set up in the Central Methodist Mission Church. The Muslim curator explained how the multi-racial vibrancy and success of District Six flew in the face of the prevailing racist ideology of the apartheid regime and led to it being snuffed out. The memories of the local people were fondly recorded in the various displays. The museum had on show a wooden church pew painted with the words, 'Europeans only'.

In 1966, PW Botha, the South African Minister of Community Development, designated District Six a 'white group area' under the Group Areas Act 1950. Over the next fifteen years, more than 60,000 people were removed to new townships on the Cape Flats. By the early 1980s, the Coloured and Indian residents had been forced out, and most of the buildings demolished.

On returning home one evening, Sibonakaliso told how she had been held up at knife point on her way to the station and asked to hand over her valuables, including her earrings. Fortunately for her, two women had approached, and a car driver stopped and chased the mugger away. The car driver offered all three women a lift to the station and warned them not to walk at that spot again. Sibo saw no point in reporting the incident to the police. The Mpofu family seemed to accept the threats to its security as part of the daily routine. Joshua pointed out that, while white people were paranoid about the crime rate, the situation was far worse for black people in the townships. The whites were protected by car travel and security gates.

Mel and Frank were taken by Ratie to visit the University of Western Cape where she was Dean of the Faculty of Community and Health Sciences. Ratie asked Mel to explain the pattern of nurse education in the United Kingdom to staff in the School of Nursing. The nurse educators present discussed the similarities and differences with the South African system of producing nurses. Most of the students in the Department were coloured or African, but a few whites were now attending too.

Under apartheid, the University of the Western Cape had been for coloureds only, but under Ratie's leadership the number of African student nurses had risen considerably. In the sixteen years she had been at the university, she had worked hard to improve African students` access to higher education and to ensure that they were treated and assessed fairly. She had to deal firmly with staff who persisted in believing that the admission of Africans would result in a lowering of standards. Under South Africa's Employment Equity legislation, which introduced a form of affirmative action for Africans and women, universities are required to reserve some senior positions for under-represented groups. This has led to a backlash, with many black staff members viewed as inferior and undeserving of their positions.

The building occupied by the School of Nursing had formerly served as the apartheid regime's 'Coloured Parliament', one of the three racial parliaments providing a semblance of representation for designated whites, coloureds, and Indians. The majority African population, however, was denied any say in government and considered adequately represented by the rurally-located 'Bantustans' which never occupied more than 13 per cent of South African territory. Two thirds of the Africans lived in urban areas and had no vote, nor say, in national or local government. The parliamentary chamber, with spectators' gallery and blue-leather upholstered benches, now provides a somewhat luxurious lecture theatre for the Department's student nurses.

On one of their regular forays to the local shopping centre for newspapers and cappuccinos, Joshua told Frank the history of how he trained as a ZAPU guerrilla fighter in the Soviet Union at a location near to Moscow. The one-year course was extremely intensive and included classes in political economy, mathematics and Russian, in addition to military instruction. In 1969, he returned as a base station commander to a camp in Zambia, accommodating about two hundred soldiers. From there, the guerrillas made periodic reconnaissance forays across the border into what was then Southern Rhodesia. Joshua described the formation of the Rhodesian defence forces which spread out across the terrain in staggered groups of sixteen. If one group was attacked, it was not long before reinforcements converged on the spot.

Back at camp, the ZAPU soldiers became more and more disillusioned with the ineffectiveness of their leaders. Many of them were not military trained and knew little of battle tactics. The politicians running ZAPU were, in effect, taking tactical military decisions. The soldiers believed that this arrangement could not be made to work and would inevitably lead to a pointless loss of life. They requested an urgent meeting with the leadership.

A conference involving a Zambian minister was eventually arranged on 11 March 1971, at which the soldiers were warned that any decision taken would be seen, not only a leadership challenge to the five senior officials in charge, but to the authority of Joshua Nkomo himself. Afterwards, the ZAPU camp was surrounded by Zambian paramilitaries.

One day, a roll call of 29 names was called out, including those of camp and platoon commanders. Joshua's name was third on the list. These officers were taken away by Zambian paramilitary forces and kept at Milima, in Kasama, north of the Copper Belt, close to the Tanzanian border. The detention order was signed by Kenneth Kaunda. Joshua was imprisoned in Zambia from June 1971 to April 1974, when he was released to travel to the United Kingdom to become a student at Fircroft College.

After their officers had been taken away, the remaining soldiers insisted that they could no longer operate. Some left to join ZANU, which was less firmly anti-tribal than ZAPU, and drew most of its forces from the Mashona. More despicably, 120 of the rank-and-file foot soldiers were taken in trucks to the Rhodesian border and handed over to the Rhodesians, where they were immediately put in prison. Later, five or six of them were sentenced to death. When the regime changed in 1980, the sentences were commuted and all prisoners released. The guerrillas who joined ZANU faired less well. Many of them suffered summary execution while serving in the Zimbabwean army in the years that followed.

Ratie reminded Frank of his contribution to the Zimbabwean Liberation Struggle in the years after Southern Rhodesia's Unilateral Declaration of Independence (UDI). Bridget, Frank's African girlfriend in 1973, had taken him to Ratie's flat in Birmingham, where he had met a number of exiled Zimbabweans, including Didymus Mutasa, later to become an apologist for Mugabi as his regime began to crumble.

Bridget first involved Frank in readdressing letters arriving from Eastern European countries to destinations in Southern Rhodesia and vice versa, adding his name and his Wolverhampton Oak Street address as the sender. He never saw the content of the letters, but was led to assume that this was a way of avoiding interception of the post by Rhodesian censors.

Soon afterwards, Ratie, Bridget and Frank set up the Campaign for the Relief of Rhodesian Political Prisoners and launched an appeal for money, clothes and books for prisoners, 'restrictees', and 'detainees'. They were supported by another expatriate, Jacob Moyo, who, before coming to Britain, spent eight years at Gonakudzingwa, one of the detention camps, and formerly a restricted area.

Ratie and Bridget, of course, were concerned specifically with the situation of the ZAPU guerrilla fighters detained in Zambia. Ratie, acting on the advice of Jacob Moyo, was determined to obtain the release of Joshua and the other guerrilla fighters. She decided to explore the possibility of bringing them to the United Kingdom to study. Joan Lester, the Minister of State for Foreign Affairs, was persuaded to provide grants to fund the education of African Rhodesians. (Kenneth Kaunda, the President of Zambia, was seen as a friend of Britain, and the British government wanted a solution that would avoid embarrassment and satisfy all parties to the dispute.)

Frank was given the job of finding university places for the detainees in Zambia. He composed a letter to the universities, suggesting that they could contribute to future African development by educating black Rhodesian students displaced by the illegal Smith regime. He was gratified when he received positive responses, promising 41 places in all. One of these places was allocated to Joshua, which he took up after finishing a preparatory course at Fircroft College in Birmingham.

Joshua and Ratie took Mel and Frank to see the African and Coloured townships of Cape Town. They drove through Manenberg, Philippi, Cross Roads, New Cross Roads, Hanover, Nyanga, Khayelitsha and Harare, and then across the extensive sandy Mitchell's Plain.

Under the apartheid laws passed in the 1950s, no Africans were allowed to settle on a permanent basis west of a line 1000 kilometres away from Cape Town. The only Africans allowed into the area were temporary migrant workers, all of whom were men. African women were banned from working in Cape Town, leaving domestic work entirely for the Coloured population. As a result men-only hostels formed the basis of township development. By the 1970s, there were ten men to every woman living in the Cape townships. Nevertheless, the apartheid laws were unable to stop the inexorable movement of people seeking jobs.

The migrants set up squatter camps built of anything they could lay their hands on. In the 1970s and 1980s, the government repeatedly demolished the informal settlements, only for them to be rebuilt again as soon as the police had left. The gangs in these areas were often encouraged by the police to harass the squatters.

Visitors cannot fail to be dismayed by the sheer size and scale of these crowded slums. Mel and Frank passed mile after mile of ramshackle huts, built mainly from corrugated iron, old wooden planks, and tarpaulins. Taps had been installed, each providing for about ten families. They saw rows of chemical toilets made of blue plastic. Most of the slums were now supplied with electricity and running water. In places, the expanse of make-shift homes - tshotshombe - was broken by stalls selling vegetables, fruit and other goods. At one spot along the road, corrugated iron shacks, the size of an English garden shed, were set out for sale, at a cost of around R2000, or £270. On another street, there were stalls with cooking pots, and spits for barbecuing meat, prepared on the spot, with the animal carcasses and skin still lying at the road side.

The townships showed signs of recent improvement. Wide new roads had been constructed, dissecting the area into manageable and accessible chunks. Rows of simple block and rendered dwellings had been built to replace the corrugated shacks but, in some cases, shacks had been erected in the space between the units. Community and medical centres and schools had been opened. Joshua showed Mel and Frank the headquarters of the health project he had helped to set up and develop.

What makes Cape Town's African townships and squatter camps so shocking, however, is the proximity of the unbelievably-affluent white areas, such as Clifton, Camps Bay, Hout Bay, and Constantia.

But even the Coloured townships on the Cape Flats close by are superior to the constantly expanding African settlement areas.

Mel asked about the HIV epidemic and the action being taken to deal with it. Of the pregnant women in the townships, 25 per cent tested positive. Anti-retroviral drugs had at last been made available to those sufferers who stood a chance of benefiting from them. Josh and Ratie pointed out two extensive cemeteries, full of new graves marked by simple wooden crosses and plastic flowers. Most of the graves were of young people under 30 years old.

One evening, Ratie organised a celebratory barbecue, or 'braai', to welcome Mel and Frank to Cape Town and invited her friends from the Faculty at the university. In South Africa, a barbecue is referred to as a 'braai' and Afrikaans word meaning 'meat grill' - a meal cooked over an open fire. The guests consisted of the Mpofus' extended family, and Ratie and Josh's friends from the university and the community health projects where they worked.

The conversation turned to South African health problems, especially HIV, and the different infection rates of the African, Coloured, and White populations. Dave, the Director of Public Health at the University of the Western Cape, pointed out that the African rate was 30 per cent, the Coloured 12 per cent, and the white rate similar to that in Europe. Among African and Coloured, the infection was primarily heterosexually transmitted, while among whites, homosexually. He attributed the prevalence of HIV among Africans to the large numbers of migrant labourers with sexual partners - often shared - in the townships, as well as in the homelands. HIV could be found throughout Anglophone Africa, wherever large numbers of male migrant labourers were required for work in mining and other industries.

"Why did you and Josh decide to leave Zimbabwe and move to Cape Town?" Mel asked Ratie.

"We made up our minds to quit long before the country's current economic crisis," Ratie replied. "We had to get out. I even thought about applying for jobs in America, but Joshua insisted we stay in Africa."

"That's why she applied for the job at the University of the Western Cape," Joshua added, "and we ended up here in Cape Town."

"But why did you have to leave Zim?" Mel persisted.

Joshua was from the Matabele tribe and Ratie from the Mashona, making them a mixed couple in the eyes of fellow black Zimbabweans, and a focus for suspicion, prejudice and discrimination. To make matters worse, Joshua had been a member of ZAPU, the Soviet-backed guerrilla army, recruited mainly from the minority Matabele ethnic group, in contrast to President Robert Mugabe's ZANU ruling party, whose fighters had been trained by the Chinese and were drawn from among the majority Mashona.

Despite her qualifications, Ratie was repeatedly passed over for promotion. Joshua found it more and more difficult to find work commensurate with his ability, qualifications and experience. In addition, Joshua was regarded as knowing too much about the dark side of Robert Mugabe's dealings, putting him at risk from the increasingly paranoid, volatile, and arbitrary regime.

In 1986, Joshua obtained permission from the Zimbabwean Deputy Prime Minister to travel around Matabeleland South, Central, and Northern districts to investigate reports of atrocities committed by the Zimbabwean army's Fifth Brigade. Because his written credentials had been issued by the government's senior command, he was allowed, despite intense suspicion by those in authority, to visit and talk with local people. He had been warned to avoid certain dangerous and influential people from whom he steered a wide berth.

Appalling crimes had been committed, all evidenced by at least two separate witnesses and his own observations. Villagers had been forced to attend meetings to denounce alleged dissidents in their midst. When they had failed to do as they were asked, some were arbitrarily selected and shot, or given clubs and ordered to beat their neighbours to death. Even when they did as they were told, they, too, were dispatched by the soldiers.

Joshua told how he had seen burnt-out huts with their doors secured from the outside with wire. Whole families had been confined and burned to death. He estimated that, in all, about 30,000 Matabele had been murdered. A separate investigation by the Catholic Church put the figure at 20,000.

On his return to Harare, Joshua submitted his report to Simon Muzenda, the Deputy Prime Minister, with the warning that continued action of this kind by government forces was likely to lead to civil war. The document was reclassified from Confidential to Top Secret and his original written manuscript and typed copy destroyed in his presence. Nevertheless, the killings were halted and the Fifth Brigade disbanded.

Joshua was still very preoccupied with events in Zimbabwe and had just written a paper making the case for a truth and reconciliation committee to be set up to help usher in a new era of democracy for his country. He asked Frank to read through his proposal, much of it an historical account of the tragedies to have befallen Zimbabwe in the last 130 years. Frank suggested that the truth and reconciliation exercise focus exclusively on the violation of the judicial process and the unlawful acts of the Mugabe regime, rather than on the draconian legislation inherited from colonial times and extended under ZANU-PF.

Ratie, Josh and Sibo accompanied Mel and Frank on a pilgrimage by catamaran to Robben Island. Six miles off the coast, Robben Island is the isolated location of the prison that once held the apartheid regime's political prisoners. It has since been made into a memorial to its victims. Its most famous inmate was Nelson Mandela, the first president of post-apartheid South Africa, who was incarcerated there for more than 23 years.

Their first stop on the island was the house of Robert Sobukwe, a former teacher who had founded the Pan-African Congress Party. He had been imprisoned here for nine years in solitary confinement. He was removed from the island in 1969 and held instead in Kimberley under house arrest until his death from cancer in 1978. Sobukwe believed in an Africanist future for South Africa, rejecting the view that it was possible for black Africans to collaborate with other racial groups, despite the country's sizeable number of non-black minorities. Unlike Nelson Mandela and the African National Congress, he saw the struggle against apartheid in terms not of social class, but of race. Mel and Frank were relieved that the strategy of the African National Congress had prevailed over that of the Pan Africanists.

Another stop was the quarry where the prison inmates had been forced to break stones in the searing heat and bright sunlight, the glare from the white limestone damaging their eyesight. The visitors were taken next to the maximum security prison with its high walls and perimeter fencing. They were shown round by a former inmate, who spoke from experience about the cruelty of the guards. He pointed out Mandela's bare cramped cell, equipped with a single blanket and bucket in exactly the same way as those of the other prisoners.

Mel and Frank sat for some time in the prison yard meditating on what they had seen and heard. Frank found himself thinking of another prison he had visited two years before: the House of Terror in Budapest. Instances of inhuman treatment, punishment and torture aimed at suppressing freedom of thought, expression, and association, were a widespread occurrence, by no means confined to the hated apartheid state.

Having crossed to Robben Island myself in 2005, I asked my parents what they thought of their visit.

"A sobering and deeply emotional experience," Dad confessed. "Your mother wept openly and I choked on the lump in my throat!" I understood only too well. The visit I made had had the same impact on me.

"What we saw there," Mom said, "was just the logical consequence of state-enforced racial separation. That jail stood for everything that we have worked all our lives to put a stop to."

"The release of those political prisoners," Dad observed, "summed up our own personal triumph against racism and bigotry, not just in the trivial contribution we made to the anti-apartheid movement, but in our struggles in Wolverhampton, too."

"We have been on a pilgrimage," Mom concluded, "and have come back home re-energised."

Postscript

What happened to the wedding guests?

It is now thirty-four years since our parents married. The cycle of birth, reproduction and death has moved onward. We three children have long since arrived on the scene, together with our cousins. Grandparents, great uncles and great aunts have passed away, leaving only Aunt Epsi as our sole surviving relative of that generation living in England. Our parents' list of wedding guests has shrunk accordingly. Some friends have remained close to the family. Many have stayed in touch with the help of an annual Christmas card. A few, however, have moved away and lost contact, or betrayed our parents' trust in them. I want to round off our family history as neatly as I can with an account of what happened to the people in the wedding photographs.

Mel and Frank, the bride and groom, are now retired from paid work, but expend just as much energy as before on volunteering in the community, writing, campaigning politically - particularly in regard to equality and human rights - and cultivating their garden, both literally and metaphorically. Mel retired in August 2007 as Dean of the School of Health and Director of Health Service Provision at the University of Wolverhampton, where she had been employed since July 2002. Frank left Race Equality West Midlands - by that time rechristened Rights and Equality West Midlands - in August 2008.

Mom still has her wedding dress, consisting of the bandana skirt, matching head wrap, and the white embroidered peasant blouse she wore in 1976. She persists in wearing this costume on important occasions, such as at dinners held to celebrate subsequent decades of Jamaican independence. The colourful outfit has also been borrowed to display at local multi-cultural events and exhibitions.

Mom and Dad have recently moved to 'Blue Roof', a pretty art-deco style property in Tettenhall, about three miles away from the house in Oak Street where we were brought up. Friends, who visit, invariably joke about my parents' 'bourgeoisification'- a word which I hope I've spelled correctly. They are correct in assuming that Mom and Dad have learned to place greater value on human rights, the rule of law, and the safeguarding of personal property, and are far more alert to the dangers posed to democracy by the power of an unbridled bureaucratic state. But our visitors are totally mistaken if they assume from the 'Blue Roof' lifestyle, with its croquet on the lawn, that Mel and Frank no longer identify intuitively with the underdog. My parents are as angry as ever about injustice, the abuse of power, inequality, plutocratic privilege, and unnecessary war. And they are still roused to energetic action by prejudice, injustice and discrimination.

In recent years, Wolverhampton has become far more racially integrated, with ethnic minority families moving gradually from inner areas to the more affluent suburbs, although the city is still palpably divided along lines of income and social class. Mel and Frank's next-door neighbours, coincidentally, just happen to be in a mixed relationship: an Indian doctor and a white nurse, with two mixed-race children, and there are Indian families living in some of the other large houses in the road.

Our parents have begun to drop hints that they would like grandchildren, and take every opportunity to remind us that our body clocks are ticking. They have started to hone their grand-parenting skills in advance on Dulce's two-year-old child, Taika.

Mel remains close to Pat, her former bridesmaid and cousin-in-law, who still lives in London, caring for Fabian, her disabled child, who is now 37 years old. Fabian is much preoccupied with playing computer games, which my brother helps select and purchase for him.

Pat and Lionel (Mel's cousin), had another child, Natalie, who went on to study sociology at the University of Canterbury and who now works in marketing in London. Natalie is in contact with my sister Toussaint.

Lionel made a lot of money in London as a builder, improving and refurbishing domestic property. He eventually divorced Pat and married another Jamaican woman, Jean, originally from Content, but living in London. He died from cancer in 2002.

Pat occasionally escapes from her home in Hanwell to spend a few days with Mel and Frank. An excellent cook and cake maker and decorator, she recently helped Mel organise a house-warming garden party at Blue Roof, preparing and serving the guests with tasty Jamaican rice and peas, and curried goat.

Carmelita, Mel's younger sister and the other bridesmaid in the photograph remains in Budapest, overseeing volunteer missionaries at different locations in Central Europe (as described in chapter 24). She returned recently to Birmingham to celebrate her fiftieth birthday party with family members and friends from the local church which sponsors her work.

Aunt Epsi, Mel's mom and our only surviving grandparent, now aged 90, still lives in her Victorian terrace house in Taunton Road, Sparkbrook. The steep stairs make her bedtime ascent increasingly hazardous. Yet she is determined to stay put until they carry her out in a box. Mel, Lloyd, and Delvin, a family friend, call by frequently. She cooks for herself, sits out in her little garden, and is taken by mini-bus to the local day centre. On Sundays, she is collected for church. Every Wednesday, when Mel visits to do her shopping and gardening, she insists on sending back a tasty Jamaican meal to Wolverhampton for Frank, her favourite (and only) son-in-law.

Fount of Jamaican family history and folklore, she is respected by her children and six grandchildren who still listen attentively to her wise words of advice. She, in her turn, is immensely proud of them. She has on display photographs of all six of her grandchildren, mostly decked out in their graduation gowns. We love Grandma Epsi very dearly and visit her whenever we can. She was delighted and touched by the poem, 'Mother-in-law thanksgiving', that Dad wrote about her. It sums up her warm-hearted character with the lines:

> 'Bless you, Epsi, your spirit is
> As light as a hibiscus flower
> Peering up to receive the Lord.'

Aunt Epsi misses her husband, Mr Son, who died in Queen Elizabeth Hospital in 2005, to the distress of us all, but especially Carmelita, his only daughter. Mr Son's wanderlust, which led him to search for his fortune in England, was the reason why Aunt Epsi, Carmelita, and later, Mel and Lloyd, came to live in England in the first place. We admired his courage, determination, and success in fending for his family in a strange and alien place, particularly in the knowledge that he never learned to read and write. Mr Son was a warm and unassuming fellow who, whenever we visited him at Clent Villas, would joke with us and dangle us on his knee.

We never knew Fitzroy Chevannes, Aunt Epsi's first partner, and father to Mel and Lloyd. Mom and Dad attended his funeral in London in 1977, five years before I was born. As is customary at Jamaican funerals, Dad joined the other male mourners in shovelling spadefuls of soil into his open grave.

Mel's brother, Lloyd, trained as a mental health nurse, marrying a fellow nurse, Bernadette, a Chinese Malay. Mel and her brother were not unusual in marrying people of a different ethnicity from themselves: in Britain around half of black Caribbean men and a quarter of black Caribbean women have partners of a different ethnicity to themselves - most frequently white. Lloyd and Bernadette have three children: our cousins, Clint, Wystan, and Sabrina. Clint and Wystan attended King Edward V1 High School, and Sabrina, King Edward V1 High School for Girls in Edgbaston, Birmingham. All three went on to medical school to train as doctors.

Our cousin, Clint, is married to Helen, who is white, and has a baby son called Harry. As to be expected, Aunt Epsi is very proud of her first great-grandchild. Our cousin, Sabrina, excelled at chess, becoming an international chess star and top girl in the British Land UK Challenge 2005. In 2007, she was selected to play for the England Women's Team in the European Team Championships in Crete. She has her own website featuring the Chevannes Chess Academy, a chess coaching programme for children. She tours schools to play chess, taking on up to 25 pupils at a time! Her strap lines are 'Will you be the last one standing?' and 'Can you face the fury?' As a fan of Chris Tucker in Rush Hour, Sabrina describes herself as ' Blackanese', and is clearly at ease with her mixed-race identity, just as we are.

Our white paternal grandparents, Norman and Phyllis Reeves, lived to a ripe old age and, like Grandma Epsi and Mr Son, showed us great affection. Grandad Norman, born in 1905, died in 2001, aged 96, when I was twenty. After his retirement, he and grandma moved from Bournville to Leominster in Herefordshire, where he took up local history, founded the Leominster Museum, and wrote a number of books about the district, the most well-known being *The Town in the Marches. A History of Leominster and its Environs.* He had a great respect for learning and showed a keen interest in our educational progress, referring to Robeson as 'the young Archimedes' in acknowledgement of his prowess at maths.

Believing firmly that God was the designer and creator of the universe, Norman was convinced that he would be rewarded in heaven if he led his life in accordance with God's purpose as interpreted by his Holy Mother, the Catholic Church. It never ceased to upset him that Frank continued to insist that human beings alone gave purpose to their lives and to their gods. Frank was putting his immortal soul at risk and that of his children, too. We attended Norman's funeral service at the Catholic Church in Leominster, where Grandma Phyllis made sure he received the full ceremonial treatment to clinch his prompt entry into the kingdom of heaven.

After Norman died, Phyllis sold the bungalow in Leominster and moved to live near to her daughter - our Auntie Maggie - in Southwell, Nottinghamshire, where she spent five happy and peaceful years. A devoted wife, she chose a Catholic funeral and to be buried in Leominster next to her husband. Auntie Maggie still misses her very much.

Grandma Phyllis was the last of that generation of the Fortey family, the daughter of our maternal great-grandfather, Edward Fortey, and great-grandmother, Florence, both born in 1876, exactly one hundred years before Mel and Frank were married. Two of Phyllis's sisters, Great Aunt Edna and Meg, were also present in my parents wedding photos. Both have since passed away.

Between them, smiling at the camera were Edna's daughter, Janet, and her husband, Eddy. Eddy, too, has died, probably from overwork as a taxi driver. Dad retains contact with his cousin, Janet, who, though retired, still works part-time as a teacher at the Children's Hospital in Birmingham. Much travelled, Janet is the only person Dad knows who has been on a cruise to Antarctica!

Frank's sisters - our paternal aunts - dressed smartly for their brother's wedding. Although they all lived at some distance from Wolverhampton, we saw and got to know them at family gatherings and at our grandparents' home in Leominster. All three of them ended up establishing enduring partnerships with white Englishmen.

Maggie met Barrie, Annie met Pete, and Philippa met John, each couple producing two children, or six more cousins for us. With the three of us, Billy (Dad's son by his first marriage), and Barrie's two children from his first marriage, Norman and Phyllis managed to accumulate twelve grandchildren, three of them of mixed race, a statistic that made them very pleased and proud. Nevertheless, our grandparents were reluctant to publicly acknowledge, and remained disappointed and ashamed, that three of their four children had undergone divorce before establishing stable partnerships, and that only one had retained her Catholic faith.

Auntie Maggie, who is three years younger than Frank, trained as a teacher on leaving school but, on completing her course, went to live in New York, where she gained a secretarial job as a secretary in the Australian consulate. She travelled widely in South and Central America, and to Iran, where Hassan, her first husband, was born. Hassan was intensely possessive and that relationship came to a premature end.

Returning to England, she settled in Nottinghamshire, where she met her husband, Barrie, and taught modern languages and English as a Foreign Language until she retired in 2010. Barrie was an athletically-built potter, making his living as a teacher. Erica, aged 27, and Theo, aged 25, are Maggie and Barrie's two children - our cousins. Erica, who is interested in politics, works in London as a civil servant, while Theo is an artist. Mom and Dad recently went to see Theo's first exhibition in Nottingham, entitled 'The Simian Crease', and declared it 'thought provoking'.

Auntie Annie has had a very varied career as a civil servant. She began in 1971 as a tax officer with the Inland Revenue and retired in 2006 from a job as an equality and diversity officer with the Learning and Skills Council. Following the breakdown of her first marriage, she met and married Pete, starting her family with the arrival of Daniel in 1980, and Thomas in 1984 - two more of our cousins.

We visited them when we were very young at Strensham, and later at Ripple in South Worcestershire, where Pete has a small holding. Pete is built like a tank and worked as an irrigation engineer, before setting up his own irrigation business. Daniel is a management accountant, while Thomas read history, took the same masters degree in international development at Birmingham University that I did, and now has a job working for a social enterprise in London.

As mentioned in the preface, Auntie Annie was an adopted child. Frank, my dad, recalls accompanying his father, Norman, on a visit to the Catholic-run Father Hudson's Homes in 1949 to bring back his new baby sister, recently weaned from her mother, a poor single Irish woman.

It is scarcely surprising that Annie's birth mother gave her up for adoption. In 1949, women who gave birth out of wedlock were stigmatised. They faced an impossible financial burden managing their child care while having to work long hours to earn their living. And intense pressure would be placed on them by institutions, such as the Church, to put their baby up for adoption, a course of action invariably regarded as in the child's best interests.

By way of contrast, in Jamaican rural communities at the time, it was perfectly normal - indeed, the norm - for an unmarried woman to raise a family on her own. There was no pressure or facility in that society for adoption. Just as well, as both Mel and her brother, Lloyd, were born to Aunt Epsi out of wedlock. If, like Annie, they'd been put up for adoption, they might now be living with an adoptive family in the United States and searching for their birth mother in Bog Walk, Jamaica.

In her later years, Auntie Annie spent a great deal of time and effort researching her origins. She deliberately sought out her birth mother and attempted on several occasions to meet her, only to be rebuffed. Annie's mother was born and raised in rural Fermanagh, in a tiny place called Eshansillogue. Annie traced and contacted other members of the family and went to Ireland to find and visit her grandparents' graves.

After her mother died in 2006, she contacted her half-sister, Linda, who had a daughter named Lisa. Annie formed the opinion that Lisa had a similar outlook on life to her son, Thomas. In common with Thomas and me, Lisa had applied for the course in international development at the University of Birmingham, but didn't take up the place because she got a job as a graduate manager in the NHS. Was it merely coincidence that two blood relatives and a non-genetically-related cousin, unbeknown to each other, had chosen to follow the same course? Surely, it is more likely to be a consequence of the milieu in which we all were brought up?

Aunt Pip took a degree in biology and trained as a teacher. She worked at schools in Telford and then Coventry, where she taught science in a secondary school. After meeting John (an engineer with Courtaulds) while on a holiday in Singapore, she married in 1980. The Catholic ceremony took place at Norman and Phyllis's church of St Ethelbert in Leominster, much to our grandparents' pleasure. One of their four children, at least, had been properly married and, as it turned out, was to be the only one never to divorce. The wedding was a traditional affair, with the bride transported to church in a carriage drawn by two white horses.

Aunt Pip is very fond of animals. She moved with John to a bungalow in Arley, North Warwickshire, which came with an acre of land on which she established a menagerie of ponies, donkeys, goats, sheep, and various kinds of fowl. When we went to visit her, she would take us for a ride along the lanes in a trap drawn by a donkey called 'Dora'. She has two children, Edwin and Roger, whom we never got to know very well because of our difference in age.

One wedding photograph shows a smartly-dressed Frank simultaneously shaking hands with his two smartly-dressed best men, Ryman Reece Roper and Sadun Perera, all three of them wearing shirts, made by Aunt Epsi, out of bandana material. My earlier chapters will have alerted readers to the subsequent course of Dad's relationships with his two best men. The picture in the album serves as a poignant reminder of how shared political ideals and intimate friendships can be abandoned or betrayed.

In the heat of the battle over the college's funding allocation, Reece announced his retirement and stood down, leaving the Further Education Funding Council to demolish everything he'd achieved with a thoroughness reminiscent of the Roman destruction of Carthage. Reece, no doubt, was dismayed by the personal attacks on him and the collapse of his life's work, but this didn't stop him blaming events on 'a tiny minority' who had let him down. Reece died in 2009, aged 71, ten years after the closure of the College. During those years, we had no contact with the Ropers, or their children, Anita and Christine.

Following the failure at the tribunal in 1989 of his racial discrimination case targeted at Reece and Frank, Sadun Perera went on teaching at Bilston Community College. He remained in employment there long after Frank had left and it merged with Wulfrun to form the Wolverhampton College.

By the time Toussaint, Robeson and I were born, my parents had left the old Bilston College of Further Education behind them, as had many of their colleagues there. I asked Dad to recall what had become of the faces in the photographs.

David Warm and his wife, Denise, went to live in Manchester, where Dave sought to reaffirm his cultural and religious identity by working as a youth leader in a Jewish youth club. Afterwards, he secured a job teaching youth studies at the University of Coleraine in Northern Ireland, later to become part of the University of Ulster. With Dave's move to Northern Ireland, contact became less frequent, confined to Christmas card exchange and the occasional New-Year's-day telephone call. Recently, Frank came across a book chapter by Dave, entitled 'The Jews of Northern Ireland', confirming that his old friend had retained his interest in ethnic relations.

Dave, like Frank, also commemorates Holocaust Memorial Day. He recently organised the showing of a film about the Kindertransport, the international effort to help Jewish children escape from the horrors of the Nazi Holocaust, and gave a talk about the child refugees of Northern Ireland. In February 1946, a transport plane with 1000 children on board took off from Prague in Czechoslovakia to land at Nutts Corner airport outside Belfast. On board were some of the few surviving orphans of Auschwitz, the extermination camp, where 1,500,000 Jews were murdered. The children were accommodated on a refugee farm at Millisle, County Down and, to their amazement, allowed to eat as much as they wanted.

Betty Simms was the Health Visitor Tutor at the college, who had encouraged Mel to pursue a teaching career, providing her with initial lecturing experience and encouraging her to obtain a Technical Teacher's Certificate, and acting as a referee for the job at the University of Central England. Unfortunately, Betty developed aggressive carcinoma and died shortly afterwards in Compton Hospice. She bequeathed Frank a portrait of Vladimir Lenin which belonged to her father. He still has it, albeit now relegated to a less prominent position in the house.

The photograph of the Bilston College guests contains two faces that we still recognise: those of Pasvil Plummer and Trevor Coote. Their Afro hairstyles have long since disappeared.

Pas is one of Frank's oldest friends and still pops round to the house for a regular discussion on current affairs, usually of a political nature. Pas is now a manager at Wolverhampton College, responsible for coordinating equality and diversity matters. Trevor Coote remains a close family friend. He and his first wife, Jackie, had two mixed-race children, Alex and Angela, who have both prospered. Trevor works for the council as an environmental health officer with responsibility for noise nuisance.

The fate of Claudette, who wasn't in the wedding photos (but peeped in at the reception to see the wedding cake that she had given to Frank and Mel as a present), is mentioned in Chapter 23. In 2009, Mel received a note from Claudette's mother in Jamaica to say she had been meaning to write for some time in response to the Christmas cards sent to her daughter. Claudette's health had indeed declined after my parents last visited her and she had eventually succumbed to the systemic lupus which had prevented her joining the wedding party in 1976.

And what of the African guests? Joshua Mpofu, his wife Ratie, and daughter Nonhlanhla returned to Zimbabwe in 1982, and now live in Cape Town. My recent contact with them, followed by parents' visit, is described in Chapter 25. The two other African guests, Herbert and Agnes Taruvinga, likewise, returned to Zimbabwe when white colonial rule was finally brought to an end. Herbert soon rose in the ranks of the ZANU ruling party, and became, Dad recalls, a minister of sport and, later, a member of the Zimbabwean embassy in Ethiopia. Disaster befell the family shortly afterwards. Herbert and children were killed in a horrific road accident near Harare, an event from which Agnes, now living in London, has never recovered emotionally.

The Banner Theatre group, which staged the play, 'Woman Kind', at the wedding, is still in business. Founded in 1973, by Charles Parker, a radical BBC Radio presenter, it was one of the first to make use of multi-media techniques, including drama, folk music, slides, and oral history tapes. In 1977, it produced 'The Great Divide', a play on racism, showing the problems faced by Asian workers at the Conygree foundry in Smethwick. In 1980s, it staged 'On the Brink', which dissected racist employment practices at the British Leyland factory at Longbridge. From time to time, my parents have gone to see Banner's productions, which are usually put on in pubs and community centres.

Finally, an update on us three children, who weren't able to appear in the wedding photographs, as we had yet to be born.

With a first class honours degree from the University of Warwick, Toussaint went on to do her PhD in molecular biology at Manchester, completing in 2005. She now works as a senior clinical research associate for a large international pharmaceutical company and flies to hospital locations in Europe to supervise drugs trials.

Robeson completed his degree in statistics, operational research and management, at University College, London, and now works as a statistician, analyst and modeller of games for Gamesys, a successful and rapidly-expanding on-line gaming company. He specialises in analysing player behaviour with a view to improving predictive models. In 2009, he helped his company win 'bingo operator of the year' and, in 2008 and 2009, 'best slots'. He is keen on gadgets, gismos, computer games, and all sports, especially football.

As for me, Spartaca, I was International Diversity Coordinator at Oxfam GB until 2008, when my contract came to an end. Based in Nairobi, Kenya, I coordinated Oxfam's international division's gender and diversity programme across its international regions so that Oxfam's diverse staff could work more effectively as teams. It involved travel to different continents and countries. Since then, I have continued to live in Nairobi, working freelance as a consultant for various charities, drafting funding proposals for them, and running capacity-building programmes on social cohesion, conflict prevention, and the safeguarding of basic human rights. I have worked with Horn Relief, an agency providing aid to Somalia and GOAL, an Irish NGO. Uncannily, my objectives and motivation seem on reflection to be identical to those of my parents, as portrayed in the course of this book

The reader can safely infer that, to date, my sister, brother, and I have led relatively normal and untroubled lives. None of us appears to suffer from 'bad blood', identity crisis, personality disorder, educational backwardness, autism, low IQ, violent outbursts, cultural confusion, anomie, rootlessness, marginality, or any of the other ills traditionally attributed to our mixed-race inheritance. On the contrary, we thrive on our ability to draw effortlessly on the rich traditions present in the multi-cultural environment in which we have grown up. We count ourselves very fortunate to have been brought up by two energetic, capable, and politically-conscious individuals from different racial groups who have instilled in us the importance of confronting injustice and insisting on our right as human beings to be treated equally.

This concludes our family history of more than half a century of racial mixing. I'll finish with a snatch from another of Dad's poems inspired when he was once asked if he were Jewish:

'What sense to give to pride or shame
In our genetic destiny?
I need to stand up every day
And say, when asked to give my name,
I'm Spartacus, I'm Malcolm X,
And just as much, I'm Abraham.'

Glossary

ackee. The ackee tree is an evergreen tree, native to tropical West Africa, which produces a fruit known as an 'ackee'. It consists of a red pear-shaped pod which opens up to display three large black seeds embedded in a soft cream flesh. In Jamaica, the flesh is separated and cooked, usually with salt-fish or bacon/salt-pork. It is said to look and taste a little like scrambled egg.

Angela Davis. Born in 1944 in Birmingham, Alabama. An American civil rights activist and member of the Communist Party of the USA. Associated with the Black Panther Party, she was tried and acquitted of being involved in the murder in California of Judge Harold Haley. As professor at the University of California Santa Cruz, she produced a number of books including her widely-read autobiography. She is commemorated in John Lennon and Yoko Ono's song, 'Angela', and Mick Jagger's song, 'Sweet Black Angel'.

Babylon. A word used by Rastafarians to describe human government and (white) institutions which are regarded as an affront to the laws of Jah (God), and which are believed to have led to the oppression and enslavement of the black race.

Bhangra. A form of Indian folk dance and music originating in the Punjab, the specific dance movements reflecting the daily activities of Punjabi farmers. Popularised in Britain by Punjabi Sikhs, Bhangra has begun to influence and fuse with Western popular music.

Black nationalism. A political ideology advocating the unity, common interests, and destiny of black people separate from, and in opposition to, a multi-cultural future and bonding with white people.

Black Power. A political movement and ideology emerging to prominence in the United States in the late 1960s. It emphasised racial pride and the need to promote black collective interests by developing institutions under black community control.

CND. The Campaign for Nuclear Disarmament was launched in London in February 1958 in response to the fear of a nuclear war between the United States, Britain and the Soviet Union.

chocho. The pear-shaped green fruit of the climbing vine, Sechium edule, eaten throughout Jamaica as a vegetable.

coco. An edible root tuber or rhizome, similar to yam.

Coloureds. In South Africa, Coloured People, or Cape Coloureds, were one of the four racial groupings defined by the apartheid laws. The Coloureds constitute a population of roughly four million people, concentrated mainly in the Western Cape Province. Mostly Afrikaans-speaking, they are the descendants of slave labourers and Dutch settlers, and of other people of mixed ancestry.

Community cohesion policy. A government sponsored initiative developed in response to fears of growing social unrest between Muslims and the local white population, following the 2001 civil disturbances in northern towns, and the 9/11 attacks in the USA.

dasheen. An edible rhizome, a variety of coco.

diva. A small clay oil lamp which is lighted along with others to form a glittering display at the Hindu and Sikh Festival of Lights, or Diwali (literally 'festival of lamps').

dojo. A place where students of martial arts gather to train or exercise. In Japan, traditionally attached to a temple.

Eldridge Cleaver. An American Black Power Leader and prominent member of the Black Panther Party, serving, while in Cuba, as its Minister of Information and Head of International Section. He was also editor of the Panther's official newsletter. While in prison, he wrote the book, *Soul on Ice* (1968).

Enoch Powell. The Member of Parliament for Wolverhampton South West from 1950 to 1974. In 1968, his 'river of blood' speech on the perils of immigration to Britain resulted in a climate of racial excitement and the vilification of immigrants from the New Commonwealth.

escovitch. A style of cooking, often of fish, using vinegar, onion, pepper, and spices. It is thought to have been introduced into Jamaica by Spanish Jews before the capture of the island by the English.

FEFC. The Further Education Funding Council (for England) was set up in 1992 to distribute government funding to further education colleges. Following the Learning and Skills Act 2000, it was replaced in 2001 by the Learning and Skills Council.

ganja. The name 'ganja' derives from the Sanskrit 'ganjika', and refers to the psychoactive plant and herbal products known also as cannabis or marijuana.

Garveyism. A political ideology and movement, deriving from the ideas of Marcus Garvey, founder of the Universal Negro Improvement Association in the USA. Garvey advocated a unified black diaspora and a powerful black state in Africa to empower black people everywhere by giving them grounds for being proud in their achievement.

gobby. Talkative, ready to answer back.

gurdwara. A Sikh temple or place of worship, the word translating into English as 'the guru's home', 'guru' meaning a person who has knowledge, wisdom and authority, in the case of the Sikhs, one of their ten great religious teachers, such as Guru Nanak.

higgler. A market trader, a peddler, itinerant merchant, a person who brings produce to sell at market. Now infrequently used in the UK, the word remains in common parlance in Jamaica.

hominy. Porridge made from maize meal with added grains of maize corn.

irie. A state of relaxation and of feeling at peace with the world, which can be induced by smoking or imbibing cannabis (marijuana).

Jamaican patois. The everyday speech of many of the common people of Jamaica, which exists in parallel with the standard forms of English spoken and written by the Jamaican educated classes. Its vocabulary and syntax are derived from both English and West African sources. It is known alternatively as 'Jamaican creole', a 'creole' being a pidgin (or language of trade) which over time has become a mother tongue, with its own native speakers.

kata. A kata is a detailed movement routine commonly used to learn and practise the martial arts and, in the context of this book, karate.

Khalistan movement. Campaign to create a Sikh homeland in the Punjab region of India and Pakistan along the lines of the 18th century Sikh Empire. In Punjabi, 'Khalistan' means 'the land of the pure'.

Malvinas. Las Malvinas is the Argentinian name for the Falkland Islands.

mandir. A Hindu temple, or place of worship for followers of Hinduism.

Marxist philosophy. Refers to the ideas of the German philosopher, Karl Marx, particularly his materialist approach to social theory, as well as to work based on, or deriving from, his writings.

National Front. A Far-Right racist political party founded in 1967, which was especially active in the 1970s and 1980s. Its policies were vehemently anti-immigrant and included compulsory 'repatriation', anti-Semitism, and holocaust denial.

NHS. 'The National Health Service' is the name used to refer to the public health services of the United Kingdom. It was created by the National Health Service Act 1946 and was based on three principles: that health care should be free at the point of use, financed from central taxation, and that everyone (even people temporarily resident or visiting the country) should be eligible.

News from Nowhere. A book by William Morris, Victorian artist and early socialist thinker, describing a utopia in which people live in an idyllic classless rural society free of private property, cities, government, judicial system, and oppressive sexual morality.

pakora. Indian snack, consisting of chopped vegetables and other ingredients formed into balls, battered and deep-fried.

Pan-Africanism. A political ideology and movement emphasising the need to liberate Africa from white European colonial and post-colonial domination in order to build a powerful Africa-wide modern economy.

pawpaw. A pear-shaped fruit, green to begin with but ripening to yellow or brown, growing on a small tree. Commonly eaten in Jamaica, it tastes like a cross between a mango and banana.

praxis. The process of translating a theory or set of ideas into practice; the application or realisation of an idea in action; moving from conceptualisation of social reality to action aimed at changing it.

Rastafarianism or Rastafari. A religious movement and way of life that emerged among the poor of Jamaica in the 1930s. Based on the doctrine that the last Emperor of Ethiopia, Haile Selassie 1, (refered to by his pre-regnal title, Ras Tafari), is an incarnation of God (or 'Jah'), taking the form of a second coming of Jesus Christ to the African continent.

REC. Racial Equality Council. A national network of local RECs, funded in part by the Commission for Racial Equality was set up in the early 1990s to work towards the elimination of racial discrimination, and to promote equality of opportunity and good relations between persons of different racial groups. RECs replaced local Councils for Community Relations which had themselves taken over from the original Councils for Racial Harmony, set up in response to the hostility shown in the 1950s and 60s towards New Commonwealth Immigrants.

samosa. A baked or fried pastry, often triangular in shape, with a savoury filling consisting of meat or vegetables, eaten in large quantities on public occasions not only in Southern Asia, but in the United Kingdom.

Sita. A Hindu goddess, and wife of Rama, the seventh avitar of Vishnu, and a principal character in the Ramayana, a Hindu epic, named after her husband, Lord Rama. For Hindus, she is the embodiment of womanly virtue and an avatar of Lakshmi. The Ramayana story is celebrated at Diwali, the Festival of Light, which occurs in November.

Stokely Carmichael. A Trinidadian-American and member of the Black Panther Party in the 1960s. He was an alumnus of Howard

University an historically-black college in Washington DC. He popularised concepts of 'Black Power' and 'Black Pride'. With Charles V Hamilton, he wrote the book *Black* Power, published in 1967. Active in opposition to the Vietnam War.

Tertiary education. A 'third stage' of education following primary and secondary, and preceding higher education. It includes traditional 16-to-19 sixth-form education and further education.

UDI. Unilateral Declaration of Independence. In November 1965, the white settler regime in Southern Rhodesia led by Mr Ian Smith, declared the country (since renamed Zimbabwe) to be independent of British rule.

Wulfrunian. A native or inhabitant of Wolverhampton, a city situated in the West Midlands of England.

ZANU. Zimbabwe African National Union, a political organisation set up to fight for black majority rule in Southern Rhodesia. It had broken off from the Zimbabwe African People's Union. In 1980, under the leadership of Robert Mugabe, ZANU won the first 'one person one vote' elections.

ZAPU. Zimbabwe African People's Union, a political organisation led by Joshua Nkomo set up in 1961 to fight for national independence shortly after the ban placed on the National Democratic Party by the white Rhodesian Government.

About the author

The child of a Jamaican mother and English father, Spartaca was born and brought up with her sister and brother in Wolverhampton in the British West Midlands, where she became involved from a young age in her parents' unremitting struggle for racial justice. After reading law at the University of Lancaster, she took temporary work and saved to go backpacking in South East Asia, Australia, and New Zealand. On her return, she was employed by the West Mercia Criminal Justice Board as its community and diversity officer, advising board members on anti-discrimination legislation, and setting up a multi-agency equality forum and a black staff support group.

In pursuit of a lifetime ambition to become an international development worker, she left to study for an MSc in Poverty Reduction and International Development Management at the University of Birmingham. As part of the course, she spent time in South Africa evaluating the Truth and Reconciliation Commission. Afterwards, she became Oxfam's diversity advisor based in Oxford, and then its international diversity officer in Nairobi, Kenya. Since then, she has worked as a freelance consultant in East Africa, advising non-governmental organisations on human rights, women's equality, social cohesion and conflict prevention.

This, her first full-length book, written with help from other family members, describes her parents' lives and marriage, and the experience of growing up as a mixed-race young woman in a zealously anti-racist household and vibrant multi-racial city environment.